NARRATIVE CHANCE

POSTMODERN DISCOURSE

ON NATIVE AMERICAN

INDIAN LITERATURES

Edited By

GERALD VIZENOR

UNIVERSITY OF OKLAHOMA PRESS

Norman

Other Books by Gerald Vizenor

Wordarrows: Indians and Whites in the New Fur Trade (Minneapolis, 1978)

The People Named the Chippewa: Narrative Histories (Minneapolis, 1984)

Griever: An American Monkey King in China (Boulder, 1987; Minneapolis, 1990)

Bearheart: The Heirship Chronicles (Minneapolis, 1990)

Crossbloods: Bone Courts, Bingo, and Other Reports, rev. ed. (Minneapolis, 1990)

Interior Landscapes: Autobiographical Myths and Metaphors (Minneapolis, 1990)

The Heirs of Columbus (Hanover, N.H., 1991)

Landfill Meditation: Crossblood Stories (Hanover, N.H., 1991)

Dead Voices: Natural Agonies in the New World (Norman, 1992)

Summer in the Spring: Anishinaabe Lyric Poems and Stories, New Edition (Norman, 1992)

Requests for permission to quote should be addressed to the chapter author.

Library of Congress Cataloging-in-Publication Data

Narrative chance : postmodern discourse on native American Indian literatures / edited by Gerald Vizenor.
p. cm. — (American Indian literature and critical studies series ; v. 8)
Originally published: Albuquerque : University of New Mexico Press, c1989.
Includes bibliographical references (p.) and index.
ISBN 0-8061-2561-6
1. American literature—Indian authors—History and criticism. 2. Postmodernism (Literature)—United States. 3. Indians in literature. 4. Narration (Rhetoric) I. Vizenor, Gerald Robert, 1934- . II. Series.
[PS153.I52N37 1993]
810.9'897—dc20   93-4116
                                                                      CIP

The paper in this book meets the guidelines for permanence and durability of the Committee on Production Guidelines for Book Longevity of the Council on Library Resources, Inc.

2   3   4   5   6   7   8   9   10

In Memory of
D'Arcy McNickle

But after the white people came, elements in this world began to shift; and it became necessary to create new ceremonies. I have made changes in the rituals. The people mistrust this greatly, but only this growth keeps the ceremonies strong.

—LESLIE MARMON SILKO, *Ceremony*

And the journey is an evocation of three things in particular: a landscape that is incomparable, a time that is gone forever, and the human spirit, which endures.

—N. SCOTT MOMADAY, *The Way to Rainy Mountain*

Representation as aesthetic semblance indicates the presence of the inaccessible. Literature reflects life under conditions that are either not available in the empirical world or are denied by it. Consequently literature turns life into a storehouse from which it draws its material in order to stage that which in life appeared to have been sealed off from access.

—WOLFGANG ISER, "Representation: A Performative Act"

Contents

Preface

In the telling of a story there are silences in which words are anticipated or held on to, heard to echo in the still depths of the imagination. In the oral tradition silence is the sanctuary of sound.

—N. Scott Momaday,
Columbia Literary History of the United States

The earliest symptom of a process whose end is the decline of storytelling is the rise of the novel at the beginning of modern times.

—Walter Benjamin, "The Storyteller"

The novel is the imaginary paradise of individuals. It is the territory where no one possesses the truth. . . . The novel is born
not of the theoretical spirit but of the spirit of humor.

—Milan Kundera, *The Art of the Novel*

Charles Newman argues that postmodern has no heroes since it is an
"ahistorical rebellion" against an "innovative information society."
He considers modernism a "retrospective revolt against a retrograde in-
dustrialism." In his critique on the inflation of criticism, *The Post-
Modern Aura*, he writes that postmodern does not idealize a "specific
historic period as an emulative model, or attempt to recapture the pu-
rity, however illusory, of some vanished age."

There are four postmodern conditions in the critical responses to
Native American Indian literatures: the first is heard in aural performances; the second is seen in translations; the third pose is a trickster
signature, an uncertain humor that denies translation and tribal representations; and the last postmodern condition is narrative chance in
the novel.

These four conditions imagine a discourse on tribal literatures, a
discourse on communal memories, popular human unities, individualism, racial separations, museum durance, tragic impostures, social
science monologues, the enervation of modernism and more; post-

modern interpretations are neotic mediations on narrative chance in a language game.

The postmodern opened in tribal imagination; oral cultures have never been without a postmodern condition that enlivens stories and ceremonies, or without trickster signatures and discourse on narrative chance—a comic utterance and adventure to be heard or read.

The immanent pleasures of an aural performance are unbodied in translation; the tribal experiences that were *heard* in stories, and natural variations on stories, are transformed in publications that are *seen* as cultural information, some with imposed historical significance. Modernism is a disguise, a pretense of individualism and historicism; postmodern is a pose in a language game that would controvert the institutional power of translation—what is seen or published is not a representation of what is heard or remembered in oral cultures. The postmodern printed word, in other words a pose, is not a source of aesthetic presence or historical modernism. The printed word has no evolution in tribal literatures; the word is there, in trees, water, air, and printed on paper where it has been at all times.

Native American Indian literatures have been overburdened with critical interpretations based on structuralism and other social science theories. Brian Swann and Arnold Krupat, editors of *Recovering the Word*, point out that structuralism, a "concern for principles of organization and function" dominated their collection; the "Indian as an individual is not much examined in these essays." Claude Lévi-Strauss and Alan Dundes have been cited more than Mikhail Bakhtin or Jean-François Lyotard in critical studies of tribal literature in the past decade. Anthropologists, in particular, are not the best listeners or interpreters of tribal literatures. "To put it brutally, but not inaccurately," Clifford Geertz writes in *Works and Lives: The Anthropologist as Author*, "Lévi-Strauss argues that the sort of immediate, in-person 'being there' one associates with the bulk of recent American and British anthropology is essentially impossible: it is either outright fraud or fatuous self-deception."

Andrew Wiget comes closer to modernism and social science methodologies than to other critical theories in his interpretations of tribal literature. In *Native American Literature* he covers the tribal world from oral narratives to the novel in six short chapters. He announces that "trying to find some clear and universal criteria for distinguishing different types of narrative has been the ever-elusive goal of folklorists and anthropologists." Wiget asserts that oral cultures are not static but at the same time he explains that "there has been no single effort to order and assess that literature."

Charles Larson studied three generations of fiction writers in his *American Indian Fiction.* Beginning with *Queen of the Woods* by Simon Pokagon and ending with *Ceremony* by Leslie Marmon Silko, Larson invented four political structures to hold tribal novelists and their publications: assimilationists, reactionaries, revisionists, and qualified separatists.

Novelists Pokagon, John Oskison, author of *Wild Harvest* and *Brothers Three*, and John Mathews, author of *Sundown* and other books, are named assimilationists because some of their characters seem to lean toward the values of the dominant culture. Larson argues that these novels are "conventional in form, traditional in subject, anything but innovative—indistinguishable from hundreds of other fictional works of the time. . . . If we did not know that these men were Native Americans we might conclude from their novels that they were white."

Larson sees *The Surrounded* by D'Arcy McNickle and *House Made of Dawn* by N. Scott Momaday as reactionary books. He points out that these novels are about tribal men who are isolated in the dominant culture and unable to return to the traditional past. "Although their present existence is individualistic, the past from which they have been severed is collective." *Seven Arrows* by Hyemeyohsts Storm and *Winter Count* by Dallas Chief Eagle are called revisionist because they "depict aggressive confrontations" between tribal and dominant cultures.

The qualified separatist books are *Winter in the Blood* by James Welch and *Ceremony* by Leslie Marmon Silko; the characters in these novels have lived in urban areas. Larson observes that these authors "often appear to be infused with a sense of urgency to proclaim the quality of contemporary Indian life. . . ."

Paula Gunn Allen overturns androcentric structuralism in her mythic meditation on the renaissance of the feminine in tribal cultures. *The Sacred Hoop* celebrates spiritualism, "woman-focused worldviews," and revisionist utopian gynocracies—a new structuralism based on esoteric tribal lesbianism. She argues that "one of the major distinguishing characters of gynocratic cultures is the absence of punitiveness as a means of social control. Another is the inevitable presence of meaningful concourse with supernatural beings." Allen asserts that "American Indian thought is essentially mystical and psychic in nature." However, she hands over tribal literatures to structures: she divides traditional literature from "genre literature of the present." Traditional literatures are further divided into ceremonial and popular, or into "canonical works and those that derive from canon. . . ." The canons are obtrusions that transvalue tribal literatures.

Structuralism and other social science theories never seem to enter stories as a language game without an institutional advantage; those unexpected cultural harmonies, those common intersections in aural performances and trickster discourse, are translated, transformed, and held to represent established modernism; they are academic tropes to power rather than tribal stories in a language game. The postmodern pose is an invitation to liberation, a noetic mediation and communal discourse.

Leslie Marmon Silko narrowed the focus of postmodern criticism; she used the word postmodern to mean separation from comunal experience in a review of *The Beet Queen* by Louise Erdrich that appeared in the *Albuquerque Journal's Impact Magazine.* The postmodern condition, however, is not literature on trial but a liberation of tribal stories. Silko is precise in one sense, that postmodern attention would "set language free," but she misleads the reader by saying that postmodern "writing reflects the isolation and alienation of the individual who shares nothing in common with other human beings but language and its hyg[i]enic grammatical mechanisms." Erdrich is a polished writer and she could be called hygienic, an unusual postmodern metaphor on grammar, but not in the sense that is implied in the review. One definition of hygiene is the promotion of health. Modernism is much more mechanical and institutional; postmodern is a situational pattern, not a historical template; an erudite riposte to tribal representations, not a disguise or formal grammar.

Silko argues that *The Beet Queen* is best when the characters explore the "depths of the subconscious . . . and turn ever inward on themselves." Later, however, she points out that "Erdrich leaves her element and tries to place her characters and action in places and points in history that are loaded with 'referential' significance. Good fiction need not be factual, but it doesn't obscure basic truth." The postmodern pose is a noetic mediation that denies historicism and representation; in particular, it denies the kitschy speculation on the basic truth.

Walter Benjamin reads the novel in the ruins of storytelling, an aesthetic modernism, but his mutable nostalgia for the past would be a misconception of tribal aural stories and literatures in translation. Karl Kroeber illustrates this problem of oral literary traditions in his essay on a tribal storyteller: "Peter Seymour may be the first 'informant' to exploit the machine to increase the recursive functions of a traditional telling. . . ."

Milan Kundera reads the novel in the spirit of humor and unheard appeals. In *The Art of the Novel* he responds with "four appeals" to the notion that the novel has come to an end: the appeal of play, or grand games, a lightness without the imperatives of realism; the appeal of dream, an aesthetic ambition to break free from verisimilitude; the appeal of thought, but not a philosophical transformation; and the appeal of time, personal memories and collective time. "If the novel should really disappear, it will do so not because it has exhausted its powers but because it exists in a world grown alien to it."

The critical essays in this postmodern collection focus on translation and representation in tribal literatures, comic and tragic world views, trickster discourse, and on selected publications by novelists N. Scott Momaday, Leslie Marmon Silko, D'Arcy McNickle, Louise Erdrich, Gerald Vizenor and other Native American authors.

Native American Indian stories are told and heard in motion, imagined and read over and over on a landscape that is never seen at once; words are heard in winter rivers, crows are written on the poplars, last words are never the end. In *The Delicacy and Strength of Lace*, a collection of letters between Silko and James Wright, she wrote to the poet, who was in the hospital with cancer, that she sensed "another present" in their friendship. "In this place, in a sense there never has been a time when you and I were not together. I cannot explain this. Maybe it is the continuing or on-going of the telling, the telling in poetry and stories." Wright died before her last letter was delivered.

Gerald Vizenor

NARRATIVE CHANCE

1

A *Postmodern Introduction*

GERALD VIZENOR

Postmodern discourse

Native American Indian histories and literatures, oral and written, are imagined from "wisps of narratives." These narrative wisps, wrote Jean-François Lyotard, are

> stories that one tells, that one hears, that one acts out; the people does not exist as a subject but as a mass of millions of insignificant and serious little stories that sometimes let themselves be collected together to constitute big stories and sometimes disperse into digressive elements.[1]

The critical attention in this collection is postmodernism: new essays on narrative discourse, authors, readers, tricksters and comic world views rather than tragic themes, individualism and modernism.

Lyotard uses the word *postmodern* to describe "the condition of knowledge in the most highly developed societies" and to designate "the state of our culture following the transformations which, since the end of the nineteenth century, have altered the game rules for science, literature, and the arts." His studies "place these transformations in the context of the crisis of narratives."[2]

The word *postmodernism* is a clever condition: an invitation to narrative chance in a new language game and an overture to amend the formal interpretations and transubstantiation of tribal literatures.

Ihab Hassan, for instance, wrote that postmodernism sounds awkward and uncouth. The word "evokes what it wishes to surpass or suppress, modernism itself. The term thus contains its enemy within, as the terms romanticism and classicism, baroque and rococo, do not. . . . But if much of modernism appears hieratic, hypotactical, and formalist, postmodernism strikes us by contrast as playful, paratactical, and deconstructionist."[3]

Brian McHale, on the other hand, asserts,

> Nobody likes the term, yet people continue to prefer it over the even less satisfactory alternatives. . . . Postmodernism is not post modern, whatever that might mean, but post modern*ism*; it does not come *after the present* (a solecism), but after the *modernist movement*. . . . Postmodernism follows *from* modernism.

He wrote that a "superior construction of postmodernism would be one that produces new insights, new or richer connections, coherence of a different degree or kind, ultimately *more discourse*."[4]

Native American Indian literatures are tribal discourse, more discourse. The oral and written narratives are language games, comic discourse rather than mere responses to colonialist demands or social science theories.

Stephen Tyler, in his essay on postmodern anthropology, considers discourse as the "maker of the world, not its mirror. . . . The world is what we say it is, and what we speak of is the world." Tribal narratives are discourse and in this sense tribal literatures are the world rather than a representation. Tyler argues that one of the constant themes in the dominant culture has been the "search for apodictic and universal method. In our own times we see the triumph of formalism in all branches of thought. . . . Form, in other words, produces form; it is both process and structure." He points out that postmodern

> writing focuses on the outer flow of speech, seeking not the thought that "underlies" speech, but the thought that *is* speech. . . . Modernists sought a form of writing more in keeping with "things," emphasizing, in imitation of modern science, the descriptive function of writing— writing as a "picture of reality."

Postmodern writing overturns

> modernist *mimesis* in favor of a writing that "evokes" or "calls to mind,"
> not by completion and similarity but by suggestion and difference. The
> function of the text is not to depict or reveal within itself what it says.
> The text is "seen through" by what it cannot say. It shows what it cannot
> say and says what it cannot show.[5]

Pleasurable misreadings

The world is a text, Vincent Leitch argues in *Deconstructive Criticism*,
and nothing stands behind this world of tropes because a literal language does not exist, except in illusions. The literal translations and
representations of tribal literatures are illusions, consolations in the
dominant culture. There can never be "correct" or "objective" readings of the text or the tropes in tribal literatures, only more energetic,
interesting and "pleasurable misreadings."[6]

Native American Indian literatures have been pressed into cultural
categories, transmuted by reductionism, animadversions and the hyperrealities of neocolonial consumerism. The concept of "hyperrealities"
is borrowed from *Travels in Hyperreality* by Umberto Eco. He wrote
that Americans live in a "more to come" consumer culture.

> This is the reason for this journey into hyperreality, in search of in-
> stances where the American imagination demands the real thing and, to
> attain it, must fabricate the absolute fake; where the boundaries be-
> tween game and illusion are blurred. . . .[7]

Tribal cultures, in this sense, have been invented as "absolute fakes"
and consumed in social science monologues. The consumers demand
more cultures and new literatures; at the same time, postmodern criticism would liberate tribal narratives in a most "pleasurable misreading."

Native American Indian literatures are unstudied landscapes, wild
and comic rather than tragic and representational, storied with narrative wisps and tribal discourse. Social science theories constrain
tribal landscapes to institutional values, representationalism and the
politics of academic determination. The narrow teleologies deduced
from social science monologues and the ideologies that arise from
structuralism have reduced tribal literatures to an "objective" collec-

tion of consumable cultural artifacts. Postmodernism liberates imagination and widens the audiences for tribal literatures; this new criticism rouses a comic world view, narrative discourse and language games on the past.

"The return to the past, to the traces, fragments, and debris of memory and history is both necessary and inconclusive," reasoned David Carroll.

> The acceptance of representation in its simple sense is a kind of bureaucratic solution to the conflicts of history, an acquiescence to the demands and false security of realism without the will or the force to maintain the potentially irresolvable contradiction of the struggle.[8]

Monologic realism and representation in tribal literatures, in this sense, is a "bureaucratic solution" to neocolonialism and the consumption of narratives and cultures.

In a recent essay on narrative and politics David Carroll wrote,

> Any narrative that predetermines all responses or prohibits any counter-narratives puts an end to narrative itself by suppressing all possible alternative actions and responses, by making itself its own end and the end of all other narratives.[9]

Narrative dissidence

Antonin Dvořák, the composer, and Oleg Cassini, the modern couturier, have in common their unusual interests in tribal cultures; now a source of "little dissident narratives" and ironic literature.[10] Separated in time by a century, these two men shared certain hyperrealities about Native American Indian cultures.

"The Americans expect great things of me," wrote Dvořák. "And the main thing is . . . to create a national music. Now, if the small Czech nation can have such musicians, they say, why could not they, too, when their country and people are so immense?"[11]

Patricia Hampl, in her sensitive meditation on the Czech composer, wrote that he arrived in Spillville, Iowa, in 1893, with his wife, six children, housemaid, and secretary.

> They stayed the whole summer, an unusually hot one, past Dvořák's fifty-second birthday, which fell on the feast of the Nativity of Mary,

September 8. He passed out cigars to the townspeople who gathered for a celebration in his honor. Two days later—quite suddenly it seemed to some people—he and his family packed up and were gone, back the long way they had come.[12]

Big Moon, the Kickapoo leader and healer, was in Spillville late that summer with other tribal people to sell medicinal herbs. Dvořák attended the tribal dances, listened to the music and even paid for a snake oil headache treatment; he consumed the hyperrealities that he believed were tribal, authentic, real and representational. A franchised composer at the turn of the last century, he was inspired and imagined a national music; meanwhile, most tribal cultures were enslaved on reservations. The tribal people he encountered were on the boundaries. Modern immigrants were surrounded by "native immigrants" that summer in a small town; their stories are narrative wisps in the national tenure on savagism and civilization.

"He believed the answer lay in the music of the slaves," Hampl wrote,

Negro spirituals, and in American Indian music, especially its insistent, patient rhythms . . . Maybe he could not perceive the American hesitation. In the old country "the peasants" were himself, his family. His people. In America there was a boundary. Black and white, red and white. We call it racism. He stepped over the line easily, perhaps thinking Indian drum beats were as accessible to white American composers as Czech folk music was to him. He didn't hear the heavier hit of the drum on the ear, the black wail it is impossible to borrow."[13]

Dvořák considered an opera based on *The Song of Hiawatha* by Henry Wadsworth Longfellow, a romantic colonialist poem. "He had read the poem in translation," Hampl wrote. "Naturally, its admiration for the indiginous culture appealed to Dvořák. So did Longfellow's lyrical, if rather didactic, restatement of landscape and the beauties of nature." But the idea "fizzled."[14]

Dvořák and his daughter Otilka, who was fifteen that summer, visited the Chicago World's Columbian Exposition. Behind the mechanical Uncle Sam on the midway, the barkers and pitch men, Otilka must have witnessed the ethnic exhibits, tribal dances and ceremonies. In 1893 the exhibits included a "Bedouin camp, a Winnebago Indian village, a Lapland village, a Persian palace, a Chinese market," and other cultural hyperrealities.[15]

Otilka returned to Spillville. Later that summer she was seen near the tribal camp on the boundaries, near the river where her father walked and recorded the sounds of water, birds and tribal music. She was seen "roaming around the woods, Big Moon by her side. Keeping company. . . . It was Big Moon with her in the woods by the Turkey River, and what of it?"[16] Dvořák was told about his daughter and the tribal leader who had danced for the composer and treated his headache. "Like so much, it depends on your attitude, your place in the story," wrote Hampl. "That night the Dvořáks started packing. They were gone the next day."[17]

Dvořák pursued the hyperrealities of tribal cultures, the structured ceremonies at the tenable borders of civilization in a small town. He imagined tribal music as an instance of nationalism and worried that his daughter was too close to savagism. This, the wilderness in flesh and bone too close to home, is where hyperrealities and dioramas transmute the landscape and narrative discourse.

"I see the rest," wrote Hampl. "Girl on a pony, gold light in the blue morning sky, a glade where a good-looking man, native to the place, puts his hand surely between two clumps of fern to expose for her the white wood mallow, a plant she had never seen before."[18]

Oleg Cassini, the personal couturier and costume designer, considered "looks and styles" and historical periods in his fashion career; unabashed hyperrealities abound in his recent autobiography. "I realized that there was one area I'd never really exploited: my lifelong obsession with American Indians."[19]

Cassini satisfied his obsession in an agreement with Peter MacDonald, the elected chairman of the Navajo Nation. Cassini announced at the National Press Club that he would build, as a joint venture with the tribal government, a "world-class luxury resort" on the reservation. The architecture and furnishings of the tourist resort would "have their base in authentic Navajo designs." MacDonald said that the designer resort would "reflect the unique culture and tradition of our people." Moreover, the tribal leader announced, "We are creating a Navajo Board of Standards for all new tourist facilities on the Reservation to assure that the Navajo name means quality."[20] Designer hyperrealities are valuable properties in a consumer culture, even on reservations.

In one instance Cassini stated his clever attention to cultural selection and tribal standards. "A good many of my American Indian dresses required intricate beading of a sort that was not available in Italy," he wrote in his autobiography.

I'd been told Hong Kong was the place to find such material. . . . And then the show began. The line was modeled by girls with dark hair and the somatic characteristics of Indians; one wore beads and head-dresses. Sometimes the models were barefoot, but generally they wore moccasins.[21]

These stories are serious and comic, numerous narrative wisps that controvert hyperrealities. Tribal literatures are burdened with colonialism and tragic world views; however, there is a curious humanism in tribal narratives on minacious consumerism. Serious attention to cultural hyperrealities is an invitation to trickster discourse, an imaginative liberation in comic narratives; the trickster is postmodern.

Mikhail Bakhtin considered consciousness and character identification in aesthetic events. In trickster discourse the trickster is a comic trope, a chance separation in a narrative.

There are events that, in principle, cannot unfold on the plane of a single and unified consciousness, but presuppose two consciousnesses that do not fuse; they are events whose essential and constitutive element is the relation of a consciousness to *another* consciousness, precisely because it is *other*. Such are all events that are creatively productive, innovative, unique, and irreversible.[22]

Tribal narratives are creative productions rather than social science monologues; the trickster is a comic trope, chance in a narrative wisp, tribal discourse and an irreversible innovation in literature.

Comic signs and holotropes

The trickster is a communal sign in a comic narrative; the comic *holotrope* (the whole figuration) is a consonance in tribal discourse. Silence and separation, not monologues in social science methodologies, are the antitheses of trickster discourse. The instrumental language of the social sciences are tragic or *hypotragic* modes that withhold communal discourse. Comic signs and tragic modes are cultural variations, the mood and humor in a language game; but they are not structural opposition.

Comic world views are communal; chance is more significant than "moral ruin." Tragic modes are inventions and impositions that attend the "discoverers" and translators of tribal narratives. The notion of the "vanishing tribes" is a lonesome nuisance, to cite one *hypotragic* intrusion, that reveals racialism and the contradictions in humanism and historical determinism. More than a century ago, when politicians, missionaries and some intellectuals argued over monogenesis and the "separate creation of nonwhite races," the commissioner of Indian affairs "asserted that 'the fact stands out clear, well-defined, and indisputable, that Indians, not only as individuals but as tribes, are capable of civilization and christianization.'"[23]

These two capabilities, however, were not acceptable to most whites at the time; those who "saw cultures with primitive technologies, engaged in some limited agriculture yet dependent to a large extent upon hunting and gathering for food and apparel." It was common then

> to refer to Indian communities as hunter societies as opposed to white societies engaged in agriculture id domestic industries. . . . They contrasted the preliterate Indian societies . . . with the accomplishments of their own society and judged the Indian languages generally worthless even though of scientific interest . . . and they saw their own rapidly multiplying population overwhelming the static or declining numbers of the Indian tribes.[24]

The paternal rhetoric of liberal politics, however, promised that peace, wealth and power would be shared; but there was no salvation in the domination, revision or transvaluation of tribal cultures. In the *hypotragic* end there are tricksters and comedies—chance, humor and at best a communal discourse in a tribal narrative. The colonists strained to tame the wild, the tribes and the environment. Now, high technologies overbear postcolonial promises and transvaluations; the tragic mode is in ruin.

Comic signs in tribal narratives, and then tragic modes in translations and imposed histories, are seldom mentioned in social science research and "discoveries." To understand these variations and the problems of interpretation we must turn to the theories of imaginative literature. Literary criticism, however, has not considered tribal narratives until the past two decades. Arnold Krupat comments that "there has been a sufficient amount of sophisticated writing about Native American literature in the last ten years or so to constitute a New Indian Criticism."[25]

Even now, serious critical attention to tribal narratives is minimal; a dubious virtue, given the instrumental possession of tribal experience by romantic adventurers, missionaries and then social science. "Prior to the twentieth century," Michael Castro points out, "literary approaches to the Indian were dominated by two opposing and distancing stereotypes, the 'brutish savage' and the 'noble savage,' each serving underlying psychic needs of Western culture."[26] These stereotypes and several others, such as idiotism and "genetic code" alcoholism, are *hypotragic* impositions that deny a comic world view—the racist denial of tribal languages and ceremonies.

Histories read the past, or the past in the historical present; criticism reads the narrative; and the trickster reads neither. Here in trickster discourse the trickster unties the *hypotragedies* imposed on tribal narratives—tribal narratives have been underread in criticism and overread in social science. The tragic mode is not in structural opposition to the comic sign. Rather, it is a racial burden, a postcolonial overcompensation at best; these burdens are a dubious triumph. "Without a sense of the tragic, comedy loses heart, it becomes brittle, it has animation but no life," asserts Richard Sewall. "Without a recognition of the truths of comedy, tragedy becomes bleak and intolerable."[27] Without a doubt social science theories are "bleak" reminders of the *hypotragic* intrusion and postcolonial domination of tribal cultures and literature.

More than fifty years ago Aldous Huxley "wondered whether tragedy as a form of art might not be doomed." He witnessed colonial durance, the intrusions of "moral ruin" and the duress of romantic and tragic modes in the translation of comic tribal literature, but his concern centered on the classics. Meanwhile, social science studies reproduced new theories and contributed not so much to the doom of tragedies, but to a new insolence in tribal literature, an outbreak of *hypotragedies*. Huxley argues in "Tragedy and the Whole Truth"[28] that tragedies are more than "mere verisimilitude" and empirical evidence, more than facts; tragedies are not the "whole truth." The trickster, a semiotic sign in a third-person narrative, is never tragic or *hypotragic*, never the whole truth or even part truth. Social science on the other hand is never comic, never a chance and never tragic in the end. Causal research strains to discover the "whole truth" or the invented truth in theories and models; these "whole truth" models imposed on tribal experiences are *hypotragedies*, abnormal tragedies in this instance. They have no comic imagination, no artistic intent, no communal signification of mythic verism.

"To make a tragedy," Huxley writes, "the artist must isolate a single element out of the totality of human experience and use that exclusively as his material. Tragedy is something that is separated out from the Whole Truth. . . ." In *The Death of Tragedy*, George Steiner holds that tragedy is dead because of the promise of salvation, which is an argument similar to the "whole truth."

In his classical studies on tragedy and comedy Walter Kerr points out that "tragedy is the form that promises us a happy ending."[29] He argues that "comedy depends upon tragedy" and that there is hope in tragedy, while in comedy "there is no way out." He would not, it seems, agree with the notion of the "whole truth." Kerr writes, "In short, tragedy should report every conceivable experience man can have as he exercises his freedom totally in the hope of arriving at a new state of being."[30] Huxley declares, "For the fact is that tragedy and what I have called the Whole Truth are not compatible; where one is, the other is not."

Social science theories isolate certain elements in tribal narratives; the construction of human experience is modular. The trickster is a communal sign, never isolation; a concordance of narrative voices. The trickster is not tragic because the narrative does not promise a happy ending. The comic and tragic, the *hypotragic*, are cultural variations; the trickster is opposed by silence and isolation, not social science. The antithesis of the tragic in social science is chaos, rumors and wild conversations. The trickster livens chaos, but as Paul Watzlawick has argued, realities in social science rest "on the supposition that the world cannot be chaotic—not because we have any proof for this view, but because chaos would simply be intolerable." The comic trickster and social science, a tragic monologue, are contradictions but not antithetical; social science is a limited language game.[31]

"The comic rites are necessarily impious," muses Wylie Sypher, "for comedy is sacrilege as well as release. . . . We find ourselves reflected in the comedian, who satisfies our need for impieties."[32] Sypher maintains that the "high comic vision of life is humane, an achievement of man as a social being," which would include trickster narratives, comic *holotropes* and concordance in discourse. "So the comic spirit keeps us pure in mind by requiring that we regard ourselves skeptically. Indeed this spirit is an agent of that civilizing activity Matthew Arnold called 'criticism,' which is essential to 'culture.'"[33]

The trickster, then, is a comic and communal sign, a discourse in a narrative with no hope or tragic promises. The trickster is neither the "whole truth" nor an isolated *hypotragic* transvaluation of primitivism.

The trickster is as aggressive as those who imagine the narrative, but the trickster bears no evil or malice in narrative voices. Malice and evil would silence the comic *holotropes*; there would be no concordance in the discourse. Neither the narrator, the characters, nor the audience would share the narrative event.

Arthur Koestler observes in "The Act of Creation" that there are various "moods involved in different forms of humor, including mixed or contradictory feelings; but whatever the mixture, it must contain a basic ingredient which is indispensible: an impulse, however faint, of aggression or apprehension. . . ."[34] He writes, "Replace aggression by sympathy," as liberal humanists and postcolonial interpreters have done with tribal cultures, "and the same situation will no longer be comic but pathetic, and evoke not laughter but pity."

Freedom is a sign, and the trickster is chance and freedom in a comic sign; comic freedom is a "doing," not an essence, not a museum being, not an aesthetic presence. The trickster as a semiotic sign is imagined in narrative voices, a communal rein to the unconscious, which is comic liberation; however, the trickster is outside comic structure, "making it" comic rather than inside comedy, "being it."[35] The trickster is agonistic imagination and aggressive liberation, a "doing" in narrative points of view and outside the imposed structures.

Jean-Paul Sartre reasoned that freedom, or comic liberation in this instance, is involvement, to be *engagé* [engager] in a free choice; "a freedom which would produce its own existence would lose its very meaning. . . ." Freedom determines "itself by its very upsurge as a 'doing'"[36] The trickster is a comic sign with no histories, no political or economic signification, and no being or presence in the narrative. The trickster is nothingness in a narrative voice, an encounter that centers imagination in comic *holotropes*, a communal being; nothingness in consciousness and comic discourse.

"Creativity occurs in an act of encounter," wrote Rollo May in *The Courage to Create*, "and is to be understood with this encounter as its center."[37] The trickster is an encounter in narrative voices, a communal sign and creative encounter in a discourse.

Tribal cultures, social science and the environment have at least three circumstances in common: science is a trope to power and rules memories; science measures humans and the earth in *hypotragic* isolation and monologues; the tribes and the wilderness vanish in tragic narratives. The wild environment and tricksters are comic and communal; science is a monologue with science not the environment, and the antitheses are silence and chaos. "In literature or in ecology, comedy enlightens and enriches human experience without trying to transform either mankind or the world," wrote Joseph Meeker in *The Comedy of Survival: Studies in Literary Ecology.* "The comic mode of human behavior represented in literature is the closest art has come to describing man as an adaptive animal."[38] The trickster animates this human adaptation in a comic language game and social science overcomes chaos in a monologue; the environment bears the comedies and tragedies.

Notes

The first epigraph on the dedication page is from *Ceremony* by Leslie Marmon Silko (New York: Viking, 1977), 126; the second is from *The Way to Rainy Mountain* by N. Scott Momaday (Albuquerque: University of New Mexico Press, 1969) 4; and the last epitaph is from "Representation: A Performative Act" by Wolfgang Iser, *The Aims of Representation* ed. Murray Krieger (New York: Columbia University Press, 1987) 227.

1. Jean-François Lyotard, *Instructions païnnes* quot. David Carroll, "Narrative, Heterogeneity, and the Question of the Political: Bakhtin and Lyotard," *The Aims of Representation*, ed. Murray Krieger (New York: Columbia University Press, 1987) 85.

2. Jean-François Lyotard, *The Postmodern Condition: A Report on Knowledge* (Minneapolis: University of Minnesota Press, 1984) xxiii.

3. Ihab Hassan, *The Postmodern Turn* (Columbus: Ohio State University Press, 1987), 87, 91.

4. Brian McHale, *Postmodern Fiction* (New York: Methuen, 1987) 3–5.

5. Stephen Tyler, "Post-Modern Anthropology," *Discourse and the Social Life of Meaning*, ed. Phyllis Pease Chock and June Wyman (Washington: Smithsonian Institution Press, 1986) 37, 40, 45.

6. Vincent Leitch, *Deconstructive Criticism* (New York: Columbia University Press, 1983) 59.

7. Umberto Eco, *Travels in Hyperreality* (San Diego: Harcourt Brace Jovanovich, 1986) 8. In *Simulations* Jean Baudrillard argues that the "hyperreal" is the product of a synthesis of "models in a hyperspace without atmosphere . . . never again will the real have to be produced. . . ." The hyperreal is "sheltered from the imaginary, and from any distinction between the real and the imaginary, leaving room only for the orbital recurrance of models and the simulated generation of differences." Indians are simulations in the social

sciences, conceivable models of tribal cultures. "For ethnology to live, its object must die." The posthumous savages, he writes, have "become referential simulacra, and the science itself a pure simulation." (New York: Semiotex(e), 1983) 3, 4, 13, 15.

8. David Carroll, *The Subject in Question* (Chicago: The University of Chicago Press, 1982) 117.

9. Carroll, "Narrative," 77.

10. Carroll, "Narrative," 75. He wrote, "Hundreds, thousands of little dissident narratives of all sorts are produced in spite of all attempts to repress them, and they circulate inside and eventually, or even initially, outside the boundaries of the totalitarian state. The importance of these little narratives is not only that they challenge the dominant metanarrative and the state apparatus that would prohibit or discredit them, but that they also indicate the possibility of another kind of society, or another form of social relations. . . ."

11. Patricia Hampl, *Spillville* (Minneapolis: Milkweed Editions, 1987) 82.

12. Hampl 9.

13. Hampl 82.

14. Hampl 90.

15. Burton Benedict, ed., *The Anthropology of World's Fairs* (London: Scolar Press; Berkeley: The Lowie Museum of Anthropology, 1983) 58.

16. Hampl 92.

17. Hampl 94.

18. Hampl 98–99.

19. Oleg Cassini, *In My Own Fashion: An Autobiography* (New York: Simon and Schuster, 1987) 359.

20. Wayne King, "Navajos Plan Luxury Resort for Tourists on Reservation," *New York Times*, October 28, 1987.

21. Cassini 360, 61, 62.

22. Mikhail Bakhtin, *Mikhail Bakhtin: The Dialogical Principle* by Tzvetan Todorov (Minneapolis: University of Minnesota Press, 1984) 99–100.

23. Francis Paul Prucha, *The Indians in American Society* (Berkeley: University of California Press, 1985) 7.

24. Prucha 8–9.

25. Arnold Krupat, *For Those Who Come After: A Study of Native American Autobiography* (Berkeley: University of California Press, 1985) 4.

26. Michael Castro, *Interpreting the Indian: Twentieth-Century Poets and the Native American* (Albuquerque: University of New Mexico Press, 1983) xiv.

27. Richard Sewall, *The Vision of Tragedy* (New Haven: Yale University Press, 1959) 1.

28. Aldous Huxley, "Tragedy and the Whole Truth," *Virginia Quarterly Review*, April 1931: 177–82.

29. Walter Kerr, *Tragedy and Comedy* (New York: Simon & Schuster, 1968) 36.

30. Kerr 135.

31. Paul Watzlawick, ed., *The Invented Reality* (New York: W. W. Norton, 1984) 63. John Berger provides an unusual distinction between opposition and separation. In *And Our Faces, My Heart Brief As Photos* (New York: Pantheon Books, 1894 89), he wrote, "The opposite of to love is not to hate but to separate. If love and hate have something in common it is because, in both cases, their energy is that of bringing and holding together—the lover with the loved, the one who hates with the hated. Both passions are tested by separation."

32. Wylie Sypher, "The Meaning of Comedy" *Comedy*, ed. Wylie Sypher (Baltimore: Johns Hopkins University Press, 1956) 223–24.

33. Sypher, 252–53.

34. Arthur Koestler, "The Act of Creation" *Bricks to Babel* (New York: Random House, 1980) 330.

35. Kerr 15.

36. Jean-Paul Sartre, *Being and Nothingness* (Secaucus, New Jersey: The Citadel Press, 1956) 461. "Adventures are stories, and one does not *live* a story," wrote Iris Murdoch in *Sartre: Romantic Rationalist*. Stories are told later, "one can only see it from the outside. The meaning of an adventure comes from its conclusion. . . . But when one is inside an event, one is not thinking of it. One can live or tell; not both at once. When one is living, nothing happens." (New York: Viking, 1987) 39–40. Trickster discourse reveals narrative contradictions in representation, simulation, comic adventures, liberation, and nothingness.

37. Rollo May, *The Courage to Create* (New York: W. W. Norton, 1975) 77.

38. Joseph Meeker, *The Comedy of Survival: Studies in Literary Ecology* (New York: Charles Scribner's Sons, 1972) 39, 192.

2

Technology and Tribal Narrative

KARL KROEBER

In 1969 N. Scott Momaday was awarded the Pulitzer Prize for fiction for his novel *House Made of Dawn*; as if the award resolved all critical issues, the novel's strangeness as novel has never been adequately investigated. It begins and ends with Jemez formulaic words for beginning a traditional story, *dypahloh*, and for concluding, *qtsedaba*, though Momaday himself neither belongs to the Jemez Pueblo nor is a speaker of its language. He is the son of a Kiowa father and a Cherokee mother who moved away from Oklahoma, first into Navajo country and later close to their jobs at the Jemez Pueblo. And, as Momaday himself has insisted, the Kiowas, whom he considers his tribal people, wandered into Oklahoma only in historically recent times. In so moving they began to conceive of themselves in a new fashion almost at the moment of their virtual destruction as a culture by white American society. Momaday's personal displacements thus echo those of his people, and one is tempted to read the protagonist of his novel as echoing Momaday's own difficulties in establishing his Indian identity. Yet that protagonist appears in a novel in English; Momaday uses a non-native language and generic form to evoke and articulate possibilities of being Indian. The culture which alienated Momaday from his people authorizes the language and form of his art.

Perhaps the simplest illustration of the complexity in which Momaday's art is entangled is the title, *House Made of Dawn*—an English translation of words from one of the Navajo healing ceremonies, another language and culture foreign to Momaday. He engages in these anomalies, I believe, so as to turn back *on itself* the form of the novel, for that form is expressive of forces that weakened and scattered the Kiowa, destroying his "native" literary heritage. Given his circumstances, especially his deprivation of a native language, Momaday was almost compelled to write the kind of novel he did. We can't seriously engage with his artistry until we go beyond clichés about "ethnic fiction" to recognize the agonistic contradictions in which *House Made of Dawn* is rooted. Momaday invents imaginatively to evoke an "Indianness" for his readers (a majority of whom presumably will not be Indians) through an Anglo-American literary structure that must prohibit any authentically Indian imaginative form.

Necessarily therefore, Momaday's fiction is ambivalently inconclusive and self-frustrating. The variety of interpretations it has provoked, from disputes about the significance of details to arguments about whether its overall effect is optimistic or pessimistic, testifies to its being a novel by an Indian dramatizing the inappropriateness of the genre for the expression of his Indianness.

Because *House Made of Dawn* is not a perfect novel, it is important to distinguish intrinsic contradictions in Momaday's complex effort at creative imagining from more superficial problems, such as stylistic flaws. The influence of writers such as Lawrence, Conrad and Hemingway, for example, is at times jarringly obtrusive, as when the Navajo Benally remembers his childhood.

> You could smell the coffee and hear it boiling in the pot, even after he took it off the fire and poured it into the cups. You could see it, how black and hot it was, and there was a lot of smoke coming out of the cups. You had to let it set a while because the cups were made of enamelware and they could burn your hands. It was hard to wait, because you were cold and you knew how good it was going to taste. But the meat cooked right away and you could pick it up and it made your fingers warm. The fat was full of juice and smoke, and sometimes there was a little burned crust on it, hard black flakes that you could feel on your teeth, and the meat was tough and good to chew. And after a while you could pick up the cup and hold it in your hands.[1]

More bothersome than this simple imitativeness is Momaday's relentless symbolizing, which constantly threatens to transform realistic narrative into schematic allegory. A spectacular instance is the Albino, the protagonist Abel kills after being humiliated by him in the rooster-pull contest. At issue is not whether there was an unusually high incident of albinism at the Jemez Pueblo, but that, given the nature of Momaday's story about Indians, no reader, red or white, can avoid perceiving the Albino as symbolically overdetermined. One must agree with Larry Evers' interpretation that the Albino represents the white man *in* Abel, but one notices also that the representation occurs through schematic symbolizing. Thus, to follow Evers, the killing dramatizes Abel's failure genuinely to confront and come to terms with alien forces inside himself. The murder makes Abel vulnerable to those forces as they press on him from outside, specifically represented in the murderous beating given him by the sadistic policeman, Martinez. The rigidity of this patterning prohibits the reader from experiencing the complicated reality of Abel's self-alienated condition. What is not realized for the reader—the very efficacy of the physical description of the murder helps to block such realization—is that Abel's assumption of a personal "duty" to kill the "evil" Albino *violates* the fashion in which the Jemez community would exorcize such a malignancy. Abel's action reduces a social or cultural evilness to the status of personal enemy. Because the Jemez community is really alien to Momaday, the only way for him to dramatize its potency is in this negative fashion that renders obscure the nature of the identity Abel seeks.

The elusiveness of the "Indianness" Abel strives to recover in *House Made of Dawn* is illustrated by Momaday's dependence on white ethnographers. The title and the central image of the novel are taken from Washington Matthews, and one crucial passage is an almost literal reprint of his translation of a prayer from the Navajo *Night Chant*,[2] Momaday's principal changes are, as Floyd Watkins puts it with revealing naivete, "leaving out prepositions and articles . . . [to gain] an effect of the starkness of a primitive language like Anglo-Saxon."[3] Momaday hadn't the least intention of representing Navajo as a primitive language, but he opens his work to such dim-witted misunderstanding by his reliance on a white translation of an Indian artistic/religious spirit he wishes to recover. Here, as with the rooster-pull ceremony drawn from Leslie White and with the very use of the novel form, Momaday is caught up in a hazardous contradiction between his theme and the means available to him for its artistic evocation.

Because the cultures Momaday represents are not native to him, he relies on reports of white ethnographers whose accuracy on specific and limited details may defeat his deepest purposes. This novel would not alert the uninformed reader to the full range of hostilities between Pueblos and Navajos. The "Indianness" Abel's story defines is thus simplified and "falsified," the full integrity of Pueblo and Navajo cultures (which creates the oppositions between them) being elided. Momaday's difficulties are representative of the frustrating self-conflicts faced by any Indian using an Anglo-American literary form to assert the validity of a native vision against the overwhelming power of Euro-American culture. Momaday illustrates his problem (implicit in the untranslated words that begin and end a novel that is *not* a Jemez traditional story) with graphic brilliance by having *House Made of Dawn* start and conclude with Abel running, not with, but *behind* the communal runners from the Pueblo.

Less successful is the figure of Tosamah, who never becomes integrated into Abel's life story. He is a clown and a Priest of the Sun,[4] ludicrous yet "full of authority."[5] His conduct of peyote ceremonies seems indebted to Weston La Barre's book, *The Peyote Cult*, and his sermon, "The Way to Rainy Mountain," is from Momaday's own book of that title describing Kiowa history. Less derivative is Tosamah's first sermon on The Word, from the perspective of the gospel according to St. John, which Tosamah interprets as leading mankind to "perish by the Word." Such words used by the Kiowa "were medicine; they were magic . . . no medicine was ever more powerful."[6]

Tosamah is an unmistakable version of Coyote, the most familiar guise of the trickster.

> the drapes parted and the Priest of the Sun appeared, moving shadow-like to the lectern. He was shaggy and awful-looking in the thin, naked light: big, lithe as a cat, narrow-eyed, suggesting in the whole of his look and manner both arrogance and agony. . . . he had the voice of a great dog.[7]

His sermons seem entirely appropriate to the trickster's role in modern discourse as defined by Vizenor:

> The trickster is a chance, a comic holotrope in a postmodern language game that unconvers distinctions and ironies between narrative voices; a semiotic sign for "social antagonism" and "aesthetic activism" in postmodern criticism and the avant-garde, but not "presence" or ideal cultural completion in narratives.[8]

But in fact Tosamah's sermons are not integral to the development of *House Made of Dawn*, as is suggested by the second sermon's derivation from another work. The words are trickster words, one might say, but the art in which they occur renders them unefficacious. For Momaday the trickster is a peripheral, distanced speaker, not the center of the agonistic *displacement* experience, which he feels as the core of contemporary Indian personal and tribal experience. Yet, one must wonder, is not the conventionally realistic form of his fiction even more peripheral to the crisis it would articulate? May it not be that Tosamah, as is suggested by his use of Momaday's *The Way to Rainy Mountain*, articulates better than Abel the mode in which the author may find that from which he has been displaced? Perhaps something like a parodic sermon, a truly trickster form, might serve Momaday's deepest purposes better than the Euro-American novel?

Instead of adapting an Indian mode of presentation, Momaday relies, as Evers has pointed out, on a sense of place. He defines the recovery of an Indian identity as coming through identification with a physical locale. In Evers' words, "following D. H. Lawrence," Momaday's "sense of place derives from the perception of a culturally imposed symbolic order on a particular physical topography."[9] But neither Abel nor Momaday possesses access to a communal existence that would permit efficacious cultural imposition of a symbolic order. This is exactly the problem at the center of *House Made of Dawn*. Abel is inarticulate, as Momaday is without fluency in any native tongue. Without language there can be no imposition of a culture's symbolic order on physical surroundings. Abel's inarticulateness reflects Momaday's generic deprivation. The very form of his work testifies to his impotence to impose a symbolic order other than one structured by the culture he would resist, or pass through, to recover a different order, an order that would not use language novelistically.

It is the agonistic nature of Momaday's novel that empowered subsequent Native American writers of fiction. Given Momaday's circumstances he could not have written a less contradictory novel than he did. But in so honestly creating a fiction whose form inevitably (not accidentally) frustrates the aspirations that brought it into being, to celebrate a native culture's resistance to the overwhelming Euro-American culture, he displayed for following Native American novelists the most fundamental problem of their endeavor.

What Momaday's so painfully but courageously confronted is made clear by a temporal coincidence. In 1968, just a few months before

Momaday was awarded the Pulitzer Prize, a linguist named Anthony Mattina sat down with a Colville Indian named Peter Seymour and tape-recorded a five-hour story Seymour told in Colville, a language Mattina did not then understand. A translation with verbatim text in Colville and commentary by Mattina, who has since learned the language, was published in 1985 by the University of Arizona Press under the title of Seymour's tale, *The Golden Woman*. It will never win a Pulitzer, but *The Golden Woman* is a marvelous story and may be regarded as a more important literary work than Momaday's novel when our society understands that such material is not merely folkloristic or anthropological or linguistic *data*, but may also be art, even art of a high order. The rest of this essay is dedicated to the development of such understanding because, until we can so perceive works such as *The Golden Woman*, we lack the basis to assess fully the difficulties faced and the successes achieved by contemporary Native American novelists.

Seymour's *Golden Woman* is more remote in language but no farther from us in time than Momaday's novel. It is no less an authentic work of art, even though linguists, folklorists and anthropologists may obscure its artistry simply by doing their proper work. By demonstrating the narrative's self-testing values critics may serve both their discipline and the cause of Native American literature. Perhaps because they are ethnographically and linguistically ignorant, critics conscious of their limitations may focus attention on formal achievements to which other specialists are professionally indifferent. In any event, as such a critic I believe that *The Golden Woman* affirms as an immediate, unique experience of telling, as a current event if you will, the self-knowledge and self-respect of Colville culture in its hour of dissolution. Here a Colville storyteller has been driven to a device worthy of the finest trickster: finding artistic viability by making use of the technology of white civilization that has marginalized the Colville. Seymour's art consists in telling *their* story into *their* recording device in a fashion that preserves *his* way of telling.

The free translation of *The Golden Woman* occupies about thirty pages and can be read in less than one-half hour, although the taping of the telling took some five hours. This ratio between speed of hearing and speed of silent reading is a fair measure of the difference between the usual speed of reception of written and oral literature, though "reception theorists" have paid little attention to the distinction. But temporal comparison is complicated and enriched in the case of *The Golden Woman* because its form is what folklorists, borrowing from music, call a "round"—a story that repeats a part or parts of itself at one or more points. Understandably, the central repetition of *The Golden Woman* is not included in Mattina's translation, since it must have taken the better part of an hour's telling. Written literature never uses so much verbatim repetition—a written text can easily be reread. In oral performance only literal repeating makes possible reevaluations analogous to those evocable through rereading.

Seymour's mammoth "round" cautions us to think carefully about the circumstances of *this* telling. Seymour, who had met Mattina for the first time only a few days before, spoke into a tape recorder operated by the linguist who, because he didn't understand Colville, couldn't know what Seymour was telling. Seymour's only audience was the tape. So what kind of a story did he tell? A round, which seems an appropriate choice of form, since he was, in one sense, talking to himself. Yet Mattina's account of his subsequent friendship with Seymour suggests that the peculiar circumstances of the telling were necessary. Mattina is positive that had he "organized a story-telling session with audience, atmosphere, the works, Seymour wouldn't have performed."[10]

Seymour, Mattina tells us, was aware that his children and grandchildren weren't interested in long stories. Other elders never listened to his tales. So one may suspect that Seymour's telling is among other things a comment on his situation as a Colville storyteller in 1968. Because *The Golden Woman* is a European fairy tale transferred into a Western American setting, it may be interpreted as depicting the intrusion upon the Colville of white culture. Both formally and substantively Seymour's *Golden Woman* tells us about the conditions in which he now must tell. Late in the story, the "king," wanting a crowd at his wedding, tells "all the telephone operators . . . You telephone operators, you telephone to all the kings like me here on earth" (44). This amusingly updates fairytale style, but the anachronism also suggests problematics of superimposing devices of modern technology on oral discourse. Telephone and tape recorder testify that the range and durability of speech have been increased by a technological civilization which jeopardizes oral literary traditions founded on the simple and direct relations manifested in fairy tales. Ethnologists and folklorists have long been congratulating themselves on the benefits of tape recorders to their work. Peter Seymour may be the first "informant" to exploit the machine to increase the recursive functions of a traditional telling, and thereby provide literary criticism with insight into how narrative art may insert itself into complexly hostile socio-cultural situations.

The recorder allows the construction of a continuous narrative out of an intermittent telling, which draws our attention to the aesthetics of time, a topic but little investigated. Seymour and Mattina discussed the potential soporific effects of storytelling, and mention is made of a story "so long that those listening to it went to sleep before it was concluded." This might well have happened had Seymour told a live audience a five-hour tale containing many repetitions. In a story that contains so much repetition will those who *don't* sleep be attentive? Wherein lies the satisfaction to Peter Seymour, speaking into a tape recorder, to repeat himself for an hour?

I suspect that such questions should consider the peculiar position of the tale teller, any teller. Mattina deserves credit for reminding us of the self-isolating aspects of artistry, even in oral performance. Even in a communal society the artist is to some degree a loner. However sustaining of his culture and supported by it, a master teller endows his stories with qualities we now term aesthetic, which are not fully defined by specific cultural restraints, coercions and inspirations. In societies that do not distinguish a separate domain of "the aesthetic" an artist's self-conscious artistry will be much more isolated. The apochryphal blindness attributed to Homer may symbolize how even the founder of a tradition works in and through an essential loneliness.

In any event, some awareness of the difficulties of his situation seem to motivate Seymour's self-deprecating references to his storytelling as "BS-ing" (2). Given the deteriorating condition of Colville culture in 1968, what can the native teller do but BS? Is he lamenting that he is now reduced to mere fairytale telling? May there not be a bitter personal irony beneath the obvious irony in telling a white man a story from the white man's culture made ludicrous by its transposition into terms and situations of white-corrupted Indian culture?

It isn't easy to answer such questions because Seymour's narrative skill conceals what is painful and probing under an easy, charming meta-commentary. He observes how, in this genre, information gets picked up quickly: "that's fairy tales for you, it travels fast, and its got no feet" (37). But one notices that the adaptations of motifs, plot devices, and formulaic situations are congenial to sharp critiques of familiar conditions of our contemporary world of telephones, airplanes and radios. At the end of his telling Seymour remarks to the tape recorder that he has been *teaching*, perhaps that a fairy tale may be utilized for aims presumably remote from those in which the genre originated. This includes comment on how the white culture in which fairy tales originated has intruded into the narrative traditions of Seymour's people.

Seymour's story constantly involves itself in problems of genre translation. It calls our attention to difficulties today in Western America of evoking a king, magic birds or seeking one's fortune—the last of which in Seymour's telling becomes finding a job as a carpenter, housepainter or dishwasher. If we knew more about how Seymour learned the tale, we could assess more usefully the significance of his transformations. He learned the tale, he told Mattina, from someone named Lisette, about whom Mattina discovered nothing. But Mattina believes that Seymour had heard the story fifty years earlier. We can only say with assurance that *The Golden Woman* is a Colville transformation of a European form only slightly and obscurely connected to any Colville tradition of telling, though our scholarship has not yet even considered the possibility of such a tradition. Yet just as the marvelous pictures on the walls of Lascaux could only have been created by people who had learned an extraordinary skill, so Seymour's narrative skill also must owe something to a traditional storytelling art.

Like most readers of the Arizona volume I do not read Seymour's language but the English translation, which is primarily that of a bilingual Colville woman, Mary Madeline deSautel. Her translations, Mattina says, "were loose—certainly not morpheme by morpheme, and never even word by word. She translated Colville into the English she normally spoke, and I wrote it the way she spoke" (9). Mattina's forthrightness and clarity in confronting the hazards of his decision to use this translation are admirable. The decision to accept deSautel's "Red English," a substandard English characteristic of many Indians, is reasonable if only because the story itself is about the penetration of Euro-American culture into Colville life. But the "continuous translation" of deSautel differs from the verbatim text taken from the tapes and difficulties arise when the two are juxtaposed. An example of detail: the

Colville word translated in the first paragraph and elsewhere as "chief" is usually (though not always, for instance, line 370) translated as "king" when applied to the protagonist's boss. A more subtle question posed by metaphors is remarked on by Mattina (65): there does seem to be the possibility of a systematic correlation in Seymour's telling, but not in deSautel's translation, of physical height and depth with psychological states of pride and envy. In general, deSautel seems to add a good deal, though some part of her additions are in fact renderings of details given by Seymour in one of his repetitions and then shifted by Mattina into the "original" narrative. Space prevents discussion of the fascinating translation problems posed by this text, and normally I cite from deSautel's rendering, although in the passage that is the narrative's climax, I use the verbatim translation of Seymour's words.

The Golden Woman tells how the youngest of four sons, with the aid of a magic horse, rescues his brothers from death after they have left home to seek their fortunes. Jealous of, rather than grateful to, their savior, the elder brothers plot to destroy him. They maneuver him into being sent to steal from the man-eater who had nearly killed them a pair of golden birds. The boy succeeds and presents the birds to the king of the country to which the brothers have come, but his siblings then have him sent to capture a strange sea creature for the king—the Golden Woman. The boy does capture her, but she falls in love with him. She schemes to have the golden birds tell a story at a gathering the king has convened to celebrate his marriage to her. The birds tell the story we have heard of the younger brother rescuing his elders. Hearing the story awakens the youngster to his worth and to the Golden Woman's love for him. She poisons the king and marries the youngest son.

Mattina identifies this as story type 531 in the Aarne-Thompson classification scheme, but analogues are less important to the tale than Seymour's ingenious interplaying of realism and humor. This serves as the ground for his implicit commentary on white-red relations, launched by his first sentences.

One tribe of people was sitting around, it's one town, one big town, but I don't know the name of the town. It's nothing but a fairy tale. And they have a chief in that town, they have a big chief, and he's important, and he's got more than one son, four of them, all boys. It's early spring and the snow is all gone, school was over, and the three oldest went to see their father (19).

The white-Indian confrontation of a "town" consisting of a "tribe of people sitting around" is self-reflexively deepened by the apparently deprecating comment, "It's nothing but a fairy tale." For the remark sets up a conscious interaction between what narratologists call *histoire* and *recit*—events told of and telling, that interplay being a central dynamic in Seymour's performance. He thus persistently brings into question the authority of his narrative. One aspect of this self-contestation is his intersecting of literal and metaphoric at crucial junctures, such as when we are told that the protagonist is "in a good track" though he is literally wandering in a storm. Beneath all rhetorical and figurative interpenetrations is the fundamental one of white fairy tale being reworked through a Colvillian telling into the white man's recording machine to teach the white man something of the red man's art.

After the father agrees to let his sons travel he orders his hired man to equip them with the best horses, saddles, spurs and so forth, and gives them money.

> "You don't know where you're going, and you don't know the country, and then you won't know the people when you get there, and maybe you might get hungry. And this is what I give you for your grub. And if you get to a town then you'll have money, and if you go to an eating place you can eat, and you can camp at a hotel, and you can put your horses in a barn. You have some money and you can pay for that. But if you don't have money you'll have a bad time" (21).

Throughout the telling this kind of practicality accompanies sardonic comments by the narrator on white ways and incongruities between the systems of contemporary Western life and their system of fairy tales. It is casually suggested that airplanes originated from the example of the magic flying horse (39). When the youngest brother gets into the saddle of the magic horse, the narrator reminds us that a few sentences earlier he had been described as too small to get into the saddle by himself (23). But the profoundest incongruities are more than just amusing.

When the elder brothers have ridden off the youngest boy is told, to his distress, that he is too little to go with them. His mother suggests to his father that he be given a lunch bag, a few pennies and an old pair of chaps and that he be set on an ancient horse that can scarcely walk. This will make the boy happy, he can't get far, and "then he won't get feeling bad, he won't get sick over it" (22). Sure enough, the old horse

barely gets over the first ridge before collapsing. In frustration the boy
beats the animal, who says to him:

> "Please have pity on me, little boy, I'm not doing this on purpose. It's
> not my fault I'm to the limit of my oldness, my breath is all out of me,
> and I'm weak-boned" (22).

When the boy, angry and crying, continues to beat the horse,

> All at once something spoke to him from above. "Leave that poor thing
> alone, pity your horse, I'll pity you." He raised his head, gee, he seen a
> beautiful horse, pretty as a picture. . . . That beautiful horse told him:
> "Hurry, get on, or you'll be too late to save your brothers. They're just
> getting to the man-eater . . . if you take your time they'll be dead. You
> keep staring at me. Let's get close to their heels. Hurry and get on. (23)

The establishment of a ground for parallelism here is adroit, as it is
whenever Seymour exploits the age-youth motif. The frustration of the
helpless boy invokes the magic horse. Later, the boy's frustration at the
failure of the horse's magic leads him to drive the horse away. From
that point on the fairy tale is not so magical. Fairy tales move fast without feet, Seymour tells us, but they carry you only so far. After having
beaten the magic horse the boy becomes bitterly self-accusatory. "I'm
disgusted with myself," he says; "it's all caused from my bad temper that
put me in bad. My horse left me because I licked him. Now I'm disgusted with myself." (40) As the boy cries and wanders off, all at once:

> he got on a good track, and then it started to rain. It rained and the wind
> blowed close to the shore, and there were waves. It was on a good track,
> and he ran into some baby eagles, just hatched, two of them. They
> didn't have a feather on their body. They were just a-shivering from the
> cold. He felt sorry for them. he started to gather pine needles, anything
> to make a fire, and he started building a fire for the baby chicks, the
> eagle babies. And they got warmed up. (40)

Once again the boy hears a sound from above. This time it is the
parent eagles returning—they had been delayed by the storm. In grati-
tude to the boy for saving their children they encourage him to try
once more to capture the Golden Woman. Taken captive at last, she
begins to take charge of the story. With her capture the surprises of

magic are replaced by more realistic wonders. She suggests, "We just as well get married. Your the one that took me" (42). She thinks, "He isn't for nothing, this little fellow is something to grow for, or he wouldn't have caught me. . . . this outstanding kid got me. He must be smart." But the boy demurs, saying, "No, I'm working. I got a boss for my job." He thinks of himself as "not qualified for nothing" (42). So he takes her to the king, who observes, "now I see you, I am a well-satisfied king" (43).

> He told all the telephone operators: "You telephone operators, you tele-phone to all the kings like me here on earth, and the important people, they'll get here also. And you send an invitation to all those around here. There's no old or young. Everybody's going to gather here to-night." (44).

Only the boy refuses to go to the party, telling the king's cook for whom he washes dishes as a regular occupation that he is too "pityful" and dirty and possessed of only old clothes. But the king wants every-body, and two sheriffs are sent for the boy, who protests. In an action that recalls his capture of the Golden Woman, "they grabbed him by the arms, he tried to squirm around, they walked off with him." (45). With everyone present, at the Golden Woman's behest the golden birds tell a story, which is exactly the story we have heard of the broth-ers' rescue from the man-eater. But this telling is marked by by-play between rooster and hen. There is a question of which should tell the story, with a sharp dig at white men's sham politeness to women (46). Of course the rooster is the one to tell the story, but he occasionally questions the hen: "Am I telling it right?" And the hen answers, "Yes, you're telling it right. That's just what you done" (47). This large round ends in a passage I cite from the verbatim translation. It is a moment at which, starting a new tape, Seymour splices his story. He connects one tape to its predecessors as the two tellings, one within the other, dove-tail. This is the crucial moment in the narrative because here the story finally breaks its repetitive patterning. And this narrative transforma-tion is expressive of the decisive maturation of the protagonist. This use of narrative form within the story is the result—within the nar-rative—of stage-managing by the Golden Woman. Her scheme is to have the boy, through hearing an account of what he has done, awaken to what he may be qualified for, not least being herself.

---

611. Well, as they say in my language, in Colville, I am going to splice my fairy tale, *The Golden Woman*.

612. That's where I stopped telling my story; he was telling his story the rooster with the hen, the golden birds.

613. and the rooster is telling a story, to all the people, and indeed that's what the boy did, that's what he's telling.

614. He's telling what he did; and the boy like he forgot what happened to him.

615. And she thought of a plan the Golden Woman, because to the boy that caught her, that's where her heart is, that's who she wants to marry.

616. And the king is too old; and that's why all of this she thought out.

617. When he's telling his story the rooster, maybe he'll wake up (and) remember the boy what happened to him, and then they'll get married.

618. That's what is told to the people, and he tells the rooster (to) the hen, "Is it true what I've done?"

619. Then she winks at him the woman, the hen, she winks at him the hen, and she says, "Yes, yes, yes, that's what you've done."

620. Certainly I know this is what you've done, and if I had told the story, I wouldn't have everything known that that you've done.

621. And always I love you. I want you to marry me.

622. The boy like he woke up.

623. "I have done that, what he's been telling about me."

624. He woke up, and he thought that's he whose deeds they're telling to all the people.

625. Not ever do birds talk to one another, or just talk; these are the man-eater's birds, that's why they talk (and) tell about themselves.

626. Well, this boy as soon as he realized that it's his deeds (being talked about) by the rooster, he disappeared.

627. They didn't realize it, and just to the birds they were listening.

628. Then they missed the boy, he's gone, he must have slipped out.

629. Then his brothers got the belly ache.

630. He told them the king: "Don't anybody go out." (208–13)

The repetition of the earlier part of the narrative becomes fully meaningful in this passage, because it is only through hearing *as a story* what he in fact had done that the boy becomes aware of the significance of his acts, the qualities he possesses. If the first decisive step into maturation was his compassionate aiding of the young eagles, the second is the subtler and more profound recognition of himself as a worthy person, above all else a person worthy of affection and qualified for love. Within Seymour's story such recognition comes from hearing the story. Implicit in the recursive pattern is a definition also of the complex preciousness of storytelling: it creates consciousness of the meaning of what has happened to us. So, too, *The Golden Woman* articulates an understanding of what has happened to the Colville culture, specifically that it now finds viability only through using the white American culture that has overwhelmed it. Seymour tells their story into their recording device so as to preserve his way of telling.

Sustaining his heritage by means of the force that is destroying it Seymour exploits a primary, if not *the* primary, function of the narrative. Events occur in the natural world, even sequences of events, but not stories. Stories are human tellings about events, their principal aim is to give a human meaning to events. The recursiveness within *The Golden Woman* reminds us that the narrative as a whole is a repetition. The longest repeat of the story is the story itself. Such repeating, which the tape recorder mechanically facilitates, is valuable because it makes possible new meanings, renewed assessments and refined evaluations. The story repeated is a means not only of sustaining but also of changing established judgments of a personal life, the life of a society, the life of our kind.

Awareness of narrative function is made a significant thematic element within *The Golden Woman* by Seymour. The boy's unwillingness to come to the king's party expresses his sense of being unqualified, even though we judge that, as the one who captured the Golden Woman, he is most qualified. He does not judge his character and behavior well because, though he has done remarkable things he has not yet defined his accomplishments to himself. Maturity, this tale implies, depends not merely on acting responsibly but also on possessing the ability to assess one's actions consciously, because only then is one's responsible behavior usable as a model and capable of being repeated and modified.

In the first part of the tale the boy follows the magic horse's directions. His actions at the man-hunter's are not described because the horse tells him beforehand in the most complete detail what he should do. These instructions are substituted for an account of the action when they actually occur. When the horse finishes his instructions we are told, "and that's what happened" (27). The proof that Seymour's repetitions are purposeful is here, where an opportunity to repeat is superseded by a gigantic prolepsis.

The proleptic telling illustrates American Indian narrators' consistent preference for prefiguration instead of suspense. They know what contemporary reception theorists usually seem to forget: stories are always retold. The important portion of a tale's audience already knows the story. For them and anyone who returns to a narrative, prefiguration takes account of this foreknowledge. It is a means by which an informed listener is enabled to reenter creatively into a familiar telling. Prefiguring allows the imagination of informed listeners to reshape what has, for them, already happened at least once. Story-telling is repeating; within narrative, prefiguration serves a function analogous to the total act of telling a story. It gives a new, retrospective order through its reiteration of events that have already occurred in a linear sequence: the telling begins only at the end of the sequence, as rehearing begins at the end of an antecedent telling.

Under the conditions of oral narration, of course, the only way the protagonist in a story such as *The Golden Woman* can arrive at self-awareness is through hearing of himself in a tale within the story. Such a narrative-within-a-narrative allows listeners to appreciate the protagonist's transformation because for them the inset is a repeated tale. yet the effectiveness of such a repetition would seem to depend profoundly on our emotional involvement with the protagonist. To someone who doesn't care about the boy in *The Golden Woman* a repetition of his adventures can only be boring. Repetition of the kind used by Seymour brings to the foreground a principle of narrative underestimated by almost all contemporary narratologists: narrative functions through emotion. Stories have affects, and all aspects of their functioning are grounded in the emotional biases they have evoked. A story functions well when the developing configurations of its plot and themes integrate with the emotional patterns it creates.

This principle is illustrated in *The Golden Woman's* development of the theme of love. One of the man-eater's baits is her "grand-daughters," and her house is, in effect, a brothel. There the "grandmother" is tricked by the boy into killing her granddaughters, the event dramatizing the house's perversion of love. Genuine love, because it involves more than sexual attraction, is best dramatized by the Golden Woman's scheme to change her wedding from the king she doesn't love to the boy she does. Her affection for him is inseparable from her assessment of his potential as a man, of which he himself is unaware. Her plot is to have the golden birds tell a story within the story which is, in fact, the first part of the story we have heard. The golden birds' collaboration is revealed when the rooster asks the hen, "Is it true what I've done." She winks at him when replying, "yes, yes, yes, yes." The put-up job climaxes with the hen's final, "And I always love you. I want you to marry me." That statement awakens the boy; the birds' dramatic representation arouses his capacity to love. Within Seymour's telling the fairy tale is used to awaken us to possible significancies, some grimly problematic, of fairy-tale telling by a Colville in 1968.

The Golden Woman represents love as impossible for the immature, as in reverse, magic is no longer available to the mature. Therefore, in the crucial passage cited from the verbatim translation, as soon as the boy "wakes up" he disappears. A few sentences later he returns as a man; the Colville words now applied to him are different from those used earlier. Thus, the boy is *ta-twìt* (Seymour, 1. 622), whereas the man who enters (with what seems oedipal speed) immediately follow-ing the king's death is *gal-tmíx* (Seymour, 1.649), the same word used by the Golden Woman about him and translated by deSautel as "hus-band," that is "my man." There is, one may observe parenthetically, a lovely touch of the returner transformed in this scene: the Golden Woman does not at first recognize the handsome young man in good clothes, the reality produced by her device for magical transformation.

Seymour emphasizes the commonplace yet mysterious process of maturing by which a boy vanishes into a man. He stresses the violence of the older brothers' reaction to the Golden Birds' telling. As the young boy vanishes the older brothers, fearing that the birds will con-tinue with the story of their career and so expose their jealous machi-nations, get what Seymour calls "the bellyache." Ready to shit in their pants they make the obvious plea to be excused, but the king denies their request telling his working man, "go and bring in the big tub. Put it right on the floor. Whoever gets the belly ache, he can use it. Don't nobody go out" (49). But the brothers are not publicly exposed; the story has stopped rounding on itself because the Golden Woman, having attained her goal of awakening the boy through the birds' story, says to the king, "There's very different in our age, you're old and I'm just a girl, and don't you think, if we get married, you'll be very sorry, you'll always be jealous, jealous hearted because you're old" (49). Ad-mitting she has a point, the king asks if she knows "a good medicine to make me young again." She sure does:

33

She pulled out of her clothes a bottle, a little bottle. She told him: "You drink this, drink it at once, and then you'll be back ten years younger towards a boy. And then we'll be even. Take it." She gave it to him, he took it down at once. Must be just a little spoonful, just one swallow, and it's gone. He did like that, the king has spasms, he let go and fell on his back, he just quivered. The people and the kings all rushed to him on both sides, there was a doctor there, but he didn't have no medicine. They rushed him to the hospital, but he never come to, he's dead. He's still dead. (49)

Among marvelous reports of the death of kings, this ranks alongside that of Babar's predecessor. But this king's fate is exemplary of a childish (as distinct from a child's) belief in magic, a foolish faith in an easy reversal of the fundamental order of things. Through the magic of fairy tale (the story retold by the golden birds) the young protagonist is awakened to the truth of his being. The truth of such narrative is truth to human desires and needs. This is why in fairy tales, as in children's make believe, magic power is not so much sought as given; magic is the validation of desire. In seeking a literal, logical, merely physical magic to make himself young again, the king asks for a lie and he gets it. He's still got it.

As Jean Paul Sartre said, we live in one direction but tell of our lives in the other, so the authentic magic of narrative art seeks not to deny natural facts but to improve on them, to transform them into a natural-human reality, to make the natural socially meaningful. Although the protagonist in our story must begin the process of his maturation, he requires help to complete that development, as we all do because we are social creatures needing the fulfillment available only through friends, a lover, community. Assistance comes to our young man through a story of his adventures. The story brings truth because it reveals, as only story can, the human significance of events it narrates.

The Golden Woman's self-reflexivity, then, is neither merely decorative, traditional nor structural, but thematically functional. Through the Golden Woman's mode of awakening her lover Seymour conveys to us what Percy Shelley articulated more abstractly in his "Defence of Poetry." He observed that "neither the eye nor the mind can see itself, unless reflected upon that which resembles itself." Shelley went on to argue that by showing us our minds literature teaches us not only self-knowledge but also self-respect.[11] Shelley was a Romantic poet. Recent critics have had little to say about art fostering self-respect, in part because they have not been concerned with how works of art make their way into processes of social development or deterioration. Recent criticism has preferred to explain the context of art from the perspective of the context and to analyze art in terms of the nonartistic. But, as this contrast of *The Golden Woman* and *House Made of Dawn* is meant to show, there is much to be learned by examining how works of art enter, unasked, into a socio-cultural context and also from evaluating the contexts of the artwork from the perspective of its act of creative intrusion.

I have tried to show that we miss the agony at the heart of *House Made of Dawn* if we ignore Momaday's struggle with a form inherently in contradiction to the profound purposes in his art. We miss an even more valuable insight (as well as another poignant experience) if we fail to recognize how Seymour's *The Golden Woman* is slyly inserted into our literature to confirm the self-respect of Colville culture even as we destroy it. In an adaptation of tricksterism to contemporary conditions, Seymour uses Western technology to exemplify how a Colville imagination could reshape one of our narrative forms. He thus teaches us that our kind of "progress" destroys diverse modes of imagining. Yet through Seymour's reworking of a European fairy tale, Colville imagining, is now a precious part of our heritage. Without even being able to operate it, Seymour used a tape recorder to save what his people could no longer save for themselves, including a critique of what destroyed them. The test of our criticism's worth is whether we can appreciate the artistic significance of that critique.

Appendix
Criticism and Translation

My comments on themes in *The Golden Woman* raise several complex issues which may be focused by asking whether, as critics now seem to take for granted, love is indeed the same the whole world over? May there not be diverse artistic forms of expression for basic feelings, relationships and conditions of being (love, maturation, a sense of self-identity, for instance) because these are experienced differently in different societies thanks to divergencies in cultural forms? In *The Golden Woman* the central intersection of affection and awareness occurs most intensely in the word deSautel and Mattina translate as "pity." Mattina calls attention to the importance of the Colville root for this word, *qwən.* He suggests a variety of possible connotations and notes that the term is significant throughout the Salishan family of languages, citing Reichard's comment on a Coeur d'Alene cognate (66). To someone not versed in Salishan, "compassion" often seems a more appropriate translation of *qwən* words, since "pity" has connotations of sentimentality. But "compassion" lacks the common adjectival forms of "pitiable" and "pitiful" that appear at critical moments in Seymour's story. A "pitiable' creature seems to be one not merely in a bad way nor begging for sympathy but one worthy of receiving the benefit of intelligent emotional investment from another and capable of responding appropriately to affection and generosity. Thus, another's "taking pity" opens the way to emotional reciprocity. Therefore, "love" might often be a truer translation than "pity," because both active and passive aspects of an emotional relation can be encompassed by the Colville usage. Specific interpretations of particular usages are tricky because our literature does not often represent characters presenting themselves as "pitiable," not merely of requiring aid or mercy but admitting they are vulnerable and therefore "lovable."

This point has special importance in *The Golden Woman* because of its bearing upon the theme of maturation. To become adult one must become aware that one is deserving of love, only then will he or she be capable of genuinely loving another. So phrased, the theme does not seem alien to non-Indian literature, yet I have difficulty thinking of a western story that deals with the topic in exactly the fashion of the Colville narrative. Maturation is a universal human phenomenon, but cultural differences in how it occurs may require that its representations so differ that description of its archetypal essence obscures, rather than clarifies, one's appreciation of the art of a representation.

I raise this point because of its relevance to Seymour's tale and also its significance to the study of American Indian texts and tellings as literary artifacts. Exactly what the word commonly translated as "pity" or its derivatives and cognates really mean can be determined only by a careful analysis of as many diverse uses as can be located, along with investigations into the contexts in which they occur. For the definition sought in a literary work is of a Wittgensteinian kind, a determination of particular usage. Speculations like mine are intended to stimulate adequate study of the data. I point out possibly directions for exploring linguistic details and urge linguists to focus on a particular problem because it appears to raise issues of interest in more than one discipline. Only detailed linguistic analysis can give the factual basis needed to evaluate such matters as those posed by Seymour's use of *gwan*. Literary critics must suggest narrative *cruxes* and *foci* of structural or thematic developments essential to assessment of a work's artistry.

Notes

1. N. Scott Momaday, *House Made of Dawn* (New York: New American Library, 1969) 141.

2. Momaday 134–135.

3. Floyd C. Watkins, "Culture versus Anonymity in *House Made of Dawn*," Chapter 7, *In Time and Place* (Athens: University of Georgia Press, 1977) 169–70.

4. Momaday 91.

5. Momaday 55.

6. Momaday 89.

7. Momaday 85.

8. Gerald Vizenor, "Trickster Discourse: Comic Holotropes and Language Games," Paper prepared for the School of American Research, Santa Fe, June 1986, and published in this volume.

9. Larry J. Evers, "Words and Place: A Reading of *House Made of Dawn*," *Western American Literature* 11.4 (1977): 297–320.

10. Anthony Mattina, ed. *The Golden Woman: The Colville Narrative of Peter J. Seymour*, trans. Anthony Mattina and Madeline deSautel (Tucson: University of Arizona Press, 1985) 2. Further references to this work appear in the text.

11. Donald Reiman, and Sharon Powers, eds. *Shelley's Poetry and Prose* (New York: W. W. Norton, 1977) 491.

3

The Way to Rainy Mountain:
Momaday's Work in Motion

KIMBERLY BLAESER

Although heralded as a work of innovative form because of its tripartite structure, N. Scott Momaday's *The Way to Rainy Mountain* has not received due recognition as a pioneer among the open works that actively engage the reader in the performance of the text.[1] In the book Momaday professes the power of the imagination to create and activates the imagination of his reader, making the reader co-creator of the literary work. He also acts out the reader/creator role as he responds to Kiowa myth and family history, he reads the past with his imagination, thus providing an example of the life-giving power of the reader's response.

Creator Imagination

Momaday has consistently verbalized his belief in the power of the imagination to act, not simply in a creative manner but as creator of our reality. In an essay entitled "Native American Attitudes to the Environment" he says ". . . we are all . . . at the most fundamental level what we imagine ourselves to be."[2] And in his oft-quoted lecture entitled "Man Made of Words" he likewise states, "We are what we imagine. Our very existence consists in our imagination of ourselves."[3]

In the prologue of *Rainy Mountain* he applies his philosophy regarding the creative power of imagination to the realms of history and literature, commenting on the role imagination plays in the physical, historical, spiritual and verbal journeys portrayed in the text. First, he describes the creative power of his Kiowa ancestors' imagination who, during their migration to Rainy Mountain, came of age as a people because they "conceived a good idea of themselves; they dared to imagine and determine who they were" (4). As a record of that coming of age, his telling of "the way to Rainy Mountain is," he says, "preeminently the history of an idea" (4). But Momaday does not see the migration history as static or timebound in the traditional sense. Although the verbal tradition that preserves the tale of the Kiowa migration has "suffered a deterioration in time," he says the "idea itself" remains "as crucial and complete as it ever was" (4). Crucial and complete here mean more than simply factually intact. They depict a vital and dynamic idea, one untouched by the deterioration of time because it is "man's idea of himself" (4), an idea that can be and has been reimagined in each new generation: by the character of Ko-sahn in the text, by Momaday in the writing of *Rainy Mountain,* by the reader as he responds to the text. "The journey herein recalled," Momaday writes, "continues to be made anew each time the miracle comes to mind, for that is peculiarly the right and responsibility of the imagination" (4). He says that the journey he records is only "the revelation of one way in which the traditions are conceived, developed, and interfused in the human mind" and he acknowledges that "there are on the way to Rainy Mountain . . . many journeys in the one" (4). Momaday recounts the Kiowa journey, describes his own voyage of the spirit and the imagination, and opens the door for the reader's journey.

In his prologue Momaday gives us some idea of what he feels must be brought to bear on the text by the reader who will make his personal journey through *Rainy Mountain.* The journey he says is "made with the whole memory, that experience of the mind which is legendary as well as historical, personal as well as cultural" (4). He wants the reader to use his imagination to look through the windows of history, legend, cultural and personal experience just as Momaday has in his creation of the text. In later comments about *Rainy Mountain* Momaday indicates still further expectations he holds for his readers or co-creators. "The commentaries," he says, "are meant to provide a context in which the elements of oral tradition might transcend the categorical limits of prehistory, anonymity, and archaeology in the narrow sense."[4] He speaks of a work unfinished: he provides "a context" but the reader must play his role by collaborating with the author to complete the work of breaking through the boxed-in categories, imagining discourse, uncovering connections and contradictions, and finally, perhaps creating meaning.

Form as Catalyst

But even had Momaday not seemed to invite the imaginative participation of his reader, the text itself demands response, participation and co-creation. Momaday presents the reader with unusual juxtaposition, contradiction, intentional gaps and ambiguity.

The most obvious demand on the reader's attention is the form of the text. Momaday first sets the scene of the historical Kiowa journey and of his own personal journey in the prologue and the introduction, respectively. Then he divides the body of the work into three movements of the journey: "The Setting Out," "The Going On," and "The Closing In." Within the three body-sections of the book there are twenty-four numbered parts. Each of these numbered sections also contains three parts separated by blank space and distinguished by different kinds of type. Momaday calls the narrative voices of these sections "the mythical, the historical, and the immediate." He further explains their significance by identifying the leading section as a "translation" of a traditional Kiowa myth and the following two as commentaries—the first is "documentary," the second is "privately reminiscent."[5] Following the body-sections is an epilogue, and bracketing the entire text are two poems. Interspersed throughout the work are captioned illustrations. Even the most naive reader would be struck by the complexity of form and wonder about the purpose of such a textual design. In his contemplation, the reader has already unwittingly gone beyond the mere text and begun to join his efforts with the author's to bring the words to life.

The paginal layout, illustrations, varieties of typesetting, textual divisions and visual contrasts between captions, poetry and prose accommodate not only the content but also the open intentions of the work. As Umberto Eco noted:

> Blank space surrounding a word, typographical adjustments, and spatial composition in the page setting of the poetic text—all contribute to

create a halo of indefiniteness and to make the text pregnant with infinite suggestive possibilities.

This search for *suggestiveness* is a deliberate move to 'open' the work to the free response of the addressee. An artistic work which 'suggests' is one which can be performed with the full emotional and imaginative resources of the interpreter.[6]

Momaday undoubtedly chose his form partly for its ability to engage the reader, to involve the reader in questions about the significance of divisions. These ponderings will ultimately lead to more creative questions about the relationships between parts and the violation of divisions and to some concept of the dynamic interaction within the text. Here his form acts deliberately as the catalyst for a reader/text relationship.

Response Theories

Only through the response of the reader can the *Rainy Mountain* text realize its full dynamic potential. As Wolfgang Iser has stated, "The convergence of text and reader bring the literary work into existence."[7] A look at the phenomenological reader-response theory of Iser will help explain the process by which text and reader co-create the literary work *The Way to Rainy Mountain,* and the "work in movement" theory of Umberto Eco will help identify the degree of openness involved in the text and the extent of reader participation.[8]

Iser describes the reader's response as a "climbing aboard" the text. The reader accepts certain perspectives offered him by the author in the component parts of the text, but he also causes these parts to interact and to move beyond what they say individually. As the reader moves through the text, Iser says he forms expectations which will likely be continually modified, and each modification will have a retrospective effect on what has gone before. The reader has already outstripped the actual text:

> Thus, the reader, in establishing these interrelationships between past, present, and future, actually causes the text to reveal its potential multiplicity of connections. These connections are the product of the reader's mind working on the raw material of the text, though they are not the text itself.[9]

In addition to this process Iser calls "anticipation and retrospection," the reader is also involved in picturing the absent or unwritten parts of the text with his imagination and in grouping together the different parts of the text to form a "gestalt of a literary text." This unified pattern or gestalt "arises from the meeting between the written text and the individual mind of the reader," according to Iser, but is not the true meaning of the text only a configurative meaning. The reader's illusion of meaning will subsequently be destroyed by "alien associations" which force him to change his interpretation. He continually seeks but does not find the true meaning for, Iser says, "any 'living event' must, to a greater or lesser degree, remain open."[10]

But in the continual making and breaking of gestalts the reader does gain something. Iser sees a moral dimension in the reading process. The reader moves beyond his preconceptions to a position where he can experience new thoughts. In order to decipher these alien thoughts he must formulate his faculty for understanding the thoughts and thus as readers we "formulate ourselves," says Iser, "bring to the fore an element of ourselves of which we are not directly conscious," or "discover what had previously seemed to elude our consciousness."[11] Put more simply, the reader not only participates in literary co-creation but he also expands his personal horizons, learns to think in new ways, achieves deeper self-knowledge and imagines or creates himself.

Although Eco also sees the text as able to "stimulate the private world of the addressee in order that he can draw from inside himself some deeper response that mirrors the subtler resonances underlying the text," Eco's discussion of the work in movement is primarily concerned with the unfinished nature of the postmodern open texts. He distinguishes between the standard open works which, although allowing for innumerable individual responses, ultimately "never allow the reader to move outside the strict control of the author;" and "works in movement" which Eco compares to "construction kits" with which the reader must "make the composition." As examples of standard open works Eco gives: Baroque form which "is dynamic . . . tends to an indeterminancy of effect;" Symbolist poetics; and the drama of Brecht, which ends in ambiguity and forces solutions to arise from the audience, not the work.[12] As examples of works in movement he gives musical pieces by Henri Pousseur and Pierre Boulez. These consist of several sections without a dictated sequence, pieces whose arrangement depend on the musician and, therefore, encourage what Pousseur calls 'acts of conscious freedom' on the performer's part.[13] In the field of literature he identifies Mallarme's *Livre* as a literally unfinished attempt at a work in movement.

Neither Iser nor Eco sees suggestive works as escaping the author's intentions, although they may allow for interpretations or gestalts that had not been envisioned. Even with the works in movement Eco says:

> The *possibilities* which the work's openness makes available always work within a given *field of relations*. . . . The invitation offers the performer the chance of an oriented insertion into something which will always remain the world intended by the author.[14]

The given text establishes what Momaday calls the "context," what Eco calls a "given field of relations," within which the number of possible readings or performances of the text still remains unlimited.

The Way of Creation

Among the infinite variety of textual interations and reader responses Momaday's *Rainy Mountain* allows for as an open text, Iser's theory helps us trace certain underlying dynamics.

The text begins with clearcut divisions: myth, history, personal experience; past, present, future; physical, spiritual, verbal; reality, imagination; writer, reader. These are the accepted givens, the component parts of the text as Momaday presents it to us. In the beginning, for example, he distinguishes between the historic Kiowa journey and his retracing of that journey, between his physical pilgrimage to his grandmother's grave and his spiritual quest for identity, between memories and present reality. The reader can easily identify with a view that divides experience in such a traditional way.

But the reader does not view one idea or narrative voice in isolation from the others. As words and space butt against one another, he notices textual arrangement, layout, gaps, ambigious words and contradictions. By his response he unleashes the dormant interactive power of the text or, as Iser says, "sets the work in motion."[15]

For example, as the reader looks at the three passages in each numbered body-section, he expects some connection between the three because of their juxtaposition; as he reads through the twenty-four sections, he anticipates some progression because of their arrangement. So he "climbs aboard" the text to find the connections and the progression. What he finds, we shall see, gradually leads him on a journey away from his preconceptions, away from the neat divisions the text allowed him to start with. He begins the process Iser calls "anticipation" and "retrospection."

In Section I, a reader may discover the verbal link "coming out" in the myth, ethnographic commentary and personal experience (16–17); in Section II, the reference to a game animal (18–19); in Section III, dogs as subject of each passage (20–21); in Section IV, the reference to mountains or land that "ascends into the sky" (22–23). In each numbered section the three passages have one or more easily distinguishable links. A reader may conclude from this that the form of the text allows Momaday to write about the same topic as it was viewed at different times or through different perspectives. He has arrived at this gestalt of the text after grouping together what he knows in search of a consistent pattern.

However, the reader's discovery of a verbal link or common subject may cause him to look more closely at how the three interact, "picturing" the unwritten text that ties the pieces together, and the defining lines between the passages begin to blur. For example, all the passages in section II refer to game animals but a closer look reveals other ideas that bridge the passages. The first passage is the myth of the Azatanhop that describes a splitting off of some members of the Kiowa tribe (18). The historical passage which follows specifically comments on the myth and admits the possibility that it has an actual event as its origin because, "There have been reports of a people in the Northwest who speak a language that is similar to Kiowa" (19). Can myth, then, also be history? Can fiction be fact? The boundaries of traditional disciplines begin to dissolve for the reader, divisions are called into question. This transgression of divisions acts as the alien association that challenges the reader's illusion of order thus breaking his gesalt of the literary text.

The reader at first anticipated clear-cut divisions between the three narrative voices, but their juxtaposition lead him to anticipate some type of link. In his search for the common thread he discovers a collapsing of the division between history and myth and must modify his expectations to include possible overlap of the two. He may also anticipate and, therefore, seek further breakdown of the divisions. He can now respond to more subtle suggestions that the text might include regarding the collapse of categories.

As he continues reading Section II the historical passage describes an antelope hunt conducted "according to ancient custom" and the passage of Momaday's personal experience describes an encounter with pronghorns "in their own wilderness dimension of time." The Kiowa performing the hunt were "reminded of their ancient ways" and Momaday in his sighting of the pronghorns "remembered once having seen a frightened buck on the run" (19). The historical passage hearkens back to still more distant times, the personal passage to an experience in Momaday's earlier life, his personal history. If a reader identifies this concept of personal history, the disintegration of conventional categories continues. Can the personal be historical? Does personal experience include history? If myth can be history and history is included in personal experience, can myth also be part of personal experience?

Not all readers will interact with the text in precisely the same way, discover the same connections, ask the same questions and draw the same notions of meaning. But suppose a reader had responded in the way described, causing the three apparently separate narrative voices to interact in such a way that he begins to question the validity of the categories. Then he comes to Section XXIII and notices that the lead passage (the passage in the narrative voice previously identified as myth) involves Momaday's grandmother, Aho (80). In Section XXIV, he sees that the supposedly historical passage likewise involves Momaday's grandmother (83). Aho had previously only appeared in the sections reporting Momaday's personal experience. What can the reader make of this crossing of boundaries, this breaking of form? Does this textual movement attack or destroy the intellectual notion of categorizing experience into genres, which includes implied judgment with value based on factual content? Does it imply a continuum in which what Momaday called the "immediate" becomes history and myth? Does it call into question the idea that Native American culture must remain static to be authentic and offer instead a view of evolving myth?

This discussion reveals the kind of dynamics involved in reader response. The process repeats itself as long as the reader remains engaged in the creative process. Regardless of what meaning he draws from his experience of the text, he does so by virtue of filling in the gaps and imagining the dynamic action of the text. Whatever gestalt the reader creates will not only affect his reading of the remaining text but, as Iser points out, will have a retrospective effect on what he has already read and on any rereading. The act of reading is neither synchronic nor completely linear because the text often hearkens back to what has already been read and foreshadows what is to come. It alters shades of meaning along the way, contributing to the making and breaking of literary gestalts.[16]

As an open text, Momaday's *Rainy Mountain* allows for any or all of the readings or inferences regarding the status and interaction of the three narrative voices, but it does not dictate a correct reader response. Whatever meaning the reader may glean from or create with the text has moved beyond a neatly categorized view of the world. Preconceptions of correct order have given way to attempts to understand the movement of experience—like finds like despite the artificial boundaries constructed by intellectual society. The reader has "formulated himself": to the degree that he has allowed himself to develop, to think in new ways about the world. This self-formulation is the moral benefit Iser sees in the co-creation of literature.

Performing the Text

In describing the dynamics of the reading process the explanations were simplified by including only the relationship between the three narrative passages in each section. Even such a limited view has illustrated the open quality of Momaday's work. There are, however, a multitude of other movements a reader can enact as he performs the text. The following examination will illustrate how far Momaday's *Rainy Mountain* goes toward fulfilling Eco's definition of a work in movement.

Momaday has constructed a work with intricate layers of text, much like Pousseur constructed the musical piece of *Scambi* with variable sections. *Scambi*, according to Pousseur:

> is made up of sixteen sections. Each of these can be linked to any two others, without weakening the logical continuity of the musical process. Two of its sections, for example, are introduced by similar motifs (after which they evolve in divergent patterns); another pair of sections, on the contrary, tends to develop towards the same climax. Since the performer can start or finish with any one section, a considerable number of sequential permutations are made available to him. Furthermore, the two sections which begin on the same motif can be played simultaneously, so as to present a more complex structural polyphony.[17]

By the very intricacy of its structure, *Rainy Mountain* seems a foil to the free-form *Scambi*. If Momaday's work remained a static artifact, perhaps it would stand in sharp contrast to Pousseur's composition, but once set in motion by reader response, the text, too, allows a considerable number of sequential permutations.

Although most readers proceed in the conventional fashion through works of literature, (top to bottom, front to back) the very text of *Rainy Mountain* seems to undermine this convention and not only allow but encourage "misreading." For example, although each mythic passage in Sections IV-IX (22–34) is followed by and, therefore, separated from the next by what Momaday called the two commentaries (historical and personal passages), each leads directly into the one in the following section. The myth in the following section picks up the tale as if they should be read in sequence. Mythic passage IV ends: "The woman looked all around; she saw that he was the only living man there. She saw that he was the sun" (22). After the intervening commentaries the next mythic passage begins, "After that the women grew lonely . . ." and ends, "it struck her and killed her, and then the sun's child was all alone" (24). The subsequent mythic passage picks up the story with, "The sun's child was big enough to walk around on the earth, and he saw a camp nearby" (26). The story continues in the next three mythic passages. This section of sequential myth suggests the authorial endorsement of at least one possible sequential permutation. Could not the personal passages likewise be read sequentially as pieces of the story of Momaday's life journey? Are not the middle passages the historic story of the Kiowa, a story that could be read sequentially? And might not the three be played simultaneously, so as to present a more complex structural polyphony? Although Momaday does not pass unpaginated textual passages on to the reader he may still intend multiple sequential possibilities.

Collapsing the Text

Momaday gives further indication of the multidirectional possibilities available to the reader when he, in essence, enacts the reader role, imagining or creating himself from the intricately layered text of his life. On one level *Rainy Mountain* is the story of that quest for a sense of personal identity—Momaday's search for the self that could integrate past, present and future. Just as the reading process in Iser's theory includes acquiring new ways of thinking, Momaday's journey as told in *Rainy Mountain* includes a transformation in his thinking.

He begins with a fairly conventional set of ideas, a standard encyclopedia of distinctions, because, as pointed out earlier, the text begins in separations. For example, Momaday tells us in his introduction that he undertook the journey because he wanted to "see in reality" what his grandmother had seen "in the mind's eye," thus illustrating his acceptance of the distinction between reality and imagination (7). We also know that he distinguishes conventionally between death and life because he tells us that his grandmother has died and now he "can have her only in memory" (10). He begins by separately describing the historical Kiowa journey to Rainy Mountain and his personal retracing of that journey. But the book records a transformation in Momaday's thinking, traces his own making and remaking of gestalts as they inform his life's text, a text that ultimately collapses in the continuum of time in what Joseph Epes Brown has called "the perennial reality of the now."[18]

If we examine the temper of the personal experience passages in the body sections (those given in what Momaday calls the "immediate" narrative voice) and read them sequentially, we can follow the modifications in Momaday's view. In the first movement of the book which is called "The Setting Out," the privately reminiscent passages seem able to talk only tentatively about the general topic touched on in both the mythic and historical sections, to say, "Yes, something like that has happened to me, too." For example, when the other two narrative voices deal with mountain imagery in Section IV, the personal voice says only, "I have walked in a mountain meadow . . ." (23). But gradually the voice begins to gain more authority. In Section VI Momaday writes, "I know of spiders . . ." (27). In Section IX he makes a judgment based on family history when he says, "The holiness of such a thing can be imparted to the human spirit, I believe, for I remember that it shone in the sightless eyes of Keahdinekeah" (35). He has come to believe in holiness of the human spirit because he saw holiness in the eyes of his blind great-grandmother; he has learned to create meaning from the text of life.

In the second movement, "The Going On," his ability to create meaning continues to develop in each succeeding section, and he gradually gains the power to know and participate in the Kiowa past through his imagination. In Section XIII he describes Cheney, an old arrowmaker his father had known and talked of. Momaday writes:

> In my mind I can see that old man as if he were there now. I like to watch him as he makes his prayer. I know where he stands and where his voice goes on the rolling grasses and where the sun comes up on the land. There, at dawn, you can feel the silence. It is cold and clear and deep like water. It takes hold of you and will not let you go. (47)

Momaday did not meet the arrowmaker, but through imagination he sees Cheney as clearly, perhaps more clearly, than his father saw him in reality. Momaday has filled in the gaps of time; he knows the past. He has become part of Cheney and the past.

Finally, in the movement called "The Closing In," Momaday not only sees the past in his imagination's eye, he feels it clearly in his heart. Section XX talks of his personal reaction to the tale of Gaapiatan, who sacrificed a favorite horse to save his people. "I think I know how much he loved that animal," Momaday writes, "I think I know what was going on in his mind . . ." (71). Talking about the tale of the man who had his special horse's bones stolen from him in Section XXII Momaday writes, "There have been times when I thought I understood how it was that a man might be moved to preserve the bones of a horse— and another to steal them away" (77). He has progressed from knowing the subjects of history and legend to experiencing the events and understanding the feelings. Myth and history have become alive in him.

Momaday has entered the text of myth and history through his imagination, but his journey doesn't end there; as reader he must yet carry myth and history with him back into the present. Convention allows parallels between past, present and future and between myth, history and personal experience; but Momaday's views grow beyond the idea that the past merely informs the present, that myth informs history. Momaday, the reader/creator, comes to the view that racial memory, like blood, passes from one generation to the next and story-telling awakens the sleeping giant of racial memory until the past lives in the present. To paraphrase Iser's terminology, Momaday "brings to the fore an element of himself of which he was not directly conscious," he "discovers what had previously seemed to elude his consciousness."

To understand this new gestalt, the final movement of Momaday's journey in the book, consider his references to the life and stories of his grandmother, Aho, and grandfather, Mammedaty. Momaday writes of his last encounter with Aho before her death saying, "She seemed beyond the reach of time. But that was illusion; I think I knew that I should not see her again" (10–11). He tells us in this line that she is dead and he will not see her again and, of course, in one sense this is true. But in passages throughout the book he does see her and he brings her to life for us.

What his telling of tales about his grandmother accomplishes becomes clearer if we consider Momaday's explanation of the Kiowa making a legend at the base of Devil's Tower. On their legendary journey, the Kiowa had come to a "place where they must change their lives," leave the mountains behind, and set out into the plains. They created a legend about seven Kiowa sisters who were borne into the sky and became the stars of the Big Dipper. "From that moment on, and as long as the legend lives," says Momaday, "the Kiowas have kinsmen in the night sky. . . . they had found a way out of the wilderness" (8). They had imagined and, therefore, created compatriots who could follow them into their new life. Their action reflects Momaday's view about the power of imagination to create. Momaday may have Aho, only in memory but, now that he has told of her she will have life as long as his tales do, as long as the reader can imagine and create (10).

But what Momaday ultimately taps in his storytelling goes beyond his ordinary memory. He tells of Aho's life before he was born and says, "I like to think of her as a child" (6). In many passages he tells of his grandfather, describing, for example, Mammedaty's encounter with the water beast and the mole. Yet in the epilogue he writes, "Mammedaty had died before I was born" (86). Momaday imagines the past based on the stories he has heard, the memories of the generations before him become his through imagination, they are what Brown has called "of eternal happening."[19] Momaday himself has written, ". . . the Indian has determined himself in his imagination over a period of untold generations. His racial memory is an essential part of his understanding."[20]

The extent to which the divisions of time collapse for Momaday as he collaborates with legend, history, family tales and personal experience to create himself can best be seen in his reading of the text of Ko-sahn's life. The epilogue of *Rainy Mountain* opens with the retelling of the Kiowa's experience of the Leonid meteor shower. Then Momaday introduces Ko-sahn and relates her tale of the Sun Dance in which an old woman brings earth for the sacred lodge. He closes the epilogue saying:

> Probably Ko-sahn too is dead now. At times in the quiet of evening, I think she must have wondered, dreaming, who she was. Was she become in her sleep that old purveyor of the sacred earth, perhaps, that ancient one who, old as she was, still had the feeling of play? And in her mind, at times, did she see the falling stars? (88)

Ko-sahn had not literally been at the meteor shower and had not carried the earth for the Sun Dance lodge, but Momaday wonders if she saw and lived those events through her racial memory? Did she carry the past with her through imagination until she sometimes became the old woman in the story like he sometimes became the people of his memory?

In the "Man Made of Words" Momaday tells of an experience he had after writing *Rainy Mountain,* an experience that suggests answers to those questions. Ko-sahn appears to him, or so he imagines, and they talk. When he protests to her that he is only imagining she replies:

> You imagine I am here in this room, do you not? That is worth something. You see, I have existence, whole being, in your imagination. It is but one kind of being, to be sure, but it is perhaps the best of all kinds. If I am not here in this room, grandson, then surely neither are you. [21]

When Ko-sahn speaks of her life it stretches back to the Kiowa "coming out" and forward to the meteor shower, neither of which she experienced in reality. We see that she, like Momaday, creates herself through her imagination for in her speech (as in Momaday's journey) a progression of power can be detected:

> There are times when I think I am the oldest woman on earth. . . . In my mind's eye I have seen . . . I have seen them so clearly. . . . I must have been there. . . . I must have taken part . . . I have seen . . . I was with those . . . when the stars fell. [22]

During the course of the book Momaday has come to understand the imagination's power to transcend time, to transport us through history. He, like Ko-sahn, not only hears and tells the tales of the

Kiowa but lives them, converses with them, finds his existence defined in them.

Passing the Code

The progression of power Momaday experiences in his role as reader of his life's text allows him to create himself outside the confines of convention in the "perennial reality of the now." The same possibilities exist for the reader as they respond to Momaday's text and co-create the literary work.

By his enactment of the reader's role within the story of the text Momaday essentially teaches the imagination. "Literary texts," as Terry Eagleton notes, "are 'code-productive' and 'code-transgressive' as well as 'code-confirming': they may teach us new ways of reading, not just reinforce the ones with which we come equipped.[23] Momaday's text begs us to transgress old codes, to collapse divisions, to create a literature of polyphony, of simultaneous performance, of "eternal happening." *The Way to Rainy Mountain* beckons: an open invitation to imagine, to create. In what is perhaps the most famous passage from the book Momaday describes a way of exploration that could apply as well to interacting with the landscape that is the text:

> Once in his life a man ought to concentrate his mind upon the remembered earth, I believe. He ought to give himself up to a particular landscape in his experience, to look at it from as many angles as he can, to wonder about it, to dwell upon it. He ought to imagine that he touches it with his hands at every season and listens to the sounds that are made upon it. He ought to imagine the creatures there and all the faintest motions of the wind. He ought to recollect the glare of noon and all the colors of the dawn and dusk. (83)

Notes

1. N. Scott Momaday, *The Way to Rainy Mountain* (Albuquerque: University of New Mexico Press, 1969). All further references to this work appear in the text and hereafter it is cited as *Rainy Mountain*.

2. N. Scott Momaday, "Native American Attitudes to the Environment,"

Seeing With a Native Eye: Essays on Native American Religion, ed. Walter Holden Capps (New York: Harper and Row, 1976) 80.

3. N. Scott Momaday, "The Man Made of Words," *Indian Voices: The First Convocation of American Indian Scholars* (San Francisco: Indian Historian Press, Inc., 1970) 55.

4. Momaday, "Man" 59.

5. Momaday, "Man" 59.

6. Umberto Eco, *The Role of Reader: Explorations in the Semiotics of Texts* (Bloomington: Indiana University Press, 1979) 53.

7. Wolfgang Iser, "The Reading Process: A Phenomenological Approach," *Reader-Response Criticism from Formalism to Post-Structuralism*, ed. Jane P. Tompkins (Baltimore: Johns Hopkins University Press, 1980) 50.

8. Iser 50–69; Eco, esp. 47–66.

9. Iser 52, 52, 54.

10. Iser 58, 57–58, 58, 59, 61, 65.

11. Iser 68, 68.

12. Eco 53, 51, 56, 49, 56, 52

13. Henri Pousseur, as quoted in Eco 48.

14. Eco 62.

15. Iser 51

16. See Terry Eagleton, *Literary Theory, An Introduction* (Minneapolis: University of Minnesota Press, 1983) 116.

17. Pousseur, as quoted in Eco 48.

18. Joseph Epes Brown, "The Roots of Renewal," *Seeing With a Native Eye: Essays on Native American Religion*, ed. Walter Holden Capps (New York: Harper and Row, 1976) 28.

19. Brown 29.

20. Momaday, "Native" 80.

21. Momaday, "Man" 51.

22. Momaday, "Man" 52.

23. Eagleton 125.

4

The Dialogic of Silko's Storyteller

ARNOLD KRUPAT

Autobiography as commonly understood in western European and Euro-American culture did not exist as a traditional type of literary expression among the aboriginal peoples of North America. Indeed, none of the conditions of production for autobiography—here I would isolate post–Napoleonic historicism, egocentric individualism and writing as foremost—was typical of Native American cultures.[1] To the extent that the life stories, personal histories, memoirs or recollections of Indians did finally come into textual form (traditional Indian literatures were not written but oral), it was as a result of contact with and pressure from Euro-Americans. Until the twentieth century the most common form of Native American autobiography was the Indian autobiography, a genre of American writing constituted by the principle of original, bicultural, composite composition, in which there is a distinct if not always clear division of labor between the subject of the autobiography (the Indian to whom the first-person pronoun ostensibly makes reference) and the Euro-American editor responsible for fixing the text in writing, yet whose presence the first-person pronoun ostensibly masks. Indian autobiography may thus be distinguished from autobiography by Indians, the life stories of those christianized and/or "civilized" natives who, having internalized Western culture and scription, committed their lives to writing on their own without the mediation of the Euro-American. In autobiographies by Indians, although there is inevitably an element of biculturalism, there is not the element of compositeness that precisely marks Indian autobiographies.

The earliest examples of Native American autobiography are two by Indians dating from the decades surrounding the American Revolution. These did not attract much attention; indeed, the more extensive of the two by Hendrick Aupaumut was not even published until 1827 and then in a journal of rather limited circulation.[2] It was only six years later, however that the first Indian autobiography, J. B. Patterson's *Life of Black Hawk*, appeared. This book did gain widespread notice, coming as it did at a time of increased American interest in Indians (the book was occasioned by the last Indian war to be fought east of the Mississippi) and in the type of writing then only recently named autobiography (in 1809 by the poet Southey). Both of these interests are developed in this earliest type of Indian autobiography, which presents the acts of the world-historical chief or (of particular concern in the first half of the nineteenth century) the Indian hero. The historical orientation of Indian autobiography persisted in some form into the 1930s and 1940s after which none of the warriors was left alive to tell his tale. By that time there had already occurred a shift of interest on the part of Euro-American editors from history to science. In the twentieth century professional anthropologists rather than amateur historians would most commonly edit Indian autobiographies.

In our time Indian autobiographies continue to be co-produced by historians and social scientists working with traditional native people, but their labors have very nearly been overshadowed by the autobiographical writing of a new generation of Indians, educated in Western literate forms yet by no means acculturated to the point of abandoning respect for the old ways. These autobiographies are not only contributions to historical and scientific record, but also works of art (particularly the autobiographies of N. Scott Momaday and Leslie Marmon Silko, whose claim to national attention came not from their relation to American religion, history or anthropology, but from their relation to American literature as previously established in their fiction and poetry).

The history of Native American autobiography could be charted thematically as a movement from history and science to art on a line parallel to the history of European and Euro-American autobiography.[3] To chart it thus would demonstrate that Native Americans have had to make a variety of accommodations to the dominant culture's forms, capitulating to them, assimilating them, sometimes dramatically transforming them, but never able to proceed independent of them. However, Native American autobiography differs materially from western European and Euro-American (though not strictly western American) autobiography through its existence in specifically individual and composite forms, or, both monologic and dialogic forms.[4]

To introduce the terms monologue and dialogue is to invoke an important recent development in literary theory: recent interest in the Russian theorist, Mikhail Bakhtin.

So much has been written on Bakhtin of late that any attempt to summarize his thought is bound to be incomplete.[5] In this country, at least, what is generally understood by reference to "Bakhtin," is very far from settled. To be sure "Freud" and "Marx" mean different things to different people as well; but there seems to be for Bakhtin, more than for these other major thinkers (and it is by no means generally agreed that comparison of Bakhtin to major thinkers is justified), a pronounced ambiguity. This openness may be functional, a practical illustration of what has been theoretically proposed. Perhaps it is not so much "openness," that Bakhtin's writing exhibits, but such inconsistency and ambiguity that it is difficult or pointless to specify the particulars of his thought. Hence, any attempt at an approximately neutral summary automatically becomes partial, a choice not between nuances but real differences. Nevertheless, the following briefly outlines what is at issue in Bakhtin and therefore at issue in any Bakhtinian reading of Native American autobiography.

Bakhtin calls human language "heteroglossic, polyvocal," the speech of each individual enabled and circumscribed not so much by language as a *system* as by the actual speech of other individuals. (In this he differs from Saussurian structural linguistics and its fascination with *langue*.) Speech is social and meaning is open and in flux, inevitably a dialogue among speakers, not the property or in the power of any single speaker. ". . . [A]ll there is to know about the world is not exhausted by a particular discourse about it . . . ,"[6] Bakhtin notes in a typical statement. Still some forms of written discourse and social practice seek to impose a single authoritative voice as the norm, thus subordinating or entirely suppressing other voices. It is the genre Bakhtin calls the "epic" that provides models of this monologic tendency in literature, while the totalitarianism of Stalinism under which Bakhtin lived provides the socio-political model of monologism. In opposition to the totalizing thrust of the epic, the novel testifies to its own (inevitable) incompleteness, its ongoing indebtedness to the discourse of others. The novel is the prime literary instance of dialogized speech.

Bakhtin seems to be committed to dialogue on empirical grounds, inasmuch as the term claims to name human communication correctly, pointing to the way speech and social life "really" are. But Bakhtin seems also to be committed to dialogue on moral and esthetic grounds; he approves of and is pleased by that which he finds di-, hetero-, poly-, and so on. For him, truth and beauty are one, but what this equivalence is to mean ultimately in a dialogic theory of language and of social life remains to be determined.

Does Bakhtinian dialogic envision a strong form of pluralism in which all have legitimate voice: truth having its particular authority, beauty having its, and both having equal (cognitive) force over other voices, which, although worthy of being heard, can be judged decidably less forceful? Or does Bakhtinian dialogic envision a kind of postmodernist free play of voices with no normative means for deciding their relative worth or authority? We do not know whether Bakhtin's dislike of what he calls monologue permits some forms of relatively stable assertion, in particular truth and beauty. Such statements as "the last word is never said,"—and there are innumerable such statements in Bakhtin's writing—may intend a radically ironic, a schizophrenic refusal (in Jameson's very particular sense)[7] of any form, however relativized, of grounded meaning. Or they may insist only that no single language act has the capacity to encompass the entire range of humanly possible meaning, as no single mode of political organization can give full latitude to human potential.

In this latter regard the issue is particularly complicated because, while we do know from Bakhtin that the novel is supposed to provide the fullest literary illustration of relativized, dialogic discourse, we do not know whether the nearest thing he gives us to a socio-political equivalent of the novel, rabelaisian "carnival," represents an actual model for social organization or an escape from too rigid social organization. In either case, we do not know what Bakhtinian carnival might actually entail for current or future social formations. To examine Native American autobiography from a Bakhtinian perspective, then, is not only to consider it as a discursive type—a kind of literature, generically closer to the epic or the novel as Bakhtin understands these Western forms—but as a social model which allows for the projection of a particular image of human community.

Let me now offer a reading of Leslie Marmon Silko's *Storyteller* in relation to these issues.

Merely to consider *Storyteller* among Native American autobiographies might require some explanation, since the book is a collection of stories, poems and photographs as much as it is a narrative of its author's life. Of course a variety of claims have been made in the recent past for the fictionality of autobiographies in general, the autobiography being recognized as the West's most obviously dialogic genre in which a conversation between *historia* and *poesis*, documentation and creation, is always in progress. And some of these claims might easily be used to justify classifying *Storyteller* as an autobiography.

Indeed, to justify the book's classification as an autobiography in this way, would not be mistaken; it would, however, be to treat it exclusively from a Western perspective, failing to acknowledge that traditional Native American literary forms were not—and, in their contemporary manifestations usually are not—as concerned about keeping fiction and fact or poetry and prose distinct from one another. It is the distinction between truth and error rather than that between fact and fiction that seems more interesting to native expression; and indeed, this distinction was also central to Western thought prior to the seventeenth century. Thus the present "blurring of genres," in Clifford Geertz's phrase,[8] in both the social sciences and in the arts, is actually only a return to that time when the line between history and myth was not very clearly marked. But that is the way things have always been for Native American literatures.

From the Western point of view, Silko's book would seem to announce by its title, *Storyteller,* the familiar pattern of discovering who one is by discovering what one does, the pattern of identity in vocation. This is useful enough as a way to view Silko's text. In the West it has been a very long time since the vocational storyteller has had a clear and conventional social role. In Pueblo culture, however, to be known as a storyteller is to be known as one who participates, in a communally sanctioned manner, in sustaining the group; for a Native American writer to identify herself as a storyteller today is to express a desire to perform such a function. In the classic terms of Marcel Mauss, person, self and role are here joined.[9]

Silko dedicates her book "to the storytellers as far back as memory goes and to the telling which continues and through which they all live and we with them." Having called herself a storyteller, she thus places herself in a tradition of tellings, suggesting that her stories cannot strictly be her own nor will we find in them what one typically looks for in post–Rousseauan, Western autobiography or (as Bakhtin would add, in poetry) a uniquely personal voice. There is no single, distinctive or authoritative voice in Silko's book nor any striving for such a voice; to the contrary, Silko will take pains to indicate how even her own individual speech is the product of many voices. *Storyteller* is presented as a strongly polyphonic text in which the author defines herself—finds her voice, tells her life, illustrates the capacities of her vocation—in relation to the voices of other native and nonnative storytellers, tale tellers and book writers, and even to the voices of those who serve as the (by-no-means silent) audience for these stories.

It is Silko's biographical voice that commences the book, but not by speaking of her birth or the earliest recollections of childhood as Western autobiography usually dictates. Rather, she begins by establishing the relation of "hundreds of photographs taken since the 1890s around Laguna" that she finds in "a tall Hopi basket" to "the stories as [she] remembers them."[10] Visual stories, speaking pictures, here as in the familiar Western understanding will also provide a voice; and Silko's developing relation to every kind of story becomes the story of her life.

Dennis Tedlock has made the important point that Zuni stories are fashioned in such a way as to include in their telling not just the story itself but a critique of or commentary on those stories, and Silko's autobiographical story will also permit a critical dimension, voices that comment on stories and storytellers—storytellers like her Aunt Susie, who, when she told stories had "certain phrases, certain distinctive words/she used in her telling" (7). Both Aunt Susie and Aunt Alice "would tell me stories they had told me before but with changes in details or descriptions. . . . There were even stories about the different versions of stories and how they imagined these differing versions came to be" (227). Silko's own versions of stories she has heard from Simon Ortiz, the Acoma writer whom Silko acknowledges as the source of her prose tale, "Uncle Tony's Goat," and her verse tale, "Skeleton Fixer," also introduce certain phrases and distinctive words that make them identifiably her own. Yet these and all the other stories are never presented as the final or definitive version; although they are intensely associated with their different tellers, they remain available for other tellings.¹¹ "What is realized in the novel," Bakhtin has written, "is the process of coming to know one's own language as it is perceived in someone else's language . . ." (365) and so, too, to know one's own language as bound up with "someone else's language." Any story Silko herself tells, then, is always bound up with someone else's language; it is always a version and the story as version stands in relation to the story as officially sanctioned myth, as the novel stands to the national epic. Silko's stories are always consistent with—to return to Bakhtin—attempts to liberate ". . . cultural-semantic and emotional intentions from the hegemony of a single and unitary language," consistent with a ". . . loss of feeling for language as myth, that is, as an absolute form of thought" (367).

Stories are transmitted by other storytellers, as Silko wrote early in her book:

> by word of mouth
> an entire history
> an entire vision of the world
> which depended upon memory
> and retelling by subsequent generations.
> . . . .
> . . . the oral tradition depends upon each person
> listening and remembering a portion. . . . (6–7)

But the awareness of and respect for the oral tradition, here, is not a kind of sentimental privileging of the old ways. Indeed, this first reference to the importance of cultural transmission by oral means comes in a lovely memorial to Aunt Susie who, Silko writes:

> From the time that I can remember her
> . . . worked on her kitchen table
> with her books and papers spread over the oil cloth.
> She wrote beautiful long hand script
> but her eyesight was not good
> and so she wrote very slowly.
> . . . .
> She had come to believe very much in books

It is Aunt Susie, the believer in books and in writing, who was of "the last generation here at Laguna, / that passed an entire culture by word of mouth. . . ." Silko's own writing is compared to oral telling by a neighbor, who, finding her "Laguna Coyote" poem in a library book, remarks:

> "We all enjoyed it so much,
> but I was telling the children
> the way my grandpa used to tell it
> is longer."

To this critical voice, Silko responds:

> "Yes, that's the trouble with writing . . .
> You can't go on and on the way we do
> when we tell stories around here.
> People who aren't used to it get tired" (110).

This awareness of the audience is entirely typical for a native storyteller who cannot go forward with a tale without the audience's response. As Silko writes:

> *The Laguna people*
> *always begin their stories*
> *with "humma-hah":*
> *that means "long ago."*
> *And the ones who are listening*
> *say "aaaa-eh"* (38)

These are the stories, of course, of the oral tradition. Silko invokes the feel of "long ago" both in the verse format she frequently uses and in the prose pieces, although perhaps only those sections of the book set in verse attempt to evoke something of the actual feel of an oral telling.

It is interesting to note that there are two pieces in the book that echo the title, one in prose and the other set in loose verse. The first, "Storyteller," is an intense and powerful short story which takes place in Alaska. The storyteller of the title is the protagonist's grandfather, a rather less benign figure than the old storytellers of Silko's biographical experience; nonetheless, the stories he tells are of the traditional, mythic type. The second, "Storytelling," is a kind of mini-anthology of several short tales of women and their (quite historical, if fictional!) sexual adventures. The "humma-hah" (in effect) of the first section goes:

You should understand
the way it was
back then,
because it is the same
even now (94).
      [aaaa-eh]

The final section has its unnamed speaker conclude:

My husband
left
after he heard the story
and moved back in with his mother.
It was my fault and
I don't blame him either.
I could have told
the story
better than I did (98).

In both these pieces ("Storyteller" and "Storytelling") we find a very different sense of verbal art from that expressed in the West in something like Auden's lines (in the poem on the death of Yeats), where he writes that "poetry makes nothing happen. . . ." In deadly serious prose and in witty verse, Silko dramatizes her belief that stories—both the mythic-traditional tales passed down among the people and the day-to-day narrations of events—do make things happen. The two pieces refer to very different kinds of stories which, in their capacity to produce material effects, are nonetheless the same.

    Among other identifiable voices in Silko's texts are her own epistolary voice in letters she has written to Lawson F. Inada and James A. Wright, the voices of Coyote and Buffalo, and those of traditional figures like Kochininako, Whirlwind Man, Arrowboy, Spider Woman and Yellow Woman—some of whom appear in modern day incarnations. In stories or letters or poems, in monologues or dialogues, the diction may vary—now more colloquial and/or regional, now more formal—or the tone—lyrical, humorous, meditative. Yet always, the effort is to make us hear the various languages that constitute Silko's world and so herself. If we agree with Bakhtin that, "The primary stylistic project of the novel as a genre is to create images of languages" (366), *Storyteller* is a clear instance of novelized discourse, Native

American autobiography of the dialogic type. It remains to say what the implications of this particular dialogic discourse may be.

I have tried to read *Storyteller* as an example of Native American autobiography in the dialogic mode, that is, against the backdrop of Bakhtin's meditations on language and society. By way of conclusion, it seems useful to see what Silko's book has to say about these important subjects, or more accurately, what projections about language and society might be made from the book. To interrogate the text in this way is not to treat it foremost as ethnic or hyphenated literature (although it cannot be understood in ignorance of its informing context), but as a candidate for inclusion in the canon of American literature conceived of as a selection of the most important work from among national texts (*American* literature) and texts (for all the blurring of genres) of a certain kind (American *literature*).

Let me review the possibilities. In regard to its understanding of language and the nature of communication, on one hand a commitment to dialogism may be seen as a recognition of the necessity of an infinite semantic openness. Here the inescapable possibility of yet some further voice is crucial inasmuch as that voice may decisively alter or ambiguate any relatively stable meaning one might claim to understand. On the other hand, a commitment to dialogism may be seen as a type of radical pluralism, a more relativized openness, concerned with stating meanings provisionally in recognition of the legitimate claims of otherness and difference. In regard to its implied model of the social, a commitment to dialogism may be seen as envisioning, "a carnivalesque arena of diversity," as James Clifford has described it, "a utopian . . . space,"[12] where the utopian exists as a category of pure abstraction, an image out of time and oblivious to the conditions of historical possibility: diversity as limitless freeplay. Or a commitment to dialogism may envision—but here one encounters difficulties, for it is hard to name or describe the sort of democratic and egalitarian community that would be the political equivalent of a radical pluralism as distinct from an infinite openness. No doubt, traditional Native American models of communal organization need further study in this regard, although it is not at all clear how the present-day Pueblo or the nineteenth-century Plains camp circle might be incorporated into models of some harmonious world-community to come.

Let me, then, name the alternative to dialogism as carnival and polymorphous diversity, what Paul Rabinow has called *cosmopolitanism*. "Let us define cosmopolitanism," Rabinow writes, "as an ethos of macro-interdependencies, with an acute consciousness (often forced upon people) of the inescapabilities and particularities of places, characters, historical trajectories, and fates."[13] The trick is to avoid "reify-[ing] local identities or construct[ing] universal ones," a trick, as Rabinow notes, that requires a rather delicate balancing act, one that the West has had a difficult time managing. For all the seeming irony of proposing that the highly place-oriented and more or less homogenous cultures of indigenous Americans might best teach us how to be cosmopolitans, that is exactly what I mean to say. But here let me return to *Storyteller*.

Storyteller is open to a plurality of voices. What keeps it from entering the poststructuralist, postmodernist or schizophrenic heteroglossic domain is its commitment to the equivalent of a normative voice. For all the polyvocal openness of Silko's work, there is always the unabashed commitment to Pueblo ways as a reference point. This may be modified, updated, playfully construed: but its authority is always to be reckoned with. Whatever one understands from any speaker is to be understood in reference to that. Here we find dialogic as dialectic (not, it seems, the case in Bakhtin!), meaning as the interaction of any voiced value whatever and the centered voice of the Pueblo.[14]

If this account of *Storyteller*'s semantics, or theory of meaning, is at all accurate, it would follow that its political unconscious is more easily conformable to Rabinow's cosmopolitanism than to a utopianized carnival. The social implications of *Storyteller*'s dialogism might be a vision of an American cosmopolitanism to come that permits racial and cultural voices at home (in both "residual" and "emerging" forms[15]) to speak fully and that opens its ears to other voices abroad. This is an image, to be sure, not a political program; and to imagine the "polyvocal polity" in this way is also utopian, but perhaps only in the sense that it is not yet imminent.

Silko's book says nothing of this, offering neither a theory of communication nor of politics. To take it seriously, however, is to see it as more than merely evocative, amusing, expressive or informative (to the mainstream reader curious about the exotic ways of marginalized communities). It is to see its art as a matter of values that are most certainly not only aesthetic.

Notes

1. For a fuller account see Arnold Krupat, *For Those Who Come After: A Study of Native American Autobiography* (Berkeley: University of California, 1985).

2. See Samson Occom, "A Short Narrative of My Life," *The Elders Wrote: An Anthology of Early Prose by North American Indians,* ed. Bernd Peyer (Berlin: Dietrich Reimer Verlag, 1982). Occom wrote in 1768; his manuscript reposed in the Dartmouth College Library until its publication by Peyer. Also see Hendrick Aupaumut, "Journal of a Mission to the Western Tribes of Indians," which was written in 1791 and published by B. H. Coates in 1827 in the *Pennsylvania Historical Society Memoirs,* II, part 1, 61–131.

3. This is William Spengemann's trajectory for Western autobiography which he sees as presenting "historical, philosophical, and poetic" forms, and a "movement of autobiography from the biographical to the fictive mode," in his *The Forms of Autobiography: Episodes in the History of a Literary Genre* (New Haven: Yale University Press, 1980) xiv.

4. An earlier and very different version of this paper was summarized as a presentation to the European Association on American Studies Convention (Budapest, Mar. 1986). It will appear in a publication of the selected proceedings of that Convention edited by Steve Ickringill, University of Ulster.

5. I hesitate to offer even a selected bibliography of recent work on Bakhtin, so voluminous are the possibilities. For what use it may be let me mention only two book-length studies. Katerina Clark and Michael Holquist's biography, *Mikhail Bakhtin* (Cambridge: Harvard University Press, 1984), is both indispensable and too-good-to-be-true in its shaping of Bakhtin's life and thought into a coherent, but largely anti-communist, whole. Tzvetan Todorov's *Mikhail Bakhtin: the Dialogical Principle,* trans. Wlad Godzich (Minneapolis: University of Minnesota Press, 1984) is a particularly subtle reading. Denis Donoghue's "Reading Bakhtin," *Raritan* 2 (Fall 1985): 107–19, offers a more sceptical account. The primary volumes in English of Bakhtin's work are *Rabelais and his World,* trans. Helene Iswolsky (Cambridge: MIT Press, 1968); *The Dialogic Imagination: Four Essays by M.M. Bakhtin,* ed. Michael Holquist, trans. Caryl Emerson and Michael Holquist (Austin: University of Texas Press, 1981); and *Problems of Dostoevsky's Poetics,* ed. and trans. Caryl Emerson (Minneapolis: University of Minnesota Press, 1984). The interested reader will find many special issues of journals devoted to Bakhtin, several with extensive bibliographies.

6. Mikhail Bakhtin, *The Dialogic Imagination: Four Essays by M. M. Bakhtin,* ed. Michael Holquist (Austin: University of Texas Press, 1981) 45. All further quotations from Bakhtin are from this volume and page references will be documented in the text.

7. See Fredric Jameson, "Postmodernism, or The Cultural Logic of Late Capitalism," *New Left Review* 146 (1984): 53–82.

8. See Clifford Geertz, "Blurred Genres: The Refiguration of Social Thought," *Local Knowledge: Further Essays in Interpretive Anthropology* (New York: Basic Books, 1983), originally published 1980.

9. See Marcel Mauss, "A Category of the human mind: the notion of person; the notion of self." In M. Carrithers, S. Collins and S. Lukes, eds., *The Category of the Person: Anthropology, Philosophy, History* (Cambridge: Harvard University Press, 1985).

10. Leslie Marmon Silko, *Storyteller* (New York: Viking Press, 1981) 1. All further page references will be given in the text.

11. In fact there *are* other tellings because many of the stories in *Storyteller* have appeared elsewhere, some of them in several places. (Pieces of Silko's novel, *Ceremony*, also appear elsewhere.) What to make of this? On the one hand it may be that Silko is just trying to get as much mileage as she can out of what she's done, a practice not unknown to both fiction and essay writers, native and non-native. On the other hand, in the context of Native American storytelling, repetition of the "same" story on several different occasions is standard procedure, "originality" or noticeable innovation having no particular value. It should also be noted that the retellings of Silko's stories are not exact reprintings. For example, "The Man to Send Rain Clouds," as it appears in Kenneth Rosen's anthology of the same name (New York: Viking, 1974), and in *Storyteller*, have slight differences. In Rosen's anthology there are numbered sections of the story (one to four), while there are only space breaks in *Storyteller* (no numbers). In the first paragraph of the Rosen version, Levis are "light-blue" while in *Storyteller* they are "light blue"; "blue mountains were still deep in snow" (3) in Rosen while in *Storyteller* "blue mountains were still in snow" (182). If we turn to the story called "Uncle Tony's Goat" in both books, we find differences in the endings. In Rosen the story ends this way:

> . . . Tony finished the cup of coffee. "He's probably in Quemado by now."
> I thought his voice sounded strong and happy when he said this, and I looked at him again, standing there by the door, ready to go milk the nanny goats. He smiled at me.
> "There wasn't ever a goat like that one," he said, "but if that's the way he's going to act, O.K. then. That damn goat got pissed off too easy anyway" (99–100).

The ending in *Storyteller* goes:

> . . . "He's probably in Quemado by now."
> I looked at him again, standing there by the door, ready to go milk the nanny goats.

"There wasn't ever a goat like that one," he said, "but if that's the way he's going to act, O.K. then. That damn goat got pissed off too easy anyway." He smiled at me and his voice was strong and happy when he said this (18).

The differences in the first example may not amount to much, while those in the second might suggest a slight change in emphasis; a systematic study of the differences in Silko's retellings (something I have not attempted to do) might tell us something about her development as a writer—or might not be all that substantial. My point here is that Silko's retellings in writing, whether she is aware of this or not (and it is always possible that different versions come into existence as a result of the demands of different editors rather than as a result of Silko's own determinations), tend to parallel what we know of the oral retellings of traditional narrators.

12. James Clifford, "On Ethnographic Authority," *Representations* 1 (Spring 1983): 137.

13. Paul Rabinow, "Representations are Social Facts: Modernity and Post-Modernity in Anthropology," *Writing Culture: The Poetics and Politics of Ethnography*, ed. James Clifford and George E. Marcus (Berkeley: University of California Press, 1986) 258.

14. This would not accord very well with what Silko said of herself in Rosen's 1974 volume, *Voices of the Rainbow* (New York: Viking Press, 1974) where she emphasized that ". . . the way we live is like Marmons . . . somewhere on the fringes . . . our origin is unlike any other. My poetry, my storytelling rise out of this source." As glossed by Alan Velie, from whom I take this quotation, this means like "mixed-blood[s] from a ruling family" (in *Four American Indian Literary Masters: N. Scott Momaday, James Welch, Leslie Marmon Silko, and Gerald Vizenor* (Norman: University of Oklahoma Press, 1982) 107). It goes rather better with what Silko put in her contributor's note to Rosen's 1975 *The Man to Send Rain Clouds*. She wrote, "I am of mixed-breed ancestry, but what I know is Laguna. This place I am from is everything I am as a writer and human being." (176)

15. These are values in relation to "dominant" values as defined by Raymond Williams in "Base and Superstructure in Marxist Cultural Theory," in his *Problems in Materialism and Culture* (London: Verso, 1980) 40ff.

5

Tayo, Death, and Desire:
A *Lacanian Reading of* Ceremony

GRETCHEN RONNOW

One of the "pleasures of the text" in Leslie Marmon Silko's *Cere-mony* is to observe that Tayo, the main character, never achieves a sense that he is a totally cohesive or unified self. What sense of func-tional being he does attain is always in relation to others or to the "Other" defined as the full possibilities of language. Thus, a new self, a changing Tayo, continually emerges in each new encounter. Tayo traverses the pages of the novel in a quest of desire across the possibili-ties of language; his quest is criss-crossed by substitutions for unity (for the lost "Mother"), which are the various texts and signs he learns to read. He learns that his existence is a series of interconnected stories which impart to him, finally, a sense of the fullness of Language rather than a primal unity itself.

Jacques Lacan, a well-known psychoanalytic theorist in the Freud-ian tradition, makes the observation: the subject is never sovereign in itself, but emerges in an intersubjective discourse with and in the pres-ence of the Other (the fullness of Language), and that this emergence is continually interrupted by the interplay of the various texts which make up the subject's history. Besides watching Tayo's continual emer-gence in this basic triptych (subject, other, and Other as presented in the language of the novel) we ultimately see (if we follow Lacan's mode of thinking as a possible heuristics) that Tayo's desire is for death rather than to "live happily ever after" as it may first appear to the casual reader. To desire death, but not to seek to die, deepens life. One prolongs life in order to extend desire and all that desire entails.

Tayo enters the novel as Other. He is fragmented, confused and disowned, alienated from self, family, land and tribal traditions. But to his credit, he soon recognizes that "Otherness" is more to be welcomed as mentally healthy than feared as pathological. At birth all humans lose unity with the mother's body, but Tayo's loss has been multiplied by too many deaths. Tayo mourns the loss of his mother, his brother, his uncle Josiah, and his connections to the land, to Mother Earth. His very existence is a constant search for the return of (or to) a nurturing mother figure. This strong desire finally leads him to search for the scattered cattle with which he and Josiah had once planned to start a herd. In searching for the cattle he finds the M(Other's) presence/even body promised in objects such as the cattle, the mountains and the woman Ts'eh. The full presence of the Other is never possible, but is always promised in these discrete objects. These fragmented objects and their stories signify the absence of fullness (a type of death), but Tayo finally learns that the promise of small presences is enough even when this peace of mind is jeopardized along the way by the witchcraft of the demented war veterans he knows. Such witchery would claim that there is nothing promised beyond the severed piece. Witchery is satisfied with mutilation; it ignores the larger life of connectedness in the universe and the knowledge that stories keep the connections alive and these infinite verbal associations can and should go on forever. Tayo transcends separations by learning that death, absence and silence promise infinite fullness; therefore, finally, his desire for death is a desire to go on living in order to perpetuate the possibilities of presence.

The structure of Tayo's quest in *Ceremony* parallels Jacques Lacan's theoretical paradigm. Lacan asserted that the infant, already estranged from the mother, passes through a "mirror stage." Upon seeing himself reflected as a coherent image in the mirror, the infant is reassured by assuming that he is a unified self, and from this sense of unity the ego is born. But a strong, rigid ego was undesirable for Lacan; inflexibility is mentally unhealthy. Besides, this mirrored unity is only an illusion, and the subject is deflected from knowing that his existence is really as a *corps morcelé* or fragment self. The sooner an individual relinquishes the illusion of unity and recognizes the infinite potential of verbal associations and of combining the fragments of stories, the healthier he will be. The impelling desire, however unconscious, in a human life is always a desire for reunification with the Mother—a primal unity which can never be reaccomplished. From Freud's *Fort! Da!* case, Lacan conjectured that the pain of severance from the mother can be assuaged by language. The child in this case threw a toy attached to a string out of his pram; it disappeared from his view, but he could pull it back into his presence with the string. With this game he consoled himself over the absence of his mother. That something could reappear promised that the mother also would eventually return. By imposing language on the situation, the child managed his own loneliness and alienation. The little language, the few stories that we have signify the total fullness of Language beyond us—the M(Other). For Lacan, as well as for Tayo, desire is born with language.

What should be emphasized is that unity with the self, with the land, with others or with the mother is never achieved; its possibility is only glimpsed. Lacan believed that what is at stake in psychoanalysis is not unity but rather the advent in the subject of that little reality which one's perpetual desire sustains in one: "our path is the intersubjective experience where this desire makes itself recognized"[1] To "feel the weight of words,"[2] to be "afflicted with language,"[3] was for Lacan both a dis-ease and a blessing since "the quest for being—the quest for the lost 'authentic' self (however interminable)—depends upon an original loss and the discovery of difference; self-knowledge depends upon an original misconstruction."[4]

Tayo enters the novel already misconstructed. He is an already dissociated self, a confusion of voices. He tosses in the old iron bed, the coiled springs squeaking, calling up dreams; loud voices roll him over and over like debris caught in a flood. Tonight the singing had come first, a man singing in Spanish; sometimes the Japanese voices, angry and loud; sometimes the wind; then Laguna voices, Uncle Josiah calling him, bringing him medicine. But before Josiah could come, the fever voices would drift and whirl—ordering voices, damp voices, women's voices, his mother's voice, loud juke box music and language he could not understand.[5]

But what Tayo learns in the duration of the novel is that these myriad voices—these language fragments which come to structure his unconscious—are not to be feared but welcomed as marks of his own uniqueness, even though these marks have scarred his unconscious and made him ill. Lacan writes:

What we teach the subject to recognize as his unconscious is his history—that is the way we help him to perfect the contemporary historization of the facts which have already determined a certain number of the historical "turning points" in his existence. . . . Thus, every fixation at a so-called instinctual stage is above all a historical scar: a page of shame that is forgotten or undone, or a page of glory which compels. But what is forgotten is recalled in acts, and undoing-what-has-been-done is opposed to what is said elsewhere.[6]

But as Spider Woman in *Ceremony* reminds Fly and Hummingbird in myth, undoing-what-has-been-done is never easy: "It isn't very easy/to fix things up again. Remember that/next time" (268). Tayo's struggle in *Ceremony* is bitter and abject, but Lacan also reminds us that "destiny is not very benevolent;" when a man sets off on the path of his desire, he goes forth alone and betrayed.[7] Tayo is alone; he has been rejected by family and society. He will be betrayed by his friends. This betrayal is a function of words which wound easily and which are always devoted to ambiguity since they have no proper meaning. Their function is to mask meaning, to "hollow out reality," make a hole in it, and thereby open the dialectic of truth and being.[8] Tayo is at first frightened and dismayed by these ambiguities and horrified by the various deaths, both actual and imagined, that he was powerless to prevent. But Lacan was fascinated with these holes in reality and with the various signifiers we use to mark and describe deaths. Lacan claims that the signifier of an empty grave, an unmourned death or an unburied body may be a ghost, a secret kept or denied by descendants, or just the proper name. The empty grave is also a subject; so the human subject is always split, split between a mark and a void.[9] Tayo is a split self, a victim of "word wounds." His endeavor is to learn to manage such deaths himself by way of "word cures" and to learn to repair his relationships to the dead. In his case this includes his mother, his father, his brother Rocky, his Uncle Josiah and the war dead that haunt him. Tayo resists acquiring this knowledge; at first he tries to survive with the living. Lacan taught that we think we can negotiate with the living; the dead, existing in Otherness,[10] are far more difficult to handle.

Such negotiation is always accomplished or at least attempted in discourse, but Lacan claimed that no single part of speech has the privilege of denominating things, contrary to the grammatical appearances which attribute this function to the substantive; meaning is never capable of being sensed except in the uniqueness of the signification developed by the discourse. . . . Thus it is that interhuman communication is always information on information, put to the test of a community of Language, a numbering and a perfecting of the target which will surround the objects, themselves born of the concurrence of a primordial rivalry.[11]

Old Ku'oosh, the Laguna medicine man called in by Old Grandmother, echoes Lacan here when he comes to talk to Tayo. Ku'oosh emphasizes the obligations to the community that come with being human and he alludes inherently to the primordial, to times immemorial and originary:

> He spoke softly, using the old dialect full of sentences that were involuted with explanations of their own origins, as if nothing the old man said were his own but all had been said before and he was only there to repeat it. Tayo had to strain to catch the meaning, dense with place names he had never heard (35).

Old Ku'oosh tells Tayo that the world is fragile:

> The word he chose to express "fragile" was filled with the intricacies of a continuing process, and with a strength inherent in spider webs woven across paths through sand hills where early in the morning the sun becomes entangled in each filament of web. It took a long time to explain the fragility and intricacy because no word exists alone, and the reason for choosing each word had to be explained with a story about why it must be said this certain way. That was the responsibility that went with being human, old Ku'oosh said, the story behind each word must be told so there could be no mistake in the meaning of what had been said; and this demanded great patience and love. (36, 27)

Much like Ku'oosh, Lacan believed that the word is instituted in the structure of a semantic world, that of language. The word never has only one use. Every word always has a beyond, sustains several functions, envelops several meanings. Behind what discourse says there is what it means (wants to say), and behind what it wants to say there is another meaning, and this process will never be exhausted[12] as it exists in a community of discourse.

After Ku'oosh's visit Tayo makes a start at learning to "read" instead of fear of his own conflation of voices: he hears Ku'oosh's explanations, eats the green-cornmeal mush the old man brings, and finds that the nausea is at least momentarily gone.

The women of Tayo's family are in no way nurturing mothers. Not only is Tayo illegitimate (a rupture of orderly ties and lineage), his mother also abandons him as a small child. Her sister, "Auntie," feeds and shelters him so that she may be seen as Christian by others, but she shuns him, denies him love, and forces upon him a separation from the family circle. Since Tayo is illegitimate and a half-breed besides, he is also denied access to the nurturing influence of Pueblo culture and religion. Tayo knows he cannot claim the place of son in the family or tribe; to do so would be to usurp the concept, to "falsify a filiation." Lacan comments that "we know what ravages a falsified filiation can produce, going as far as the dissociation of the subject's personality. . . . It is indeed the confusion of generations which . . . is an abomination."[13] Auntie exacerbates the disintegration of Tayo's personality by reminding him constantly of how much shame and disgrace he has brought upon the family. It is a triple dose of shame for Tayo because he inherits the "texts" and memories of his mother's shame. She was "shamed by what they taught her in school about the deplorable ways of the Indian people," shamed by the truth in the fists and "greedy feeble love-making" of the white men, and shamed by the pain of what she was doing with her life. "The feelings of shame, at her own people and at the white people, grew inside her, side by side like monstrous twins that would have to be left in the hills to die" (71).

Lacan writes that the "demon of shame" strikes the signified (in this case, Tayo), "marking it as the bastard offspring of the signifying concatenation" such that the "subject [Tayo] designates his being only by barring everything he signifies." Of course, to himself and to Auntie who never lets him forget, he signifies nothing. So far, for Tayo, the universal or the "Other is the site of a lack of satisfaction."[14] But, as we shall see, "lack of satisfaction" is ultimately desirable and healthy; it is the locus of desire which produces action.

Thus Tayo's situation for most of the novel is the situation of the *corps morcelé*, the fragmented mind and self or the fractured image; but to be aware of one's real dissolution, as Tayo is aware, is a positive start on the healing process. Being aware of one's fragmentation allows one to avoid the illusion of harmony promised by a mirror image. Lacan writes that even:

the image of the proper name evokes the fantasy of the *corps morcelé*. We are made to realize how easily the psyche is punctured by image, photo, phantasm, or phrase. The terrible rigor of psychic, like logicistic, process sets this human vulnerability in a perversely radiant frame, one that may extend toward infinity. . . . Psychoanalysis, in this light, reveals once more the unresolvable ambivalence of passion as both suffering and ecstasy.[15]

Tayo's suffering at least is manifested in the Veteran's hospital where he exists only as "white smoke" and vague outlines:

For a long time he had been white smoke . . . faded into the white world of bed sheets and walls; sucked away by the words of doctors who tried to talk to the invisible, scattered smoke. He had seen outlines of gray steel tables, outlines of the food they pushed into his mouth, which was only an outline too. . . . He walked . . . watching the outlines of his feet. . . . He inhabited a gray winter fog on a distant elk mountain where hunters are lost indefinitely and their own bones mark the boundaries (14)

Even after he leaves the Veteran's hospital his world is a kaleidoscope of outlines: "He leaned against the depot wall; sounds were becoming outlines again, vague and hollow in his ears" (21). At home there was the "outline of his lie in the dim light," the "concave outlines" that Rocky's body had made in his bed (32). And he remembers the "dismembered corpses and the atomic heat-flash outlines where human bodies had evaporated" (38). Tayo is already starkly situated in and aware of Otherness; he is not deluded by the illusory unity, the seeming cohesive substance of the mirror image. He has no rigid ego to impede understanding.

As white smoke Tayo seems to himself to be invisible, transparent and fading—an ironic reversal of the usual sense a conscious subject has of self, imagining that there is easy access to a transparent, readable self. We usually think we can "know ourselves." Lacan affirms a skewed awareness such as Tayo's:

The unconscious is both immanent and transcendent to individual subjects and marks the frontier beyond which the traditional subject, presumed to be "transparent" to himself, loses the self-transparency and begins to "fade," with all the consequent effects that lead to those characteristic manifestations of unconscious processes.[16]

In ordinary thinking a fading self is cause for alarm; the person seems to be "losing his grip" on himself. In Tayo's case, to acknowledge a sense of fading, even fading into smoke, is to acknowledge an awareness of the constant sliding of the subject under the metonymic chain of signifiers which is language. Existing in outlines is a type of affirmation: "Feared loss of self produces a new self-affirmation," as Geoffrey Hartman rephrases Lacan,[17]

Tayo begins to reaffirm his existence when the nausea of otherness is replaced by an acceptance of and familiarity with fragmentation. At a place his dead Uncle Josiah had often visited, Tayo

> leaned back against the wall. . . . He picked up a fragment of fallen plaster and drew dusty white stripes across the backs of his hands, the way ceremonial dancers sometimes did. . . . It was soothing to rub the dust over his hands; he rubbed it carefully across his light brown skin, the stark white gypsum dust making a spotted pattern, and then he knew why it was done by the dancers: it connected them to the earth (109).

At this place and with this marking gesture, he is "visible" again. Later he goes to another medicine man, Betonie, a Navajo, a race foreign and fearsome to the Pueblos, outside of the sphere of Pueblo familiarity. Betonie "keeps track of things" by collecting bits and pieces of what might otherwise be called junk, but which mark the traces of human passage: bundles of newspapers, piles of telephone books "with the years scattered among cities," old calendars, "the sequences of years confused and lost," skin pouches, painted gourd rattles and "deer-hoof clackers of the ceremony (125–26). "All these things have stories alive in them," old Betonie said (127). Betonie teaches Tayo that the world of bits and pieces is a world of stories. It is a world to be desired even though it comes to us only in disconnected, disjointed signs, traces and marks. Betonie gives Tayo a fragment of his own story. (Lacan would approve the ambiguity of the pronoun referent.) Tayo adds to his story "the black of the sandpaintings on the floor of the hogan; the hills and mountains were the mountains and hills they had painted in sand," the medicine man drawing in the dirt with his finger. "Remember these stars' [Betonie] said. 'I've seen them and I've seen the spotted cattle; I've seen a mountain and I've seen a woman'" (152, 160). For Tayo "the world [outside] and the sandpaintings inside became the same that night. The mountains from all the directions had been gathered there that night (152).

Lacan could have spoken for Betonie:

> Symbols in fact envelop the life of man in a network so total that they
> join together, before he comes into the world, those who are going to
> engender him "by flesh and by blood"; so total that they bring to his
> birth, along with the gifts of the stars, . . . the design of his destiny; so
> total that they give the words which will make him faithful or renegade,
> the law of the acts which will follow him right to the very place where
> he *is* not yet and beyond his death itself.[18]

But Lacan cautions that:

> once installed within the symbolic order, we cannot contemplate or
> possess any object without seeing it unconsciously in the light of its pos-
> sible absence, knowing that its presence is in some way arbitrary and
> provisional.[19]

By now Tayo has learned to find fulfillment in absences. His appreciation of the "arbitrary and provisional" is subtly demonstrated as
Silko describes him watching a mountain lion:

> The mountain lion came out from a grove of oak trees in the middle of
> the clearing. He did not walk or leap or run; his motions were like the
> shimmering of tall grass in the wind. . . . The eyes caught twin reflec-
> tions of the moon; the glittering yellow light penetrated his chest and
> he inhaled suddenly. Relentless motion was the lion's greatest beauty,
> moving like mountain clouds with the wind, changing substance and
> color in rhythm with the contours of the mountain peaks: dark as lava
> rock, and suddenly as bright as a field of snow. When the mountain lion
> stopped in front of him, it was not hesitation, but a chance for the
> moonlight to catch up with him. (204)

To shimmer like grass in the wind, to reflect the moonlight, to be
relentless motion, to change substance and color with each breath is to
exist in an almost strobe-light presentation—shadowed as often as lit,
absent to the viewer as often as present.

Another graceful passage in *Ceremony* captures the sense of permanence behind the fleeting impression and the indelibility underlying
the erasable. Tayo comes upon a "she-elk, painted in pale lavender
clay on the south face of sandstone. Her great belly was swollen with
new life as she leaped across the yellow sandrock, startled forever

across the curve of cliff rock, ears flung back to catch a sound behind her. . . . But the rain and wind were overtaking her, rubbing away the details of her legs; the sun was bleaching her hooves into faint outlines, merging into the cliffs." Tayo remarks that it is almost gone, but Ts'eh, the woman with him, reminds him that "as long as you remember what you have seen, then nothing is gone. As long as you remember, it is part of the story we have together." (241–42).

For Tayo the "word" or signifier is a presence made of absences; Lacan would say that "it is the world of words that creates the world of things" in the sense that it renders them present, that is, meaning-full, in their absence.[20] And Stuart Schneiderman suggests that what interested Lacan ultimately was not the subject's assimilation or possession of objects, but rather his gaining of ex-istence, of "ec-stasy" which rejects stasis. This implies an ability to occupy the place of the Other, to be able to sense the fullness of language from the position of being outside of or alien to that fullness, a position Tayo certainly has been forced to occupy. Since Tayo is beginning to appreciate absences and to sense that speech and stories (signifiers and denominators) indicate the realm of the Other, the absent and the dead, and since Tayo is even beginning to welcome the familiarity of the Other, he now emerges from his initial paralysis "not to luxuriate in being but to face the real and to act according to his desire."[21] Action was an important concept for Lacan. He writes that "it is by way of the gift of the Word that all reality has come to man and it is by his continued act that he maintains it."[22]

But before Tayo can take meaningful action he must transcend developing a rigid ego. For Lacan the ego is born in the mirror stage when the child first assumes that he is represented by an image external to himself. The image appears unified to the child, but unity is an illusion. The child must eventually learn that he is always an "alienated subject" and that his "true subjectivity" is only "restored to him in the universal (that is in the world of language) by his learning to speak."[23] In the novel's scenes that could be construed as mirror scenes, Tayo is never seduced by the unity of his own reflection. He is always already reminded that he exists as part of the universal— as language.

One of Tayo's favorite places is a pool in a canyon. Cottonwood trees crowd the canyon, their leaves catching the reflections of the afternoon sun, "hundreds of tiny mirrors flashing" (46). Significantly, the mirrors would obviously fracture any conceivably coherent image into a myriad of fragments. Tayo then kneels "on the edge of the pool and lets the dampness soak into the knees of his jeans. He closed his eyes and . . . tasted the deep heartrock of the earth, where the water came from, and he thought maybe this wasn't the end after all (47). He does not see his own image; he uses senses other than visual which somehow reach deeper into the Other—the heartrock of Mother Earth with M(Other) representing the real Other—the fullness of language. On another occasion before he had gone to war he had come to the pool. He had shaken pollen from long yellow flowers over the water, a gesture which acknowledges fecundity, insemination and the random scattering of seed and possibility. Again, instead of seeing his own reflection he had watched a spider: "She drank from the edge of the pool, careful to keep the delicate egg sacs on her abdomen out of the water. . . . He remembered stories about her. . . . She alone had known how to outsmart the malicious mountain Ka't'sina who imprisoned the rain clouds" (98–99). The little spider becomes Spider Woman of the old stories in Tayo's mind: "Thought-Woman, the spider, named things and as she named them they appeared" (1). Then, as Tayo begins to think about science teachers' textbook explanations of causes, effects and origins, the "time immemorial" stories and the text explanations begin to war in his feelings. Kneeling at the pool he experiences the conflict of words rather than the unity of explanation.

In these mirroring events Tayo's image is never unified. He is always aware of the conflict and alienation engendered by language; but a sense of self is nonetheless born and it is a sense which inspires action. He decides to refind and regather the half-wild cattle his Uncle Josiah had bought to start a herd, which have been lost and scattered since Josiah died and Tayo went off to war.

Lacan speaks of desire as the impetus to action:

> I always find my desire outside of me because what I desire is always something that I lack, that is other to me. However, judgment should lead to action, and I should act according to my desire. . . . The subject who desires is always an other subject. Once the judgment is made, I act. . . . The desire I judge to be mine is not discovered by feeling or intuition; it never becomes a function of Self, and there is never an absolute certainty that it is mine. The action taken does not resolve the splitting of the subject; it enacts it.[24]

To breed wild cattle with Herefords producing hardy but heavier range cattle had always been Josiah's desire. Tayo finally learns that to desire as Josiah desired is enough to reinstate Josiah into his on-going story. His desire impels Tayo to the action of searching for the cattle. Tayo in action is still a split Self, alienated from the living but becoming more comfortable in the presence of the dead. Tayo is motivated to find the cattle for several reasons: the cattle are missing, Josiah is dead and the regaining of the cattle substitutes for him by displacement or metonymy, and Tayo himself has felt empty and purposeless until he decides to regather the cattle. Lacan asserts, in Terry Eagleton's paraphrase that:

> all desire springs from a lack, which it strives continually to fill. Human language works by such lack: the absence of the real objects which signs designate, the fact that words have meaning only by virtue of the absence and exclusion of others. To enter language, then, is to become a prey to desire: Language is what "hollows being into desire" where we spend all our time trying to attain the mother's body. We have to make do instead with substitute objects—"Object little a," with which we try vainly to plug the gap at the very centre of our being.[25]

Interestingly, in the search for the cattle, Tayo symbolically reenacts the search for a mother substitute, as does the child in the *Fort! Da!* case. Josiah has been a nurturing mother figure for Tayo and Josiah is now absent, but Tayo can regain the comfort of his presence by "pulling in" the cattle on the "string" of their instinct to head south. This locates them geographically even though they have disappeared from view. Tayo has only to begin at the place Josiah had brought them and from where they had escaped, then go south where he will eventually cross their trail or some other sign of them:

> When he turned away from the sun to mount the mare, he saw the spotted cattle, grazing in a dry lake flat below the ridge. . . . Their memory of people endured long after all other traces of domestication were gone; and he was counting on another instinct: the dim memory of direction which lured them always south, to the Mexican desert where they were born (205).

Whenever he glimpses the cattle, however infrequently, Tayo feels himself most able to cope, most mentally healthy. Lacan writes that an object that may or may not be found in reality is, as Freud says, one that provided a "real satisfaction" which has been lost. Thus, he declares that it is not so much a question of finding an object as of refinding it, "to convince oneself that it is still there."[26]

On the journey of refinding the cattle, substitutes for mother/Josiah, Tayo also refinds the body of the M(Other) in Mother Earth and in the woman he meets. In the search he first encounters the mountain lion and, lying on the ground afterwards, he feels the magnetism at the center of the earth "pulling him back, close to the earth, where the core was cool and silent. . . . and he knew how it would be: a returning rather than a separation (210). If he died there "he would seep into the earth and rest with the center, where the voice of the silence was familiar and the density of the dark earth loved him" (211). But he does not die; he meets a woman and she loves him. She does not stay with him; she only promises to return. But the promise and her remembered presence is enough: "the terror of the dreaming he had done on the bed was gone, uprooted from his belly; the woman had filled the hollow spaces with new dreams (229).

Paula Gunn Allen explains that "love can cure him—Love in the form of the mountain spirit Ts'eh"—the woman Tayo meets. Allen writes that the "water (Ts'e) woman (Nako) is the creatrix of the waters of love that flow from a woman and bless the earth and the beloved with healing."[27] From the Keres tradition the Thought Woman story tells that in the beginning "Tse-one-nako, Thought Woman, finished everything, thoughts, and the names of all things . . . and then our mothers, Uretsete and Naotsete, said they would make names and they would make thoughts. Thus they said. Thus they did."[28] Obviously there are close connections made in the novel among Ts'eh, the mountain Tse-pi'na and Thought Woman (Mother of us all). Allen continues, "It is clear that the land is female." The nature of Woman is associated with the creative power of thought. Nor is ordinary thinking referred to in connection with Her. "The Thought for which She is known is that kind that results in physical manifestations of such as mountains, lakes, creatures and philosophical/sociological systems."[29]

Tayo realizes that he is surrounded by women, by mothers (the real Other) who love him: the encircling mountains, "Tse-pi'na, 'the woman veiled in clouds'"; Ts'eh, who is also a "mountain," surnamed Montaño; the cattle, signs of Josiah's presence and desire; and Mother Earth into whom he is drawn. "He dreamed he made love with her there. He felt the warm sand on his toes and knees; he felt her body and it was as warm as the sand, and he couldn't feel where her body ended and the sand began" (232).

Juliet MacCannell describes Lacan's idea of love between man and woman:

> the love of 'man' for 'woman' is not, historically, poetically or otherwise, for *the* or *a* woman in her particularity . . . but for her *generality*, for her gender, or more precisely for what her gender reinforces in his gender. As a 'gender' she can be the complementary 'one' to his own oneness.[30]

Tayo and Ts'eh are complementary signifiers in the larger story that is still being told.

In *The Language of the Self* Lacan writes that "one sees clearly that the realization of perfect love is not a fruit of nature but of grace—that is to say, the fruit of an intersubjective accord imposing its harmony on the torn and riven nature which supports it."[31] Tayo of the "torn and riven nature" has felt love, glimpsed the elusive cattle, even experienced the presence of the body of the M(Other). These experiences have been made possible by first knowing alienation, absence and conflict. Paula Gunn Allen adds, "So Tayo's initiation into motherhood has been completed." He bridged "the distance between his isolate consciousness and the universe, because he has loved the Woman who brings all things into being."[32]

Lacan cautioned that:

> in a universe of discourse nothing contains everything, and here you find again the gap that constitutes the subject. The subject is the introduction of a loss in reality . . . the subject takes the place of the lack, a loss is introduced in the word, and this is the definition of the subject.[33]

Lacan calls this gap or rupture a "cut" in discourse. But Geoffrey Hartman writes that in much of his work Lacan interprets a blessure (wound) that is so ambivalently a "blessing" as the symptom that acts out whatever is human in us. He summarizes Lacan in saying that the wound makes "distinct the very breach" that renders the psyche visible. It is a movement of desire that cannot define itself except as a desire and possession of another: a desire that may not be appropriated by the self, and so cannot build up a stable self.[34] Besides the fragmentations and dissociations already discussed, there are a series of cuts, wounds, castrations and breaches (some benign and some malignant) in Tayo's penultimate experiences.

The old medicine man Betonie initiates Tayo's healing ceremony, his induction into the world of stories and of fragmented discourse, by actually cutting Tayo's head. After making the cut with a flint knife, Betonie prays signifiers of pure sound, 'Eh-hey-yah-ah-na! eh-hey-yah-ah-na!" as the blood oozes along Tayo's scalp (150). Tayo glimpses in a dream the wild speckled cattle running from him, but still heading predictably south (152). The dream is born of the knife cut and of the irruption of unintelligible signifiers.

Finally Tayo corrals the cattle and inspects them: "occasionally a calf bolted away, bucking and leaping in a wide arc, returning finally to its mother when it tired of playing. Tayo's heart beat fast; he could see Josiah's vision emerging; he could see the story taking form in bone and muscle" (236). According to Lacan parts such as these "coalesce to form the body schema serving as paradigm for the fantasies that become 'stuff' through which the speaking I manifests itself as it fades."[35] These parts represent the drive/desire of the subject; in this case of the dead Josiah or the living Tayo, it is the same.

But the reader cannot help but be struck by other prominent metaphors of cuts and cutting in *Ceremony*. There are evils (not a Lacanian word, but one that points to a Lacanian notion) in the universe. Lacan indicates that as long as we remain in an imaginary realm of being seeing our own identities as fixed and rounded we misrecognize reality as immutable.[36] The notion of immutability was, for Lacan, scandalous. Hartman writes that the ability to see "language as the foundation process of differential meaning is *arrested* by the premature assumption of a 'fixating ego image.'"[37] Toward the end of the novel, Emo, a demented war veteran with a fixated ego, succumbs to these evils and seeks Tayo's life. In their perversions and psychoses, witches like Emo has become seek to "gut human beings while they are still breathing, to hold the heart still beating so the victim will never feel anything again. When they finish you watch yourself from a distance and you can't even cry (240). These victims have become walking cadavers. And these witches prefer the immutability of the severed piece to the vitality of constant change.

Lacan taught that some people can be identified as dead, as the residue or waste product of life, as ambulating cadavers. He suggested that being dead is not the same as being a corpse since corpses are only the "imaginary representation of death and thus not the entire story."[38] Emo refuses to leave the Imaginary where he is in control. His is a fixed and rigid ego, "a nondifferential, glassy essence". . . . Being only a fixed ego his power is "not an adaptive or synthesizing power, but something that rises up and smites language,"[39] a wound that is not a blessing. Emo and his cohorts mark and cut Harley's body, substituting it for Tayo's whom they cannot capture. They slice off Harley's fingertips and the skin whorls of his toes; they excise his testicles and penis tip, all body parts that mark individual identities and claim to signify. But Harley dies, probably bleeding to death under their hands; his wounds are too rigidly fixed to open "the womb of signification." Significantly, his death occurs at an abandoned mining site, a cut in the earth from which uranium was mined for the first atomic bombs and close to the Trinity Site where the tests were made for the atomic bombs dropped on Hiroshima and Nagasaki. These produced death too real to be handled by the symbolic, and probably too real even to be handled by language. These evils destroy the sense of "blessing" engendered by the "cuts" Lacan speaks of.

Lacan asserts in the *Écrits* that the moment of cut (*coupure*) as blessing appears to be related to the death or absence on which desire "is borne." But the cut on Tayo's head is a symbolic castration. It becomes "the signifier of signifiers making possible the entrance into symbolic order."[40] His body is "cut up" by erotogenic zones—signs of desire moving across him signifying the phallic unity of all possible sign systems. Lacan reminds us that the notion of phallic unity forces us to

> consider that which is at the same time the least known and the most certain fact about this mythical subject which is the sensible phase of the living being: this fathomless thing capable of experiencing something between birth and death, capable of covering the whole spectrum of pain and pleasure in a word, what in French we call the *sujet de la jouissance.*[41]

In *Ceremony* Tayo also discovers this fathomless jouissance:

> He cried the relief he belt at finally seeing the pattern, the way all the stories fit together—the old stories, the war stories, their stories—to become the story that was still being told. He was not crazy; he had never been crazy. He had only seen and heard the world as it always was: no boundaries, only transitions through all distance and time. (258)

Tayo knows that the stories are not new stories; he has only relearned their patterns. He has, as Lacan would say, "always known the answer," but the distinction between knowledge and truth repeatedly emphasized by Lacan points out the function of *méconnaissance* and *reconnaissance* in human life. Truth is not knowledge but recognition. Mental illness is the refusal to recognize that the mechanisms of negation, disavowal, rejection and isolation flow from such *méconnaissance*.[42]

Tayo has learned to read the irruptions of truth from the unconscious. Lacan wrote that "the unconscious is that chapter of my history which is marked by a blank or occupied by a falsehood: it is the censored chapter. But the Truth can be found again; it is most often already written down elsewhere." That is to say:

—in monuments: this is my body—that is to say, the hysterical nucleus of the neurosis where the hysterical symptom reveals the structure of a Language and is deciphered like an inscription.
—in archival documents also: these are my childhood memories;
—in semantic evolution: this corresponds to the stock of words and acceptations of my own particular vocabulary, as it does to my style of life and to my character;
—in traditions as well, and not only in them but also in the legends which, in a heroicized form, transport my history;
—and lastly, in the traces which are inevitably preserved by the distortions necessitated by the linking of the adulterated chapter to the chapters surrounding it, and whose meaning will be re-established by my exegesis.[43]

Tayo has learned to assimilate these texts: bodily symptoms and urges, childhood memories, the idiosyncrasies of life style and culture, tribal traditions and myths, and the other distortions and fragments of his existence.

Finally, as a survivor Tayo has a debt to pay to the dead. He must attempt to reestablish some sort of continuity for the living. This continuity is maintained by revitalizing the language and reviving the myths.[44] In *The Language of the Self* Lacan quotes Schiller, "What is to live immortal in song must perish in life."[45] Tayo sees that the story must be told, the dead mourned and placed in the symbolic order.

In the beginning of the novel Tayo's brother Rocky is killed in the war and Tayo believes that "it was him, Tayo, who had died, but somehow there had been a mistake with the corpses, and somehow his was still unburied" (28). At that time Josiah's death was also unmourned.

When Tayo dreams of Josiah, who had loved him with "all the love there was" (33), he wakes to emptiness and loss, but he learns to "re-situate them in a discourse" where "only the reference to the discourse will prevent that grief from becoming chronic." Further, as Stuart Schneiderman writes, when we give the dead over to the symbolic order their fate is not left in the destructive hands of anyone's ego. The case where the ego finds the justification for its work of mourning is precisely that in which someone has "died" but is not dead. Someone is dead-to-me, no longer loved or loving. But that someone, being dead-to, is not dead-too. When the experience of love is primary, the ego's dominion is extended and death is reduced to a loss of love. The ego denies death by idealizing love and life; the dead remain alive in the strong ego, still loving and beloved.[46] Since Tayo does not have a rigid ego, he will not deny death nor continue to be obsessed by loss. Schneiderman writes:

> A living memory ought not to remain in the ego to captivate and fasci-
> nate, but this does not mean that nothing remains. From the point of
> view of the ego, a failure to remember does mean that nothing remains;
> thus the ego is the seat of nihilism. The image of the beloved is not the
> same as the trace of that person's passage. Someone who has been bur-
> ied leaves a mark behind, a trace of his passage through our world, and
> that trace is inscribed indelibly in the unconscious.[47]

The marks of Tayo's dead exist in his unconscious, in his genetic in-heritance, in the cattle and in the mountains—all marks of their de-sires which are now his desires.

Tayo has also learned that staying alive is easy "now that he didn't care about being alive any more" (40). And when they come upon a dead calf, the woman Ts'eh teaches Tayo that "death isn't much. . . . Sometimes they don't make it. That's all. It isn't very far away. . . . There are much worse things, you know. The destroyers: they work to see how much can be lost, how much can be forgotten. They destroy the feeling people have for each other" (240). And so Tayo learns to "desire death" as separation and silence for such absences signify a fuller presence than the actual thing itself. He has accepted death's presence and just before the encounter/escape from Emo he stops to listen to death's presence:

> He listened, and there was nothing but the sound of the wind, like a
> hawk sweeping close to the ground whirring wings of wind that called

back years long past and the people lost in them, all returning briefly in a gust of wind. The feeling lasted only as long as the sound, but he wanted to go with them, to be swept away. (253–54)

Tayo desires death and a reuniting with all his dead loved ones, but to maintain a strong desire for death one must continue to live. Lacan wrote,

> When we wish to attain in the subject what was before the serial articulations of the Word, and what is primordial to the birth of symbols, we find it in death, from which his existence takes on all the meaning it has. It is in effect as a desire for death that he affirms himself for others; if he identifies himself with the other, it is by fixing him solidly in the metamorphosis of his essential image, and no being is ever evoked by him except among the shadows of death.[48]

The shadows of death, of course, are words and the Otherness of language, even just the momentary voice of the wind which is so evocative for Tayo. Or it is the language which is maintained in dialogue with others and in recounting the old stories, thereby evoking the presence of the dead. Schneiderman reminds us that the desire to die does not translate into suicide. If, as Lacan put it, one ought to sustain desire and not seek an object that will gratify it and thereby erase it, the desire to die is best enacted when death is kept at a distance.[49] He continues to say that what is important about desire is how to sustain it, how to protract it in time, how to put off the satisfaction of that desire in order, strangely enough, to make the experience of desiring more satisfying. "Actual and final satisfaction is equivalent to dying. . . . [Therefore] the desire for death means that the desire is cultivated to the extent that death is kept at a distance, ultimately to be experienced not as a real death but as *jouissance*.[50]

Tayo recognizes that existence is best inscribed in a ring. The old stories, his story and the stories of his dead loved ones have come full circle. Old Grandmother remarks, "It seems like I already heard these stories before . . . only thing is, the names sound different" (273). At first Tayo's "dreams had been terror at loss, at something lost forever; but nothing was lost; all was retained between the sky and the earth, and within himself. He had lost nothing" (229). Tayo also realizes that

> The mountain could not be lost to them, because it was in their bones; Josiah and Rocky were not far away. They were close; they had always

been close. And he loved them then as he had always loved them, the feeling pulsing over him as strong as it had ever been. They loved him that way; . . . The damage that had been done had never reached this feeling. This feeling was their life, vitality locked deep in blood memory, and the people were strong, and the fifth world endured, and nothing was ever lost as long as the love remained. (230)

Lacan also felt that things had to come full circle; that Being was best inscribed in a circle or ring: "To inscribe [such *jouissance*] it is necessary to define it in a circle, what I call the Otherness of the sphere of language."[51] For the reader, one of the pleasures of *Ceremony's* text is to see that Tayo has learned that Otherness contains the fullest possibilities of presence. What promise could be more irresistible?

Notes

* I would like to thank Professors Jerrold E. Hogle and Herbert N. Schneidau of the University of Arizona English Department for their help and advice on conceptualizing and organizing this essay.

1. Jacques Lacan, *The Language of the Self* (Baltimore: Johns Hopkins University Press, 1968) 42.
2. Juliet Flower MacCannell, *Figuring Lacan* (Lincoln: University of Nebraska Press, 1986) xv.
3. MacCannell 46.
4. Lacan 166.
5. Leslie Marmon Silko, *Ceremony* (New York: Signet, 1977) 5. All further page references to this work will be given in the text.
6. Lacan 23–24.
7. Stuart Schneiderman, *Jacques Lacan* (Cambridge: Harvard University Press, 1983) 17.
8. MacCannell 45.
9. Schneiderman 6–7.
10. The Other for Lacan has a functional value, representing both the significant other to whom the neurotic's demands are addressed (the appeal to the Other), as well as the internalization of this Other (we desire what the Other desires) and the unconscious subject itself or himself (the unconscious is the discourse of, or from, the Other). Sometimes the Other refers to the parents: to the mother as the real Other, to the father as the Symbolic Other,

yet it is never a person. Very often the term seems to refer simply to the unconscious itself, although the unconscious is most often described as the locus of the Other. See Anthony Wilden's explanation in his notes to *The Language of the Self,* pages 263–264.

11. Lacan 123.

12. MacCannell 47.

13. Lacan 40.

14. MacCannell 102

15. Geoffrey H. Hartman, *Saving the Text* (Baltimore: Johns Hopkins University Press, 1981) 97.

16. John P. Muller and William J. Richardson, *Lacan and Language* (New York: International Universities Press, 1982) 359.

17. Hartman, *Saving,* 58.

18. Lacan 42.

19. Terry Eagleton, *Literary Theory* (Minneapolis: University of Minnesota Press, 1983) 186.

20. Muller and Richardson 79.

21. Schneiderman 103.

22. Lacan 86.

23. Lacan 172.

24. Schneiderman 99.

25. Eagleton 168.

26. Schneiderman 101.

27. Paula Gunn Allen, "The Psychological Landscape of *Ceremony,*" *American Indian Quarterly* (Spring 1979): 8.

28. Allen 9–10.

29. Allen 10.

30. MacCannell 108

31. Lacan 26.

32. Allen 12.

33. Jacques Lacan, "Of Structure As an Inmixing of an Otherness Prerequisite to Any Subject Whatever," *The Structuralist Controversy* (Baltimore: Johns Hopkins University Press, 1977) 193.

34. Hartman 99.

35. Muller and Richardson 370.

36. Eagleton 186.

37. Hartman 58.

38. Schneiderman 62.

39. Hartman 27.

40. Muller and Richardson, cited, 325.

41. Lacan, "Of Structure," 194.

42. Lacan, *Language,* 165.

43. Lacan, *Language,* 21.

44. Schneiderman 160.
45. Lacan, *Language* 120.
46. Schneiderman 151–152.
47. Schneiderman 152.
48. Lacan, *Language*, 85.
49. Lacan, *Language*, 23.
50. Lacan, *Language*, 86.
51. Lacan, "Of Structure," 193–194.

6

Textual Perspectives
and the Reader in The Surrounded

JAMES RUPPERT

When D'Arcy McNickle wrote and rewrote *The Surrounded*, he was clearly working with a set of conventions he knew his audience would understand. As he revised and edited to satisfy each potential editor, he made a virtue of necessity and richly layered his narrative closer to what he perceived to be a publishable novel.

McNickle's experience and the published text of *The Surrounded* is used here to illustrate Wolfgang Iser's insight that fiction differs from ordinary discourse because it provides several channels of communication governed by different intentions, which create different perspectives. Ultimately, the convergence of these intentions, these perspectives, is in the reader. While the perspectives construct a text that encourages the reader to respond in prestructured ways, the reader must participate in the changes of perspectives bringing about the convergence. Thus, when Iser looks at a text he concludes that meaning comes into existence only in the act of reading. Criticism of McNickle's work has lacked insight into the dynamic relationship between the four textual perspectives (implied author, plot, characters and implied reader) and the meaning of the text which the reader takes away from the novel. A close exploration of this dynamic relationship illuminates the quality of McNickle's art and the fullness of his meaning.

Iser has theorized that since the act of reading is sequential, the careful reader must view one perspective at a time, letting the new material modify his view of the text's meaning. As the reader does so, each character constructs a specific viewpoint which becomes a momentary, central theme, to be viewed against the horizon of what has gone before. The reader must readjust his understanding of past action and form new expectations concerning the future. However, since the perspective on the meaning shifts from one viewpoint to another and modifies what has come before, the reader is constantly being set up only to have the ground of his perceptions pulled out from under him. This process whereby the reader sets up new conventions and expectations encouraged by the writer and then continually modifies them has been referred to as "misreading." As the reader progresses through the text, he eliminates partial and inadequate understandings of meaning, leaving a series of possible viewpoints. The impetus is always present for the reader to discard attitudes inadequate to the understanding of the text, and he may shed some of those very conventions with which he began to read the text. By following the four textual perspectives (implied author, plot, characters and implied reader), then, the reader changes, grows, transforms.[1] Thus, the reader is always a potential being in a dynamic relation to the text, a being that the act of reading has created.

In *The Act of Reading* Iser explains the first perspective, that of the implied reader, by clarifying the tension created between "the role offered by the text and the real reader's disposition."[2] It is clear to Iser that the role offered to the reader by the text is not simply one of receiving a definitive message. The reader starts with a set of conventions about society, fiction and the text. McNickle works against these assumed values by manipulating the four perspectives on meaning. Iser refers to the role given to the reader by the text as the "implied reader."

For McNickle, the implied reader was the conventional reader who held the values of the white, literate public of the early 1930s, a public with limited preconceptions of Indian life and values. But the text manipulates the implied reader's role, working it against the other perspectives. The reader is placed in a variety of roles such as a storyteller's audience, confidante, synthesizer of the "clash of values" and interpreter of allegory. McNickle's task is to transform that typical reader of

1936 into one aware of Indian cultural values and the fallacies of white attitudes toward Indians.

The plot offers a second perspective on the meaning of a text since the series of events may undercut, transform or reinforce the conventions understood by the reader. In *The Surrounded* the events which portray hope, conciliation, entanglement and despair create an accelerating, tragic vortex where event undercuts emotion.

A third and easily accessible perspective on the meaning of the text is offered by the main character or characters. As characters think, speak and act, each of them presents a view on meaning, a view the reader can accept or reject. The thoughts and words of Archilde, the young half-breed protagonist; Max, his Spanish, rancher father; Catherine, his Salish, religious mother; Grepilloux, the benevolent, paternal missionary; and Modeste, the old Salish medicineman, embody distinct viewpoints on meaning expressed in the text.

The fourth and final perspective on the text is that of the implied author. Readers form a conception of the author based on style, manner of telling and selection of material. These may or may not have relevance to the person described on the dust jacket. Many critics follow Wayne Booth's suggestion that we refer to this persona as the implied author. As McNickle offers the reader a role, so he creates a persona for himself. While writing of the boy Archilde who grows up much as he did but who dies tragically in Montana, McNickle is not writing of the young man living the literary life of Depression New York. Critics must not fuse the narrator of *The Surrounded* and McNickle the man too quickly. For the tragedy of the novel to work for the reader, the implied author must believe in Archilde's inevitable destruction, a belief that McNickle need not necessarily hold.

The implied author believes that Archilde is enmeshed from the beginning, but he reveals this attitude to the reader slowly. He does not believe that Archilde is the hope of the future as do some characters and as Archilde later in the novel starts to believe. As Archilde struggles to accept his Indian past, the implied author embeds his own wide-ranging, discouraging insights into the text. Even while Archilde feels free and strong, the implied author structurally counteracts Archilde's hopeful outlook by presenting the perspectives of the powers-that-be (such as the Indian Agent and the Sheriff) that will eventually destroy Archilde. The implied author strives to destroy any hope; his perspective is that human action and volition are ineffectual. Yet this obstacle allows the reader to create a synthesis and ultimately see that Archilde's actions and newly found wisdom are valuable human efforts. For the same reasons, the actions of protagonists of American Naturalism, such as those in the novels of Dreiser, Crane and Norris, embody the human spirit and create value.

In the book's first chapter, Archilde returns home from the white world (Portland, Oregon) after a year's absence. He plans to do the pleasurable things of his youth one more time and maybe settle some old antagonisms before he goes out into the world forever. He intends to reach back and touch the good things of his youth, unifying memory and reality to form a solid base of past experience and family relationships to remember as he travels off. Here the distance between the perspectives of the implied author and the implied reader is very slight. The reader's preconceived mores are reinforced and exploited. It is only right that a young boy leave his family and find his fortune in the big world. He is a dutiful son because he returns and wants to make peace before he goes off. He tries to remain neutral, yet becomes concerned when faced with family distrust and "warfare." When Archilde refers to an endless round of fighting and stealing, the reader agrees with his perspective that he should get away and "make something of himself."

In this chapter the implied author, implied reader, and plot only vaguely credit the comments of the old woman, Katherine, whose knowledge of the world is severely limited and who seems locked in her own routine and archaic ritual relationships. Neither the implied author nor the implied reader seem to understand or appreciate these. Max, her husband, is more accessible but unsympathetic. He seems cantankerous and unloving, yet he offers to save Louis' neck. It is clear that the young boy should be off on his own with people of his own age, people who hold values similar to the reader's. Archilde's good motives are presented with great sympathy and his perspective merges with that of the reader. Consequently, the plot seems to be a straightforward return-of-the-native, and the implied reader settles into a comfortable return-of-the-native pattern of response (though that pattern is one that writers since Hamlin Garland had been deconstructing). The plot also suggests a subplot through Louis: where is he and what will become of him?

The average white, literate reader of the 1930s is encouraged to adapt a conventional viewpoint on textual meaning, one which reinforces the white patterns of cultural expectations. The unity of viewpoints in this chapter creates a clear foreground to which one small disturbing fact is backgrounded. True, Archilde seems to be coming home for a vacation: he wants to relax, to go fishing and riding and to climb a mountainside. But it seems that no one wants to fish anymore; the pieces of Archilde's neat construct do not easily fall into place. Much of Archilde's memory world remains the same; yet Archilde's young nephews want him to buy hooks. When Archilde offers to help them fish in an older, more Indian way, they decline his pastoral vision. It seems as if the rosy sense of memory and the joyous sense of the experience of nature do not motivate anyone except Archilde. The naive pastoral romanticism with which the implied reader has been encouraged to identify is already under revision. Also, the culturally correct ideas of revering one's mother and father begin to dissolve when one is faced with their reality, and Archilde's desire to flee takes on a deeper epistemological questioning in which the reader participates.

The next few chapters begin to assail the perspective asserted in the first chapter. The desirability of material progress is questioned by Max, then the paternalism and self-centered superiority of the priests becomes evident. Archilde also begins to question assumed white values, and because the reader has identified with him, the reader begins to question also. The plot continues to create situations which force Archilde to confront the contradictory perspectives of Max and Catherine, and later Modeste and Grepilloux. Since the main characters express motivations which do not find easy support in the conventional morality or cultural code, the plot entangles Archilde in what appear to be insoluble problems and encourages his disaffiliation.

Conventional morality is again questioned through the introduction of Grepilloux's diary and Modeste's story. The private motivations of both the whites and the Salish clearly express misunderstanding of each other. Grepilloux reads his diary to Max and the reader, but the protagonist, Archilde, is not allowed to see it. The implied reader is offered privileged insider information and sees more completely than any character, including Archilde. The plot and character interaction stop completely at these two points, while the implied author interjects material which creates non-personal, historical and mythic background and ironically comments on the plot and characters in order to create an allegorical parallel. As a result, the implied reader is presented with historical and mythic stories as if he were an audience at the foot of a story-teller. The total effect is that of foregrounding the questioning of the conventional morality: since the reader can not assume the perspective of either story (they are so obviously in contrast, and each admits many erroneous assumptions) he must create a perspective that is a synthesis.

While the reader revises his understanding of "what is right" in Indian/white relations, Archilde becomes more relaxed with his people, his past, and their strivings and limitations. As the first half of the book concludes, the characters reveal the bankruptcy of the white idea of progress for the Indian as well as the ruinous effect of white religion and education on the social and personal structure of Salish life.

When the double murder takes place, the reader is ready to revise his understandings or cultural code. The plot makes it clear that Archilde is not responsible for the murder though he appears to be in the conventional world of white morality, and he is supposed to report the killings though his family and cultural ties keep him from doing so. Love of family, a value that is foregrounded at the beginning, is now in conflict with observance of the law. Archilde and his mother have begun placing Salish code over white cultural code, yet neither can see what the future will bring. Archilde sees her and the old people as "shells and husks of life forms that had once possessed elastic strength." The implied author is skeptical of either code's efficacy and certain of the misunderstanding that the conflict creates, but the implied reader is torn. The plot pushes toward entanglement and tragedy as a consequence of misunderstanding good motives.

Furthermore, the perspective of the plot is drastically separated from that of Archilde; it predominates. While the plot's complications become foregrounded, the implied reader must revise his perspective as Archilde revises his understanding and actions. It is clear that he must believe in the value of reconstructing the Indian identity, yet that requires giving up the values of white society and its laws. Because Archilde continues to feel like an outsider, ineffectual to change the despair he sees, the reader must supply suggestions for actions and values. Iser explains this movement to a position of insight when he writes:

> We call this meeting place the meaning of the text, which can only be brought into focus if it is visualized from a standpoint. Thus, standpoint and convergence of textual perspectives are closely related, although neither of them is actually represented in the text, let alone set out in words. Rather they emerge during the reading process, in the course of

which the reader's role is to occupy shifting vantage points that are geared to a prestructured activity and to fit the diverse perspective into a gradually evolving pattern.[3]

In the episode of the Indian dance, the value that the dances had and may have again for the Salish is expressed in the way the old people are shown turning away from the white world. While their action creates meaning, it is a reactionary, stop-gap measure, one which the reader recognizes as a dead-end. The reader must place his hope in the young like Archilde. But the white dance section which follows the Indian dance introduces Elsie, a desperate young Indian and product of a boarding school. The view of whites and Indians at the dance effectively discourages any easy conclusion by the reader about the beneficial influences of white culture on young Indians. Presented with two opposing, parallel views of white/Indian interaction, the reader must synthesize a perspective that is separated from Archilde's confusion, the plot's increasing entanglement, or the implied author's belief in inevitable tragedy.

Iser explains how the reader's changing perspective is created by new information from the wandering perspective: "Thus the reader's communication with the text is a dynamic process of self-correction, as he formulates signifieds which he must then continually modify."[4] The reader's expectations and revised understanding of previous events in the text, or misreading, are a necessary part of endowing a text with meaning.

In chapter twenty-six, Archilde contemplates the misery and poverty around him and the implied reader again is tempted to follow Archilde's perspective, but the reader's perspective has been permanently separated from that of any character. In the story of the mare, Archilde's good motives are attacked by the implied author, but the conventional, white reformist attitudes that Archilde expresses are also denied the reader. In this episode the implied author cuts out the characters' perspectives and talks directly to the reader. By challenging the perspective of the reader, a perspective that has been so carefully encouraged, he foregrounds again the conventional mores that had formed the foreground of the first chapter and the background of the intervening chapters, but now they are assailed critically.

Archilde's perspective is not that of his people who want to return to the past or to hide from the present. Neither is it that of the implied reader. Archilde's perspective, which has functioned as the theme, is questioned at this point and the reader must reassess Archilde's good motives (fortunately Archilde will learn from this encounter as he does from all the encounters in the book). The reader is encouraged to find a new viewpoint from which he can reconstruct meaning and good action. To do this he must reassess and reject prior viewpoints that encouraged white cultural superiority or espoused reformist attitudes. As a consequence he adopts one which values Indian autonomy yet recognizes that the present system is not working and something new must be created. Here the reader's viewpoint is decidedly different from Archilde's who is not ready to give up white reformist values, from the plot's which will entangle him if he does or does not, and from the implied author's who is telling the implied reader a tale—the allegory of the mare with its despairing prediction of disaster. After this story it is clear that Archilde wants something better, but he is not sure what it is or how it will come about.

His answer seems to come at his mother's death bed when he becomes stronger, almost a leader. Since Archilde is not sure what he must do to make things better, the implied reader must figure out how to do that. Archilde acts because the emotions feel right, but the reader is encouraged to develop an independent understanding. Because the reader can't completely accept any perspective presented, he must begin to question social values that determine federal Indian policy, questions that are deeper and more practical than anyone in the book is asking. Archilde punctuates the implied reader's position by continuing to question him and compel him to answer, such as, "How could he really help Mike and Narcisse. . . . there ought to be something better."[5] The reader must create meaning for the novel out of the confluence of the perspectives. As Iser explains:

> . . . the observer finds himself directed toward a particular view which more or less obliges him to search for the one and only one standpoint that will correspond to that view." By virtue of that standpoint, the reader is situated in such a position that he can assemble the meaning toward which the perspectives of the text have guided him.[6]

Near the end of *The Surrounded*, when the narrative voice moves to the Indian Agent, the forces that precipitate the tragedy are developed. By shifting to a previously unused narrative voice the implied author helps the reader believe in the inevitable tragedy, but the reader is further pushed to question social forces and values. He sees the flaws in the white social machinery, flaws which will ensure tragedy. His position of superior knowledge reveals the petty, uninformed and unimaginative perspective of the agent and even of the best of white society. He is pushed even more strongly to a synthesis outside of the text, one which will make sense of the tragedy and eliminate the inevitability of the tragedy by creating cross-cultural understanding.

In the final chapter the reader's perspective is further separated from Archilde's. If he is to create a progressive synthesis from the various perspectives, the reader clearly must reject Archilde's lethargy and the vague flirtation with "paganism" that motivates Archilde's trip into the mountains with Elsie. It is Archilde's questioning that makes him a worthy protagonist and thus tragic, and it is his questions that encourage the reader to find answers and his own perspective. After the idyllic moment with Elsie, Archilde starts to question again. He becomes active and exercises his volition. However, at this point the plot and the implied author's perspectives diminish his centrality to the action. Both perspectives imply that Archilde's volition is ineffectual and will lead to ruin.

The final chapter is often reduced by critics to a single perspective— that of the plot which entangles or of the implied author who weaves this tale of lost chances (perhaps to suggest that Archilde should have gone away and retained white values as the nagging voice of conventional morality might suggest to the reader). For critics today, perhaps the desire to emphasize the tragic ending is a function of a heightened liberal conscience. In 1987 many readers express a belief in Indian self-determination that white audiences of 1936 did not generally share. Some readers tend to identify with such perspectives as Modeste's or even Archilde's. However, these perspectives are clearly incomplete and it is unlikely that McNickle intended the reader to unconditionally adopt them. While pessimistic, absurdist tragedy is a common artistic stance today, more can be gained in understanding the ending from the perspective of naturalism. Here human value is created by the protagonist's struggle, not his victory.

To create the meaning of the text, all perspectives must be merged and each redefined by the others. If the reader follows the shifting perspectives he is exalted by Archilde's quest and illuminated by what Archilde learns. The reader realizes that conventional white mores will not serve the Indians. The Indian agent voices conventional wisdom with which the reader would have agreed at the beginning of the book, but by the end of the book the reader is transformed and that transformation is positive. His standpoint is outside the text and the meaning of the text is created by him. The textual structures direct the reader to the only standpoint that will correspond to the confluence of the various perspectives; at this viewpoint he can assemble the meaning toward which the perspectives of the text have led. He has seen the history of misunderstanding on both sides; he knows that while the return to tradition and the past which Modeste and Katherine represent sustains Indian identity, it will not serve to avoid the tragedies of the present. While the character Archilde is doomed, the lasting transformation of *The Surrounded* is in the reader as he adopts new attitudes and adds them to his store of experience. Or as Iser concludes: "The text must therefore *bring about* a standpoint from which the reader will be able to view things that would never have come into focus as long as his own habitual dispositions were determining his orientation."[7]

In *The Surrounded* McNickle has richly structured his text. The struggle and tragedy of the text have led the reader to new understandings through a process similar to the way that Archilde begins to understand Max only after the tragic killings, and Archilde perceives his strength and relation to his people only as his mother dies. Through the use of questioning the reader moves background concerns with social values into the foreground. Likewise McNickle uses doubling to encourage the implied reader not to identify with any one character's perspective. Ultimately his use of allegory and storytelling sets the implied reader into the position of a synthesizing audience through which the reader connects with the external world.

Notes

1 Wolfgang Iser, *The Act of Reading* (Baltimore: Johns Hopkins University Press, 1978), p. 35.

2 Iser 37.

3 Iser 35.

4 Iser 67.

5 D'Arcy McNickle, *The Surrounded* (1936; rpt. Albuquerque: University of New Mexico Press, 1978) 273.

6 Iser 38.

7 Iser 35.

7

Opening the Text:

Love Medicine *and the Return*

of the Native American Woman

ROBERT SILBERMAN

Louise Erdrich's *Love Medicine* opens with June Kashpaw, middle-aged Chippewa woman, wasting time in the oil boom town of Williston, North Dakota while waiting for a bus that will take her back to the reservation where she grew up. She allows herself to be picked up by a white man in a bar; after a short, unsatisfying (for her) bit of lovemaking in his pickup, she takes off, cutting across the snowy fields as a storm begins to hit. There is a narrative break and then we learn that she has frozen to death.

This opening immediately establishes a relationship between *Love Medicine* and a well-known group of works by Native American authors: D'Arcy McNickle's *The Surrounded*, N. Scott Momaday's *The House Made of Dawn*, Leslie Marmon Silko's *Ceremony*, James Welch's *Winter in the Blood* and *The Death of Jim Loney*. These works are central texts in Native American literature, bearing a striking family resemblance to one another.

Reduced to bare essentials, they tell of a young man's troubled homecoming. The opening line of *The Surrounded* sounds the theme: "Archilde Leon had been away from his father's ranch for nearly a year."[1] The book's title proclaims the outcome; in the final line of the text Leon extends his hands to be shackled. From *The Surrounded* a clear line can be drawn to the later works by Momaday, Silko and Welch, in effect defining the backbone of contemporary Native American fiction.

Given this closely related body of texts, Native American literature seems made to order for recent developments in literary criticism and critical theory. The writings of McNickle, Momaday, Welch, Silko and others seem especially amenable to the analytical and interpretive preoccupations of such broad movements as structuralism and deconstructionist criticism. The many shared elements in the works, as well as the equally telling differences, make them a perfect case study for the analysis of combinations, oppositions and inversions beloved in structuralist criticism. Though not engaged in a technical, philosophical debate, Native American writers reveal an obsessive concern with the relation between speech and writing that is worthy of the deconstructionist critics. Finally, this body of literature incorporates among its major social and political concerns a preoccupation with origins, marginality and otherness that would have delighted Foucault. Notwithstanding the focus in these books on a central individual, the writers address broad historical relations between groups as well as individual psychology, dramatizing for example the conflicts between tribal peoples and institutional authorities such as the police, the Bureau of Indian Affairs, and the church. In such a context questions of language and discourse—Indian language(s) versus English, native forms of expression versus nontribal literary forms such as the novel—are inevitably questions of power.

It is possible to speculate on the reasons that the narratives of Mc-Nickle, Momaday, Silko and Welch take the form they do and hold such a central place in Native American literature. One could consider McNickle and Momaday in relation to Harold Bloom's theories of influence, or the relation of the works to the broader tradition of the *bildungsroman*, a common enough form for writers of first novels. One could consider the problem sociologically and historically, with McNickle first and then Momaday, Welch, and Silko marking a distinctive point in assimilation and education, moving in the crosscurrents between oral tradition and the Western literary tradition. Then there are obvious practical reasons: using a young man's rite of passage (or failed rite of passage) provides a central dramatic conflict that makes the individual's dilemmas representative of tensions shared by the larger community.

With such a clearly defined tradition, it is not difficult to see any new Native American novel as a response to the assumptions governing these books, different as they may be in detail. To write a historical novel like James Welch's *Fools Crow* may mean entering or criticizing an alternative tradition such as the historical romance, which like the *bildungsroman* has its own genealogy, in this context running from James Fenimore Cooper and Karl May to *Hanta Yo*. Similarly, Gerald Vizenor's decision to write satirical trickster narratives, short stories in length only, is implicitly a comment on the mainstream tradition in Native American writing. That tradition is marked by a relatively conservative brand of literary realism in spite of its unmistakable discomfort with the conventions of realism and its occasional experimentalism and pursuit of a transcendental frame of reference.

The beginning of *Love Medicine* therefore signals a recasting of the tradition represented by the other works even as it partly continues to work within the older conventions and share many of the same concerns: the consequences of an individual's return or attempted return to the reservation, the significance of home and family, the politics of language and the relation between speaking and writing. *Love Medicine* has its own distinctive style characterized by the use of multiple narrators and a relaxed, informal approach that is, like June Kashpaw herself, good-humored and graceful yet hard-bitten. *Love Medicine* has little of the violence and stark, tough landscape that characterize the work of McNickle, Momaday, Welch and Silko; perhaps that can be ascribed to a Midwestern, as opposed to a Western sensibility. All the same, if in its opening *Love Medicine* suggests a move away from McNickle, Momaday, Silko, Welch and company, in the end (perhaps understandably) it moves more centripetally as the similarities with the other authors becomes increasingly evident. Yet *Love Medicine* remains a striking achievement, in part because of its subtle balance between a willingness to present a new approach marked by a narrative openness and the need to address important if familiar topics and find a satisfactory form of closure.

The narrative at once departs from the earlier novels in several key ways. The central figure is a woman, not a man. The return, the first step, does not lead to a prolonged series of encounters and soul-searching that make up the body of the work and ultimately prove defeating or redeeming; instead June's first step is her last. The narrative does not develop directly out of the problems caused by a return; it arises out of questions raised by the failed return. Somewhat in the manner of a murder mystery, the death becomes a means of exploring not only the victim's life but the lives of those around her. *Love Medicine* could have been called "Who Killed June Kashpaw?" or rather "What Killed Her?" since the responsibility and guilt are shared by many individuals embedded in an entire way of life, a complex mesh of biographical and historical factors. The remembrance of the death wells up from time to time, as when June's son King in the middle of a fight with his wife suddenly breaks into sobs and screams at his father, "It's awful to be dead. Oh my God, she's so cold."[2] The sadness observed in the young June's eyes by the woman who took her in as a child (68) underlies the entire text. It is its fundamental subtext, even with Erdrich's wonderful comic sense: June's presence, that is, her absence, haunts the book. The oppressive weight of her death is not exorcised until the final page.

With June Kashpaw's death, more lyrical but no less surprising in terms of narrative conventions than the murder of Marion Crane (Janet Leigh) in the shower in *Psycho*, Erdrich immediately decenters the novel; unlike the earlier novels *Love Medicine* has no sustaining central consciousness or protagonist. Part of the shock arises from the fact that the narrative begins neutrally but then clearly leans toward Jean's point of view:

> She was a long-legged Chippewa woman, aged hard in every way except how she moved. Probably it was the way she moved, easy as a young girl on slim hard legs, that caught the eye of the man who rapped at her from inside the window of the Rigger Bar. He looked familiar, like a lot of people looked familiar. She had seen so many come and go. . . . She wanted, at least, to see if she actually knew him. (33)

While the descriptions of the man's actions and statements remain objective, the narrative keeps moving toward the woman's point of view: "She couldn't help notice. . . . He could be different, she thought. . . . It was later still that she felt so fragile" (3–4). Though identified as "Andy," the man remains "he," while the narrator refers to the woman familiarly as "June."

Following the embarrassing experience in the pick-up, bordering on comedy but too unpleasant for laughs, the first section ends with a dream-like poetic figure: "The snow fell deeper that Easter than it had in forty years, and June walked over it like water and came home" (6). Abruptly, the second section undercuts the redemptive imagery:

After that false spring, when the storm blew in covering the state, all the snow melted off and it was summer. It was almost hot by the week after Easter, when I found out, in Mama's letter, that June was gone, not only dead but suddenly buried, vanished off the land like that sudden snow. (6–7)

This statement in the first person—the speaker is June's niece Albertine Johnson—establishes the narrative style for the novel: a collection of interlocking narratives each focusing on a different narrator or major character, yet all ultimately related to that original event—the death of June Kashpaw. The characters often tell their own stories, not only explaining their relationship to the dead woman but also spinning out a larger web of relationships that appear as a comment on her death, thereby providing the context in which it can be understood. June Kashpaw is referred to occasionally in these personal narratives but she is rarely central until the concluding section. Although some characters are deliberately prevented from taking over the narrative voice—for instance June's unsympathetic son, King, and her sympathetic lover, Gerry Nanapush—there is neither a continuous omniscient narration nor a central character. Instead, the role of narrator moves freely from character to character, moving forward and backward in time as well. The opening chapter takes place in 1981, the second in 1934, the fourteenth and final one in 1984. Thus the novel takes on the character of a jigsaw puzzle; different areas are filled in at different times. Spatial and temporal order follows a logic of development apart from simple chronology or the existence of any individual character; for example the chapter describing June's husband, Gordie, appears past the book's midpoint, though it picks up only a month after June's death.

Michael Wood once remarked that Faulkner was a key figure for many of the Latin American writers of the "Boom" (Vargas Llosa, Donoso and above all García Márquez) because he demonstrated that novels could be formally experimental works of modern art while not abandoning the traditional concern with social description.[3] Faulkner after all wrote family sagas, historical novels portraying communal life from generation to generation. Faulkner is a favorite author of Erdrich's; *Love Medicine* has more than a passing resemblance to *As I Lay Dying*, *Absalom, Absalom* and *The Sound and the Fury*.[4] Whether or not Erdrich was directly influenced by the Latin Americans, and in particular, by García Márquez, her work uses some of the same methods and at times a similar tone. The constant shifting of point of view and the chronological jumps in the narrative make divergent versions of a single event possible, introducing a modernist sense of relativism and discontinuity as well as a good deal of ironic humor.[5] The attempt to hang June as a child appears twice, once in Albertine's narrative (19–20) and once in Marie Kashpaw's (67–68); the appearance of Beverly Lamartine at Lulu Nanapush's house is told first by a neutral narrator (75–6), and later by Beverly's rival for Lulu's affections, Nector Kashpaw, who describes Beverly as "a slick, flat-faced Cree salesman out of Minneapolis . . . a made-good shifty type who would hang Lulu for a dollar" (102). As this bit of invective suggests, the language used in *Love Medicine* is not radical at all. Though not without some poetic passages, as one would expect from the author of *Jacklight*, the text generally avoids the difficulty characteristic of so much modern literature; the language used to tell the story is a lively combination of down-to-earth colloquialism and occasional literary flourishes. Throughout *Love Medicine* one of Erdrich's key concerns is narrative agility and speed, as in García Márquez; confronted by alternative narrative media such as television and movies these authors resort to an armory of devices that would make Dickens proud. Like García Márquez, Erdrich uses the artful proleptic tease:

> At the time her [Lulu Lamartine's] hair was still dark and thickly curled. Later she would burn it off when her house caught fire, and it would never grow back. (83)

> It would not surprise Bev to hear, after many years passed on, that this Gerry grew up to be both a natural criminal and a hero whose face appeared on the six o'clock news. (85)

And she delights in making the story seem more immediate by shifting the narrative from the past tense into a dramatic present tense. This technique is used with Nector Kashpaw, who loses his memory thereby becoming the perfect embodiment of a conflation of past and present: "Anyway, once I got to town and stopped by the tribal offices, a drunk was out of the question. An emergency was happening."

And here is where events loop around and tangle again:

> It is July. The sun is a fierce white ball. Two big semis from the Polar Bear Refrigerated Trucking Company are pulled up in the yard of the

agency offices, and what do you think they're loaded with? Butter. That's right. Seventeen tons of surplus butter on the hottest day in '52. (95)

Or again, later in the same chapter: "No sooner had I given her up than I wanted Lulu back. . . . It is a hot night in August. I am sitting in the pool of lamplight at my kitchen table." (104)

Such devices date back at least to Victorian melodrama, as do some of the thematic concerns such as the fascination with matters of paternity and maternity. These are serious matters: The novel concludes when a sympathetic character, Lipsha Morrissey, discovers the true identity of his mother (June Kashpaw) and his father (Gerry Nanapush). His meeting with his father is as important for the narrative as some of the great recognition and reunion scenes in classical literature, such as the recognition of Odysseus' scar and his reunion with Telemachus in the *Odyssey*. But typically for Erdrich, this climactic scene is played in a low-key comic fashion. It takes place in a kitchen in the [Twin] Cities, over a card game. The father and son recognize their shared kinship in part because they both learned to cheat at cards from their mother/grandmother, Lulu Lamartine. The comic side of the scene is complemented, however, by their intense awareness of the missing mother and lover, June Kashpaw. They are playing with her other son, King, for a car purchased with the insurance money from her death; as the game progresses Lipsha (the narrator for this section) reviews the life of father, mother and son before bringing the story full circle:

I could see how his [Gerry's] mind leapt back making connections, jumping at the intersection points of our lives: his romance with June. The baby given to Grandma Kashpaw. June's son by Gordie. King. Her running me off. Me growing up. And then at last June walking toward home in the Easter snow that, I saw now, had resumed falling softly in this room. (262)

With the family history clear at last, the disruption caused by the death can now be overcome. And so the meeting of father and son leads to a fairytale, Hollywood ending: the son helps the fugitive father escape to freedom across the Canadian border, and the father tells the son of a genetic heart defect, so that Lipsha is freed from the need to either make good on his enlistment into the Army or continue his flight from the authorities.

This resolution suggests how Erdrich takes apart and puts back together the traditional narrative. Instead of a man it is a woman returning home at the beginning. She dies immediately; but the traditional dilemma of the individual—home as freedom versus home as trap—reappears tied to a mystery of identity which is resolved favorably. The son meets his father who successfully escapes, while the son resolves an identity crisis and returns from his wanderings with a newly found peace of mind. The last word of the novel, significantly, is "home."[6]

Georg Lukacs described the novel as the form "like no other," expressing a "transcendental homelessness."[7] In *Love Medicine* the concern with home informs the entire narrative, as Erdrich rings the changes upon the term, which is by no means always identified with a condition of bliss. Albertine (in some ways a double for her Aunt June) is both ambivalent and matter-of-fact in describing her return to the reservation after her aunt's death: "Just three miles, and I was driving down the rutted dirt road, home" (11). But she immediately finds herself in the middle of a squabble between her mother and her Aunt Aurelia:

> "June was all packed up and ready to come home. . . . She walked out there because . . . what did she have to come home to after all? Nothing!"
>
> "Nothing?" said mama piercingly. "Nothing to come home to?" She gave me [Albertine] a short glance full of meaning. I had, after all, come home, even if husbandless, childless, driving a fall-apart car. (12)

The family get-together sours. Near the end of Albertine's narrative King and his wife have a massive fight; as they go out leaving the kitchen a shambles the wife says, "You always get so crazy when you're home. We'll get the baby. We'll go off. We'll go back to the Cities, go home" (39). There's no place like home—but which one?[8]

Clearly, home in *Love Medicine* is an embattled concept, as ambiguous as June Kashpaw's motives in attempting her return. When Lipsha tells his father that at last he's "home free," Gerry Nanapush immediately contradicts him: "No," he said . . . I won't ever really have what you'd call a home" (268). As his son realizes, Gerry is a man on the run. But he is strong and self-confident, unlike Henry Lamartine, Jr., a tragic figure whose return from the Vietnam War makes him an updated version of earlier figures such as Tayo in *Ceremony*. His brother, Lyman Lamartine, says, "When he came home . . . Henry was very different, and I'll say this: the change was no good" (147).

Like *House Made of Dawn* and *Ceremony*, *Love Medicine* seems to fall on the optimistic, ultimately upbeat side of the great divide governing the Native American novels of homecoming.[9] Yet Erdrich's multivoiced, multicharacter narrative method enables her to establish a complicated system of narrative balance. Thus, if two favored figures escape in a kind of romantic fantasy, another perishes; Henry Jr. drowns before he can sort out any of the confusion caused by his war experiences. The gentle Lipsha benefits from discovering the identity of his father, regaining his special "touch" in both healing and card playing; but Lyman Lamartine gains nothing from the knowledge that Nector Kashpaw was his father. His mother, Lulu, sees his problem:

> "You know what," he sighed after a while. "I don't really want to know."
> Of course, he did know that Kashpaw was his father. What he really meant was there was nothing to be done about it anymore. I felt the loss. I wanted to hold my son in my lap and let him cry. Even blind, a mother knows when her boy is holding in a painful silence. (233)

Writers such as McNickle move in the direction of high tragedy. Their world is oppressive and fatalistic, a throwback to the naturalism of Wharton's *Ethan Frome* or Zola's *La Bête Humaine*. At times the declarative sentences make the prose seem carved from blocks of stone: the narrative provides an immutable record of an implacable fate. Momaday and Silko, in contrast, see ceremony as a means of escaping nature, of leading life and art toward transcendence. With her poet's voice Erdrich often moves away from the mundane and the matter of fact, but she rarely explores exalted realms of the spirit: a vision of the northern lights shared by Lipsha and Albertine is perhaps the one notable exception. Indian ritual has no place in *Love Medicine* except in the "touch" of Lipsha, presented satirically when he replaces goose hearts with store-bought frozen turkey hearts, and watches his "patient" choke to death. Filtered through the survivors' point of view, the ghost returns as a melancholy apparition, not a horrific incubus from the afterlife. (Here is one more similarity with the tone and manner of García Márquez, who favors an equally sad image of the afterlife.) Erdrich seems to find the profane more interesting if not more desirable than the sacred; she is a worldly author and it is difficult not to suspect that she agrees with Lipsha, possibly the most sympathetic character of all, when he says:

"Our Gods aren't perfect . . . but at least they'll come around. They'll do a favor if you ask them right. You don't have to yell. But you do have to know, like I said, how to ask in the right way. That makes problems, because to ask proper was an art that was lost to the Chippewas once the Catholics gained ground. Even now, I have to wonder if Higher Power turned it[s] back, if we got to yell, or if we just don't speak its language." (195)[10]

This is an ambivalent attitude to say the least: one part faith and two parts doubt and disappointment. Lipsha's brief comment about Catholicism is not elaborated upon except as Catholicism is presented in a broadly satirical manner, especially in the character of an intimidating hell-fire and brimstone nun, Sister Leopolda, a figure out of Fellini. (I am thinking in particular of Juliet's childhood experience in the convent in *Juliet of the Spirits*.)

Erdrich, on balance, is essentially a comic writer. Most of the key moments in *Love Medicine* are comic ones, from the fateful encounter between Nector Kashpaw and Marie Lazarre, played out as a love scene complicated by the presence of two dead geese tied to Nector's wrists, to the card game between King, Gerry and Lipsha. Even a houseburning is grotesquely comic, an accident perhaps, but certainly not the mean-spirited Snopes vengeance in Faulkner's "Barn Burning." Erdrich's characters often move into melancholia or wistful reminisce, as when the high-spirited and assertive Lulu Lamartine (i.e., Libertine), the novel's version of the Wife of Bath, admits that "It's a sad world, though, when you can't get love right even after trying it as many times as I have" (218). With the death of June Kashpaw, Erdrich immediately establishes her awareness of the bleak side of existence; even sweet-natured Lipsha comments that the marked deck was appropriate for "the marked men, which was all of us" (259). Yet the story never lingers on the tragic, returning again and again to a bemused, ironic view of the comic incongruities of parents and children, friends and lovers. In the end, though the love medicine proves fatal to Nector, there is a reconciliation between the rivals, Marie Kashpaw and Lulu Lamartine, Nector's wife and his mistress, in the senior citizen's home. All passion spent, Luly says, "for the first time I saw exactly how another woman felt, and it gave me deep comfort, surprising" (236). The passage ends with a sweet—perhaps too sweet—vision of harmony as Marie puts drops in Lulu's eyes: "She swayed down like a dim mountain, huge and blurred, the way a mother must look to her just born child" (236).

In Walter Benjamin's famous essay on Leskov, "The Storyteller," Benjamin proclaims that the death of storytelling and its replacement by the novel represented the death of true human communication and wisdom.[11] The villain is the book, which replaces the companionship that exists between teller and listener with the distance between the isolated writer and the equally isolated reader. In most Native American literature the book is not embraced but accepted as a necessary evil: story and storytelling are the ideals. In "The Storyteller's Escape" Silko writes, "With these stories of ours / we can escape almost anything / with these stories we will survive."[12]

Setting the oral against the written, storytelling against novel-writing, indicates a romantic approach to art and life, a literary vision of a fall from a Golden Age to an impersonal present. After all, storytelling might be regarded as a representation of experience with no special status. Nevertheless it is the impression of presentness and of presence, of social intimacy and communion that matters, and in *Love Medicine* Erdrich subtly shapes the narrative to create a sense of immediacy. The characters themselves almost at once demonstrate the effects of storytelling, for it is storytelling that animates the women in the kitchen after June's death: their recollection of the youthful hanging episode, a playful yet symbolic anticipation of her fate, brings them all to life, giggling and "laughing out loud in brays and whoops . . . waving their hands helplessly" (21).

The opposition between speech and writing in Native American fiction may not exist in the same conceptual framework as the opposition between speech and writing in the philosophical and theoretical discourse of Derrida and contemporary literary theory. Still, the problem of language and an appropriate language for writing about Native American experience remains fundamental in these works. Thus in *Ceremony*, Silko frames her narrative with sections that are poetic and ritualistic. Similarly, Momaday frames *House Made of Dawn* with traditional ceremonial introductions and conclusions. These mixed forms straddle Native American and Western forms of expression. There are other signs of the central problems of language and form in the incorporation of episodes involving historical texts, such as the journal in *House Made of Dawn* and the repeated play between characters who speak English and those who speak tribal languages.

In *Love Medicine* Erdrich takes a different approach to the relation between native forms and the Western literary tradition. Her work, like the work of Silko and others, seems at times to aspire to the status of "pure" storytelling. This goal would make the literary text appear to be a transcription of a speaker talking in the first person present tense, addressing a clearly defined listener. Thus in several of the narratives the speaker addresses a "You." This can become too insistent, a tic rather than a sign of sincerity, as when Lipsha remarks, "I told you once before" (195), or Lulu Lamartine plays confidante with the reader by saying, "Nobody knows this" (218). Yet the attempt at seeming intimacy does move the text in the direction of an informal, colloquial prose. The liveliness of *Love Medicine* has less to do with some formal notion of speech as utterance than its success as dialogue capturing just plain talk—kitchen-table talk, bar talk, angry talk, curious talk, sad talk, teasing talk.

But in a printed text, the return of the literary is inevitable; all the devices that stylistically mark the pursuit of immediacy are in the end visible as literary devices.[13] Using the first person present tense as a substitute for third person past tense "omniscient" narration, or using colloquial diction and sentence structure as opposed to more elaborate, artificial forms must be judged within the context of a range of possibilities that govern all "realistic" prose. Erdrich's artfulness is evident for example in several beautifully sustained metaphors which appear independently in the narratives of different characters, notably a fishing image connected to Nector Kashpaw's failing memory that first appears in Albertine's narrative and then migrates into Lipsha's (193, 208, 209).

The naturalness of Erdrich's characters is as much a construction as the skill at creating a convincing voice that led Hemingway to see in Twain's *Huckleberry Finn* the start of a genuine American literary tradition—an anti-literary, seemingly informal American style based on colloquial expression.

There are precedents of sorts for much of what Erdrich accomplishes in *Love Medicine* in the Latin Americans, in Faulkner, in Edgar Lee Masters and Thornton Wilder, in the fascination during the past three decades with oral history—from Studs Terkel, to the Vietnam oral histories, to *Black Elk Speaks*—and in the Raymond Carver-Bobbie Ann Mason school of writing, with its seemingly affectless but extremely stylized tragi-comic glimpses of lower middle-class life. In each case literature attempts to free itself of the literary, as if any intervention or mediation by an author were inevitably a falsification, and only a supposed transcription could capture the truth. This literary antinomianism seems distinctly American.

Love Medicine, as its title suggests, is centered in the relationships between lovers and families. Yet because Erdrich moves away from the narrow focus of the earlier novels toward the historical novel and the family saga, she is able to touch upon economic and political matters in an extremely effective way. There are characters who can make money and characters who can't; and since at least one character is engaged in tribal politics there are some sharp things said about how things get done on the reservation. More pointed are some observations made in passing by the characters in the course of their dramatic monologues, beginning with Albertine Johnson's bitter remark in the aftermath of her aunt's death on "rich, single cowboy-rigger oil trash." To these types she says, "an Indian woman's nothing but an easy night" (9). Shortly thereafter Albertine's notes that "The policy of allotment was a joke" (11). Such asides run through the multiple narrative without ever coming to a head in the action. In *Love Medicine*, the Native Americans speak and after the appearance of the unfortunate Andy right at the start the whites are all but invisible, pushed to the margins, except for the caricature of the rich lady who makes Nector Kashpaw famous as a naked warrior in a painting, "The Plunge of the Brave." There are no political confrontations perhaps partly because the skepticism is directed internally, as in the case of Lulu Lamartine's battle with the tribal council to keep possession of her house. Even Gerry Nanapush, a colorful, sympathetic and rebellious desperado leader of the American Indian Movement, is presented by his son, Lipsha, with more than a touch of amusement: "Gerry Nanapush, famous politicking hero, dangerous armed criminal, judo expert, escape artist, charismatic member of the American Indian Movement, and smoker of many pipes of kinnikinnick in the most radical groups. That was . . . Dad" (248). (The passage where Lipsha addresses the question of his father's guilt in relation to the killing of a federal agent at Pine Ridge is one of the few unconvincing sections in the novel, a too-neat cop-out (269).)

One of the peculiar aspects of Erdrich's writing, even more evident in *The Beet Queen*, is her presentation of history. In *Love Medicine* individual sections are dated and tied to various before-and-after events in the convoluted sexual/personal relations linking the many characters, but there is little sense of an outside historical framework. With the exception of a few historical references, the episodes of the thirties could take place in the fifties or eighties. This may show that Erdrich is not interested in circumstantial social realism. But *Love Medicine* becomes historical and political through the personal, such as when Henry Jr. goes to Vietnam and Gerry joins the American Indian Movement.

Such a concentration on personal, family matters may be intentional, but the sense of being removed from political events is a powerful statement about marginality and disenfranchisement while also suggesting a preferred concern with the personal and private life of the community. Lulu Lamartine, a tough political commentator, mentions the forced migrations of the Chippewa from the far side of the Great Lakes, but she says only that the story her grandmother used to tell "is too long a story to get into now" (222). She then returns to her own refusal to move from her house. This is a typical Erdrich maneuver; she has inserted a broad political and historical point, then channeled the narrative back to a seemingly personal issue. The focus in *Love Medicine* on family may reflect an eighties concern with domesticity and "roots" and personal heritage; King's wife, Lynette, "with a quick burst of drunken enthusiasm," says to one of the older Kashpaws, "Tell'em. . . . They've got to learn their own heritage. When you go it will be gone!" (30) Much later Lipsha refers to his search for his father as his "quest" saying, "I had to get down to the bottom of my heritage" (248).

Erdrich, however, does not present a rose-colored view of an ideal nuclear family in the manner of television series such as *Little House on the Prairie* or the Depression-era drama *The Waltons,* but rather a completely unsentimental view, both affectionate and angry, of an extremely complicated extended family. And central to that vision of the family is a history that is largely unspoken in *Love Medicine* but that appears at times in personal terms through memory: the memory that exists in the hands of June's husband leading him to drink when they remind him of the feel of her body (172); the memory that plagues Gerry Nanapush and makes him go see her son King so that he can be reminded of her through King's features (262). In the final turn to memory and history Erdrich opens up her text, and not only by using multiple narrators, multiple narratives. The move is temporal as well. Storytelling brings everything into the present. But Erdrich hints at a more comprehensive truth that goes back beyond the death of June Kashpaw to a larger source of woe: one that explains why the Chippewa move west of the Great Lakes to a home on the reservation that drives them into a cycle of departure and return.

By the time Erdrich concludes the story of the Kashpaws, Lamartines and Nanapushes (the extended story of the tragedy of June Kashpaw), it is clear that she has circumscribed her story temporally, no matter how relatively open it may seem in terms of narrative technique and range of feeling. In a sense all Native American writers are historical writers, their kinship based on the shared assumption that history holds the key to understanding contemporary Native American life. Behind the immediate problems of home, family and paternity (or maternity) stands the unanswerable past. Max in *The Surrounded* proclaims to Archilde, "We've got to plan something. We won't let it end for you, like you thought. We'll make a new beginning!" But the last spoken lines in the book are those of Parker, the agent, scornfully telling Archilde, "It's too damn bad you people never learn that you can't run away. It's pathetic." What they can't run away from is less a physical location than a historical situation. That accounts for the pain in Jim Loney when he realizes that there is no place where "pasts merged into one and everything was all right and it was like everything was beginning without a past. No lost sons, no mothers searching." He adds, damningly, "There had to be that place, but it was not on this earth." The individual stories of the protagonists in Native American fiction meet in the collective history. They embrace Tayo's awareness in *Ceremony* that "His sickness was only part of something larger" as well as the bitterness at the end of *Fools Crow* when the title character realizes that change, loss and unhappiness are to be the fate of his people, and that their only consolation will be in stories telling them of "the way it was."[14]

In *Love Medicine* Erdrich is concerned with the experience of the Chippewa in the mid-twentieth century. The story leaves largely untold the parallel story of the whites and the historical background of events. It is not at all surprising that, having concentrated in *Beet Queen* on the German side of her heritage and the bleak beauty and twisted emotional universe of the Plains, Erdrich wrote *Tracks*, a historical novel on an older generation, the ancestors of the characters in *Love Medicine*.[15]

Notes

1. D'Arcy McNickle, *The Surrounded* (Albuquerque: University of New Mexico Press, 1964) 1. cf. *Winter in the Blood* (New York: Penguin, 1986), where the main character observes right at the start, "Coming home was not easy anymore," 2.

2. Louise Erdrich, *Love Medicine* (New York: Bantam Books, 1984), 33. All page references are to this edition and will hereafter be provided in parentheses in the text.

3. Professor Wood made his remarks as the featured speaker at a meeting in the late 1970s of The Columbus Circle, the organization for graduate students in American Literature at Columbia University.

4. In the retrospection of *As I Lay Dying*; in the idea of the novel as conversation of *Absalom, Absalom*; in the expressionistic use of point of view in *The Sound and the Fury*, and more. Erdrich expressed her admiration for Faulkner's early writings in an interview with Amy Ward, "The Beet Generation," *University of Minnesota Daily*, October 29, 1986: 18.

5. The only real exception occurs in pages 237–239 when the narrator is Howard Kashpaw (also "King Junior" and "Little King"), whose impressionistic, youthful point of view recalls Joyce's experimentation in adopting the point of view of the young Stephen Daedalus at the beginning of *A Portrait of the Artist as a Young Man* or Faulkner's method in using Benjy Compson as a narrator in *The Sound and the Fury*. But Erdrich's style is not as extreme.

6. The last line, Lipsha's "So there was nothing to do but cross the water, and bring her home" (272) picks up on the final line in the opening section as June walks over the snow like water. Since the passage contains no clear antecedent for "her," there is a kind of echo of June's presence as well as a play on a colloquial phrase (as in "let 'er rip"). The fusing of antecedents is also used in Henry Jr.'s narrative when Albertine merges in his mind with a Vietnamese woman: "She was hemorrhaging" (138). (Albertine seems to be something of a loose strand in the plot; she disappears from the action after her encounter with Henry Jr. in Fargo, though she is mentioned in a bit of conversation between Lipsha and Gerry, with Lipsha referring to her as "the one girl I ever trusted" (270). One of the characteristics of "open" form is a refusal to tie up loose ends and account for all the characters in the manner of the "classical" nineteenth-century novel; but in this case it seems simpler to regard Albertine's absence as a result of Erdrich's method, which brought together short stories as the basis for the novel.)

7. Georg Lukacs, *The Theory of the Novel*, trans. Anna Bostock (Cambridge: MIT Press, 1971) 41. Lukacs is deliberately playing upon a statement by Novalis, "Philosophy is really homesickness" (quot. 29).

8. Erdrich's poem "Family Reunion," *Jacklight* (New York; Henry Holt, 1984) offers a brief glimpse of a gathering similar to the one that greets Alber-

tine when she returns home following the death of her Aunt June. But it is the first line of the next poem in the volume, "Indian Boarding School: The Runaways," that expresses the essential idea: "Home's the place we head for in our sleep" (11). The line recalls the dialogue between husband and wife in Robert Frost's "The Death of the Hired Hand":

> "Home is the place where, when you have to go there,
> They have to take you in,"
> . . . .
>   "I should have called it
> Something you somehow haven't to deserve."

(*The Poetry of Robert Frost*, ed. Edward Connery Lathem [London: Jonathan Cape, 1967] 38).

The relation between Erdrich's poetry and her fiction is a fascinating one (as is the relation between the short stories as individual entities and as sections of *Love Medicine*). *Love Medicine* goes far beyond the poem "A Love Medicine" in *Jacklight*, a good poem marred by the overwrought description of masculine violence ("she steps against the fistwork of a man. / She goes down in wet grass and his boot plants its grin / among the arches of her face" (7); male mistreatment Erdrich handles in a more complex and subtle fashion with Andy and others in the novel.

As a revision and expansion of the sequence of poems "The Butcher's Wife" *Jacklight, The Beet Queen* (New York: Henry Holt, 1986) seems less than successful. In this case the poetry goes beyond the novel, especially in the dark, bitter quality in a line like "Something queer happens when the heart is delivered" (in "That Pull from the Left," 41–42). I suspect that one reason the book founders is that it is not really about characters and events but about what one character, Karl Adare, describes as "the senseless landscape" (318), that is, about the unreal existence induced by living in the kind of place described so prosaically by another character, Wallace Pfef: "I live in the flat, treeless valley where sugar beets grow. It is intemperate here. My view is a flat horizon of grays and browns" (160). In *Love Medicine* the fields are described as "casual and lonely" (79); in *Jacklight* Erdrich repeatedly stresses an almost metaphysical aspect of the landscape, as when she has the speaker in "Clouds" note that "The town stretches to fields" (43) and goes on to proclaim:

> We lay our streets over
> the deepest cries of earth
> And wonder why everything comes down to this:
> The days pile and pile.
> The bones are too few
> and too foreign to know.
> Mary, you do not belong here at all.

> Sometimes I take back in tears this whole town.
> Let everything be how it could have been, once:
> A land that was empty and perfect as clouds (44–45).

This lament for "this strange earth / we want to call ours" (45) suggests both the strong response to the landscape and the failure of *The Beet Queen* to present an adequate picture of the relation between character and environment, to capture the emotional tension bred by such surroundings. As a dark satirical portrait of small town life, *Omensetter's Luck* by William Gass seems more successful; as an image of life on the Great Plains—heavenly, hellish, beautifully empty—Terrence Malick's film *Days of Heaven* suggests more convincingly the haunted mood induced by the vast expanses. *The Beet Queen*, in a character like Karl Adare, seems to be caught between the quaintly idiosyncratic ironies of a work like *Ragtime* and the more compelling concern with evil that marks the writings of Flannery O'Connor.

9. *Winter in the Blood* is something of a special case. Alan Velie, in *Four American Indian Masters* (Norman: University of Oklahoma Press, 1982) 90–103, discusses the book as a comic novel, using "comic" in a slightly unusual sense, one concerned with notions of character (i.e., with the non-heroic) as well as with a humorous tone. I basically agree with his reading of the novel as a work that uses a sense of irony to play comedy against tragedy with unsettling results. It may be a comedy, but it's not a happy book.

10. In this passage, Lipsha also states that June was "left by a white man to wander off in the snow" (195). This would no doubt be how the incident appeared to June's relatives. Lipsha's statement presents another demonstration of the effect of multiple perspectives, though in this case the reader has been given an apparently privileged, "correct" view. It is also another example of the subtle introduction of essentially political issues and assumptions into a book that appears focused on personal matters.

11. Walter Benjamin, "The Storyteller," in *Illuminations*, trans. Harry Zohn (New York: Schocken Books) 83–109.

12. Leslie Marmon Silko, *Storyteller* (New York: Seaver Books, 1981) 247.

13. In "Writing and Revolution" *Writing Degree Zero*, trans. Annette Lavers and Colin Smith (London: Jonathan Cape, 1967), Roland Barthes discusses the artificiality and "convention of the real" in the Naturalist aesthetic, which he describes as "loaded with the most spectacular signs of fabrication," and "a literature which has all the striking and intelligible signs of its identity" (73, 74, 76). Native American writing, in its efforts to attain the condition of speech, has developed a set of what might be called "conventions of the oral," including the use of the present tense and the use of the first person with "you." These are signs of fabrication and therefore of the literary status of the text, especially when occasional statements assigned to a character suggest the consciousness of the hidden narrator. This is most obvious when the author is

most literary—usually by introducing the kind of metaphorical language that, as Barthes never fails to point out, constitutes one of the most obvious signs of a literature straining to affirm its identity. (See, for example, "Is There Any Poetic Writing?" *Writing Degree Zero*, (New York: Hill and Wang, 1967) 47, where he speaks of "the ritual of images.")

For a sharp dissection of the "epidemic" use of the present tense in contemporary fiction, see "A Failing Grade for the Present Tense" William Gass, *New York Times Book Review* October 11, 1987: 1, 32, 36–38.

14. *The Surrounded*, 159, 296–97; *The Death of Jim Loney* (New York: Harper & Row, 1979) 175; *Ceremony* (New York: Penguin, 1986) 125; *Fools Crow* (New York: Penguin) 358–60.

15. Erdrich represents not the death of the author but, in her collaborative efforts with her husband, Michael Dorris, the birth of authorial twins. I don't wish to discuss at length the third product of their collaboration, the novel published under his name, *A Yellow Raft in Blue Water* (New York: Henry Holt, 1987); but in the context of the discussion of *Love Medicine* a few observations are in order. The multiple narratives, moving back in time from youngest to oldest, from the present to a deep secret buried in the past, seems less lively than the comparable overlapping in *Love Medicine*. The duplication of episodes is not entirely compensated for by the insights gained from different perspectives. The use of the first person once again provides immediacy, but at the price of keeping the reader's understanding anchored within a narrowly defined consciousness; the characters' reliance on soap opera as a standard form of references suggests both an attempt at a realistic portrayal of contemporary working class life and a lack of sureness in defining a point of view toward the melodramatic plot, which seems part *I Love Lucy* and part *Peyton Place*. As a story of three women, the book continues the Erdrich/Dorris righting of the literary balance the sexes initiated in *Love Medicine* and continued in *Beet Queen;* but the male characters are once again less interesting than the women. Finally, the book displays a fascination with the idea of storytelling, here regarded not so much as some grand social ritual but as an instrument of survival. For example Rayona, the youngest of the three narrators, tells an inquisitive priest that her mother is dead and her father is an airplane pilot, neither of which happens to be true. (The most outrageous of all the examples of this kind of story-in-a-pinch-operators in the novels is Sister Leopolda in *Love Medicine*. She saves herself after she has skewered Marie Lazarre by proclaiming the girl's wounds the results of a divine miracle.) Dorris has the last, oldest narrator, Aunt Ida, announce at the beginning of her narration that she will tell the story her own way, then add:

> "And though I can speak their English better than they think, better than most of them, I prefer my own language. I use the words that shaped my construction of events as they happened, the words that followed my

thought, the words that gave me power. My recollections are not tied to white paper. They have the depth of time" (273).

A powerful statement of the antiliterary position, but a curious one to read on a printed page, in English.

An article in the *New York Times* for July 24, 1988 announced that Erdrich and Dorris had sold the rights to a proposed novel about Christopher Columbus's discovery of America for $1.5 million. Apparently the historical impulse I observed in their work has not yet run its course. See Edwin McDowell, "Outline of Novel About Columbus Brings $1.5 Million" (sec. 1, p. 24, col. 2).

8

The Trickster Novel

ALAN VELIE

Even in the eighties, when fewer and fewer Indians speak the old languages, Trickster tales remain a popular part of a living oral tradition. However, there exists simultaneously another tradition that is dependent on the first but separate from it, that of the trickster novel. Since the trickster is the most important mythic figure in most tribes it is not surprising that he would be a major archetype in contemporary Indian fiction. Quite a few protagonists in recent Indian novels bear a resemblance to the trickster. Some well known Indian novels with prominent trickster figures are, *House Made of Dawn, Winter in the Blood, Love Medicine,* and *Darkness in Saint Louis Bearheart.* This discourse will focus on *Bearheart,* and examine what happens when trickster leaves the oral tradition and enters the novel.

Since the focus of this discourse is postmodern criticism, the theories of M. M. Bakhtin will be applied here. Although Bakhtin lived until 1975, he did most of his writing in the thirties and forties. However, because of his political unacceptability in the Soviet Union, the consequent suppression of his works for years, and the general ignorance of Russian criticism in the West, his works were largely unknown in Europe and America until recently. Because Bakhtin's ideas were well ahead of his time and he has recently had a great effect on postmodern critics like Julia Kristeva and Tzvetan Todorov, it is appropriate to recognize him as a sort of proto-postmodernist.

The tribal trickster is not a single figure; tricksters differ greatly from tribe to tribe and even from tale to tale in the repertoire of the same tribe. Sometimes trickster is human, such as the Winnebago Wakdjunkaga and Blackfeet Napi; among other tribes trickster takes the form of Coyote, Raven or Hare. Whatever his form, trickster has a familiar set of characteristics: he plays tricks and is the victim of tricks; he is amoral and has strong appetites, particularly for food and sex; he is footloose, irresponsible and callous, but somehow almost always sympathetic if not lovable.

Trickster figures in contemporary Indian fiction differ a good deal also.[1] However, whatever their superficial differences, they are essentially what you would expect if you put the trickster in the trans-Mississippi West in the sixties, seventies and eighties: Footloose, amoral drifters with strong appetites for women and wine, they play tricks, are the victim of tricks, are callous and irresponsible, but essentially sympathetic to the reader.

Abel in *House Made of Dawn* is certainly footloose, amoral and fond of sex and wine. He doesn't play tricks, but the incident in which the Albino beats him with a rooster has resonances of the sort of humiliation that trickster customarily suffers in tribal tales when he is tricked.

The narrator in *Winter in the Blood* does play tricks. He tells his mother that he is married to Agnes, then leaves Agnes at home while he runs to town on a toot which lasts several days. Agnes gets her revenge by stealing the narrator's rifle and razor, and having her brother beat him up. The narrator is, of course, footloose, amoral, fond of wine and women, and sympathetic to the reader.

Although there is a resemblance between these figures and the trickster, admittedly stronger in the case of the narrator, it would be stretching a point to call *House Made of Dawn* and *Winter in the Blood* trickster novels. A book that comes closer is Louise Erdrich's *Love Medicine*. Gerry Nanapush is clearly a modern avatar of the trickster. Not only is he the consummate player of tricks (his miraculous escapes, for instance), but Nanapush is the name of the Chippewa Trickster Hare. The only reservation one might have in calling *Love Medicine* a trickster novel is that Gerry Nanapush is not really the central character. In fact, the book does not revolve around any one character; it is a collection of short stories all of which deal with the same set of characters.

Gerald Vizenor's *Darkness in Saint Louis Bearheart* is clearly a trickster novel. It has two trickster figures, each representing one aspect of the Anishinaabe trickster Manabozho (*naanabozho*). Proude Cedarfair, the hero of the novel represents the trickster as culture hero; Benito Saint Plumero, or Bigfoot, represents the trickster as buffoon and menace.

The best way to begin discussing the relationship of tale and novel, archetype and avatar, is with Bakhtin's conception of the chronotope. The term is a neologism Bakhtin coins to cover a concept he borrows from Einstein and applies to fiction, the "inseparability of time and space."

> In the literary artistic chronotope, spatial and temporal indicators are fused into one carefully thought-out, concrete whole. Time, as it were, thickens, takes on flesh, becomes artistically visible; likewise, space becomes charged and responsive to the movements of time, plot and history.[2]

Bakhtin uses the chronotope to compare the phenomenological worlds of different works; as a result, what initially looks like an examination of little more than setting becomes a key to understanding the essential nature of a work. As Todorov has pointed out, chronotope and genre are essentially synonymous to Bakhtin.[3] His clearest statement on the relationship of genre and chronotope occurs in his essay "Forms of Time and of the Chronotope in the Novel":

> The chronotope in literature has an intrinsic *generic* significance. It can even be said that it is precisely the chronotope that defines genre and generic distinctions, for in literature the primary category in the chronotope is time. The chronotope as a formally constitutive category determines to a significant degree the image of man in literature as well. The image of man is intrinsically chronotopic.[4]

Bakhtin's concept of the chronotope is essentially phenomenological in that each genre develops a model of the world in terms of a particular treatment of time and space. Examining the chronotope of a particular work, one asks whether time is represented in terms of quotidian reality, which most of us experience in our daily lives, or the "adventure time" that exists in romances, where no one seems to age. Spacially, are the settings abstract, so that wherever the hero goes the landscape remains the same, or are the surroundings depicted in careful detail? Are the laws of nature observed or suspended? Finally, is man larger than life, an insignificant worm, or somewhere in between?

The first observation one would make about the chronotope of tribal trickster tales is that they take place in an age before ours, in a time we might call with Vizenor "mythic time."[5] It is a world not only separated by years, but in a different sort of time, long past and inaccessible. What Bakhtin says about the epic as opposed to the novel serves as a distinction here also, the epic belongs to an "absolute past": "it lacks any relativity . . . any gradual, purely temporal progressions that might connect it with the present. It is walled off absolutely from all subsequent times . . ."[6]

In fact the difference in chronotope is even more marked between tribal tales and contemporary Indian fiction than between European epic and novel. In tribal tales animals not only spoke but were brothers to men, and spirits or *manidos* appeared constantly to humans. The closest thing in Western tradition is the legend of prelapsarian life in Eden: time stood still, there was no death or illness and the lion lay down with the lamb. One Anishinaabe tale puts it: "Now you must know that in the time of long ago, there was no sin nor war nor suffering on earth, for everything was good, as the Great Spirit made it, and animal and man walked and talked together as brothers."[7]

Time in tribal tales is usually static. Although the chronotopes differ in other important ways, the mythic time of tribal trickster tales is like what Bakhtin describes as "adventure time" in the Greek novels of the Hellenistic period, the earliest ancestors of the contemporary novel. Adventure time has no biological or maturational duration.[8] Characters do not age or develop. Although the novels are full of events, they are separated not by time that brings mutability, but by what Bakhtin calls an "extemporal hiatus."[9] Because the characters do not develop there is little continuity to adventure-time novels; they are composed of "short segments that correspond to separate adventures,"[10] another similarity to the chronotope of tribal tales.

However, whereas in the Greek novel there is not even a trace of biological or maturational duration, in the Anishinaabe tales there is a rudimentary sense of it. In the tale of Manabozho's birth, for instance, the tribal narrator states that Manabozho is a baby, but in the next sentence he says that Manabozho was curious about his parents. Next we hear that he is a warrior capable of defeating a powerful enemy.[11]

In their daily lives tribal people divided time much the way Europeans do: their histories and memoirs refer to "the Moon When the Calves Grow Hair"[12] and "The Winter when the Four Crows Were Killed."[13] They also said such things as "it was in the summer of my twentieth year."[14] Yet tribal stories generally ignore the divisions of time; there are scattered references to seasons, but generally hour, day, month and year are ignored. Most stories do not take place early or late, in spring or fall, in one year or another; they just happen.

Space in Anishinaabe tales is abstract. Occasionally there is a reference to a geographical feature like Lake Superior—Gichigami as the Anishinaabe called it (Gitche Gumee to Longfellow in his story of Hiawatha, a version of Manabozho)—but more often the narrator says, "Nanabozho [*naanabozho*] went on his way down the river, had to cross some mountains," or even more vaguely, "Nanabozho had traveled a long way."[15]

There is very little description for its own sake. Trees are occasionally mentioned as belonging to a particular species, but hardly ever described beyond a simple adjective like "tall."

While these generalizations are true enough and will prove useful in making comparisons with contemporary fiction, it is important also to examine the chronotope of particular versions of tales. Today, we encounter tribal tales primarily in libraries; we read tales told by a native informer and transcribed by a white recorder. The recorder or collector leaves an indelible imprint on the tale, usually bringing the chronotope closer to modern fiction. Time and place become far more specific. For example, Sister Laurina Levi concludes a tale of Manabozho and the beaver: "This ancient dam is known as Long Island, a natural breakwater for the harbor of Ashland, Wisconsin. Ore boats and other commercial carriers now pass through Chequamegon Bay at the place where the beaver broke through and escaped."[16]

This coda is a highly obvious addition to the tribal original, more obvious than most accretions; but fundamental changes affecting the chronotope are the rule rather than the exception. To detect them Bakhtin's remarks about polyglossia are helpful. Polyglossia refers to the different voices that appear in a work. Bakhtin is very sensitive to shifts in language in fiction; in fact he defines the novel in terms of its use of speech types and languages.[17]

Tribal tales, being communally authored and told by a number of narrators over time, would naturally have a degree of polyglossia even before Indians met whites; but the degree of polyglossia increases significantly as white myths mingle with tribal myths and whites transcribe tales for publication.

For instance, although Victor Barnouw is much more of a purist than Levi and has no glaring additions like hers, the difference between the language of expository passages and dialogue in his version of the tales indicates conscious or unconscious editing. Passages in which the narrator (ostensibly one Tom Badger) is telling the story are in correct and formal English with a heavy preponderance of simple declarative sentences. Badger often sounds like a Chippewa Hemingway: "The sky has four layers too. In the top layer of the sky there was a manido who is equal in power to the manido at the bottom of the earth. It is always day there. It is never night."[18] Yet when an Indian woman speaks, she speaks in pidgin English; her aboriginal nature is expressed by her ignorance of English tenses: "No, I never see anybody. I'm all by myself all day."[19]

Before examining how Vizenor puts the trickster into a novel it is interesting to see what he did as a teller of tribal trickster tales. *Summer in the Spring* is a collection of Anishinaabe songs and tales "edited and reexpressed by Gerald Vizenor." Vizenor got the tales from *The Progress*, a weekly newspaper published on the White Earth Agency. Vizenor's great uncle, Theodore Beaulieu, editor of the paper, printed the tales between December 1887 and May 1888. Beaulieu did a great deal of editing and reexpression himself, putting the tales in a highly solemn and formal English:

After Wainahboozho [*naanabozho*] had returned to Nokomis, and had refreshed himself with the soothing comforts of sleep and food, he related to her the incidents attendant on his journey and of the authority and power vested in him by the All-wise as "lord and master of the Earth."[20]

Beaulieu also arranged the tale into a connected series of adventures with a beginning and a middle, although surprisingly no end. They begin *ab ovo* and end abruptly *in media res*. However, each tale is clearly linked to the one before it by strong transitional phrases, and the whole narrative reads like a seamless story, not an unconnected series of tales centering on one character, which is how most collections of tales appear.

Vizenor changed only a word here and there in Beaulieu's text, most notably *naanabozho* (which Vizenor doesn't capitalize) for *Wainahboozho*. The saga begins with the birth of Naanabozho, develops his relationship with his grandmother, Nookomis, and climaxes in the middle of his showdown with the Great Gambler, Gichi Nita Ataaged. The tales are closely linked together. Where many narrators begin Manabozho tales with some variant of "One day as Manabozho was going along. . . ." Vizenor and Beaulieu begin the tales with links to previous tales such as, "After the conclusion of the narrative of *nokoomis*. . . ," "After his release. . . ," or "When *naanabozho* awoke. . . ."[21] The transitions make the tales seem like chapters in a unified narrative. The emphasis on Naanabozho's development changes the chronotope from the nondurational adventure time of the tribal tale into something closer to the chronotope of the modern novel. However, because the stories are brief, the change is subtle rather than radical.

The saga builds to a melodramatic showdown between the great gambler and Naanabozho, a gambling context in which the loser dies. the contest involves spinning a dish in which figures either stand or fall; if they stand the player wins. Beaulieu ends the narrative as the Gambler spins the dish and the figures fall. Manabozho grabs the dish and says, "Now it is my turn, should I win you must die." The next line is "to be continued,"[22] but Beaulieu never finishes the tale or prints any others. Vizenor ends his tale the same way.

The traditional ending in Anishinaabe myth, as well as the tales of other tribes, is for the trickster to win and the gambler to die. Whether Beaulieu aborts for the sake of drama or mystery like Frank Stockton's "The Lady or the Tiger," or to tease and frustrate the reader is hard to tell. When Vizenor retells the tale in *The People Called the Chippewa* he ends it with Manabozho's spin, but when he adapts it for *Darkness* he continues the action to the death of the Evil Gambler.

Beaulieu moves the tales closer to novelistic fiction in the way he depicts characters. His changes are subtle rather than radical, but they are a move towards specificity. In "Naanabozho and his Father," Beaulieu writes: "In blind frenzy Wainahboozho rushed at his father, who calmly stood, erect and firm, with arms folded across his massive chest, and his snowy locks trailed the ground . . ."[23]

Through the use of a few adverbs and adjectives Beaulieu moves the tale perceptibly in the direction of the chronotope of modern fiction. We learn from *Summer in the Spring* that, although Vizenor heard Naanabozho tales from his grandmother as a child, he read the tales in Beaulieu's version before he wrote his trickster novel and reedited them for publication in substantially the same form.

Although critics generally agree that the novel is the most amorphous and hardest form to define, there has been a critical consensus that what Ian Watt calls "formal realism" makes a novel a novel as opposed to a romance, the chief form of prose fiction which preceded it. Watt is aware that long before the novel writers considered literature mimetic; he states that realism chiefly consists of a series of conventions designed to convey "a full and authentic report of human experience" and an "air of total authenticity,"[24] a variant of Henry James' "air of reality."[25]

The conventions that establish this air of total authenticity are cynical tone, detailed nature of characterization, and specific description of time and space.[26]

Discussing a novel like *Darkness in Saint Louis Bearheart* is problematic in terms of Watt's definition. *Bearheart* is set in the future and full of bizarre and violent events. Some of these may occasionally happen or have happened in our violent country, but they do not have an "air of total authenticity." In the dinner at the Scapehouse of Weirds and Sensitives, a group of women poets who have secluded themselves in a remote survival center sit down to a meal of stuffed kitten while one of the trickster clowns, Bigfoot, performs cunnilingus under the table. Lilith Mae Farrier burns herself to death with her canine lovers when she loses to the Evil Gambler at the spinning figure game. Finally, in what one might call the Anishinaabe apotheosis of Proude Cedarfair, Proude leaves this world through a window at Pueblo Bonito and ascends to the world above this.

Instead of seeing *Bearheart* or other postmodern novels as deficient or deviant novels, however, we should realize that the realistic novels Watt describes belong to the major chronotope determined by a bourgeois way of looking at the world. Novelists and critics in our culture call this view realistic because they think that such fiction describes the world as it "really is," rather than describing a culturally determined construct.

Bakhtin's definition of the novel is much broader than Watt's; he groups romances with novels although he makes distinctions between their chronotopes. He demonstrates that many conventions of the Greek novel remained alive long after Cervantes, Defoe and Richardson.[27] In Watt's terms, *Bearheart* would deviate from the novelistic mainstream since it hardly has the necessary air of total authenticity. However, if one looks at Watt's criteria rather than his conclusions, *Bearheart* is clearly novelistic in its meticulous rendering of the details of space and time. In fact, *Bearheart* falls squarely into several traditions of the novel: The gothic, particularly American frontier gothic; American picaresque, the novel of the road from *Huckleberry Finn* to *On the Road* and *Even Cowgirls Get the Blues*; the postmodern tradition of Barthelme, Coover, and others; but most importantly, the tradition of Rabelais that Bakhtin describes as "fantastic realism,"[28] and that Vizenor calls "mythic verism."[29]

In describing the chronotope of the Rabelaisian novel Bakhtin cites a description of Gargantua's birth through his mother's ear as an example in which "grotesque fantasy is combined with the precision of anatomical and physiological analysis."[30]

Bakhtin also quotes detailed descriptions of Friar John's battles: "He beat the brains out of some, broke the arms and legs of others, disjointed the neckbones, demolished the spines, split the noses, punched out the eyes. . . ."[31] This is very like Vizenor's description of the dismemberment of Little Big Mouse by cripples:

> Sun Bear Sun climbed over dozens of crippled bodies. When he was near his little woman in the center of the pile he saw them pulling at her flesh with their teeth and deformed fingers. . . . The lusting cripples slapped their fists, thrust their beaks, pushed their snouts and scratched the perfect flesh with their claws and paws . . .[32]

The resemblances between Bakhtin and Rabelais are not gratuitous; both are engaged in battles against the values and perceptions of the dominant cultures of their time, and both use the same weapons: hyperbole, violence and scathing satire. Bakhtin describes Rabelais' task as:

> to purge the spatial and temporal world of those remnants of a transcendant world view still present in it, to clean away symbolic and hierarchical interpretations still clinging to this vertical world, to purge it of the contagion and "antiphysis" that had infected it. In Rabelais this polemical task is fused with a more affirmative one: the re-creation of a spatially and temporally adequate world able to provide a new chronotope for

a new, whole and harmonious man, and for new forms of human communication.[33]

. . . Amid the good things of this here-and-now world are also to be found false connections that distort the authentic nature of things, false associations established and reinforced by tradition and sanctioned by religious and official ideology.[34]

Rabelais was rebelling against the medieval world view, feudal and religious; this world was (at least in official propaganda) a vale of tears, a brief, nasty interlude which paled in comparison to the world to come. Rabelais fights to change his readers' way of viewing the world by presenting a different sort of world in fiction, a new world in the sense of a new chronotope. Specifically, according to Bakhtin, Rabelais operates in two ways: "on the positive side Rabelais relies on folklore and antiquity. . . . In prosecuting his negative task, the foremost device is Rabelaisian laughter—directly linked to the medieval genres of the rogue, clown and fool . . ."[35]

Vizenor utilizes both of these approaches. Where Rabelais used European folklore Vizenor uses Anishinaabe tales; and like Rabelais, Vizenor uses "laughter linked to genres of rogue, fool and clown," in the form of the discourse of trickster, who combines all three.

Vizenor's battle and rebellion are directed against mainstream American culture and ideology. Like others writing in the postmodern tradition of the novel he uses violence, hyperbole, surrealism and humor to develop a new sensibility. Gerald Graff states:

This new sensibility manifests itself in a variety of ways: in a refusal to take art "seriously" in the old sense, the use of art itself as a vehicle for exploding its traditional pretensions and for showing the vulnerability and tenuousness of art and language; in the rejection of the dominant academic tradition of analytic and interpretative criticism, which by reducing art to a set of intellectual abstractions tends to neutralize or domesticate its potentially liberating energies; in a generally less soberly rationalistic mode of consciousness, one that is more congenial to myth, tribal ritual, and visionary experience, grounded in a "protean," fluid and undifferentiated concept of the self which is opposed to the repressed, "uptight" Western ego.[36]

There are important differences between Vizenor, Barthelme and Coover, but Graff's point is certainly accurate in regard to Vizenor's fiction, especially in regard to what it says about "exploding traditional pretensions," being less "soberly rationalistic," and being congenial to myth, tribal ritual and visionary experience. In fact, what Graff says fits Vizenor more closely than it does any of the other postmoderns.

However else one might categorize *Bearheart*, it is first and foremost a trickster novel. And whether in the tribal or modern world, trickster means different things to different people. To Vizenor trickster is first and foremost a sign in the semiotic sense, a sign in a language game, a comic holotrope. This means that Vizenor conceives of trickster as a product of language, who must be seen in a linguistic context; trickster is not a reified social urge, fitting neatly into the model of a social scientist.

By "holotrope" Vizenor means whole, freestanding, both signified and signifier.[37] Quoting Bakhtin, Vizenor describes the comic holotrope as a "dialogism," meaning that trickster can only be understood as part of a greater whole, the "collection of 'utterances' in oral traditions . . ."[38] To Vizenor the tribal world view is comic and communal; the comic spirit is centered in trickster, a figure created by the tribe as a whole, not an individual author. Vizenor argues that, "The opposite of a comic discourse is a monologue, an utterance in isolation, which comes closer to the tragic mode in literature and not a comic tribal world view."[39]

Vizenor sees the postmodern chronotope in fiction as a way to attack the dominant bourgeois postcolonial world view, his chief weapon being trickster, the "agonistic liberator":

> The Trickster and comic liberator craves chance in agonistic imagination to lessen the power of social science and bourgeois humanism . . . the comic liberator is a healer in linguistic games, chance, and postmodern imagination; the trickster, as a semiotic sign, "denies presence and completion," that romantic "vital essence" in tribal representations, and the instrumental language of social science.[40]

Vizenor sees the concepts of postmodern criticism, with its linguicentric bias, as a method of demonstrating that trickster is not a reductive symbol as formulated by social scientists. Rather, he is a culturally centered, communally created, highly complex, comic figure who cannot be isolated from or understood outside of the context of his discourse.

The chronotope of *Bearheart* may be best described by using Vizenor's term "mythic verism." Vizenor states in "Trickster Discourse" that "Verisimilitude is the appearance of realities; mythic verism is discourse, a critical concordance of narrative voices, and a narrative realism that is more than mimesis or a measure of what is believed to be natural in the world."[41]

What this means is that *Bearheart* combines wild and bizarre doings and characters with a meticulous rendering of detail, a carefully created, highly specific time and place that is essentially novelistic in its graphic nature as well as its antiromantic and antisentimental tone. For instance, there is the route that the pilgrims take across Minnesota, Iowa, Oklahoma and New Mexico: they take Rt. I-10 to Minnesota, 56 through Leroy, Iowa, 218 to Cedar Falls, 63 to Montezuma, a numberless road to What Cheer, Iowa, 21 to 92 through Winterset, Macedonia and Dumfries. There is a gap through Nebraska and Kansas filled only by the Bioavaricious Regional Word Hospital before the route picks up at Ponca City, Oklahoma. They then head west on Oklahoma 60, south on 283, enter New Mexico at Clovis on 60, and end up at Pueblo Bonito on New Mexico 57. Vizenor has driven all of the route at one time or another, and this is reflected in the specificity of the chronotope.

Time is as specific as space; although the narrative is full of gothic horrors the novel does not take place in the adventure time of Greek and subsequent romances, but in a time that has what Bakhtin calls a "natural, everyday cyclicity." The temporal settings are as specific as the geographic ones; mornings and evenings are vividly described. For instance:

> Scintilla Shruggles shoved the watersoaked circus punt into the morning brume on the dark river. The slow current turned the pilgrims around and around until Matchi Makwa raised the oars and started rowing slow with the flow down toward the evil cities. . . . The first strokes of sunlight burned through the leaves on the oak and cottonwood river trees like *tchibai nopiming* woodland phantoms dancing over the faces of the passing pilgrims.[42]

Unlike the static time of myth and romance, time in the *Bearheart* chronotope rolls on inexorably and irreversibly. And Vizenor is very careful to transmit the sense of duration it takes to get from one place to another. In this chronotope the adventures may be highly bizarre, even supernatural, but the life of the novel is anchored in a world whose time and places are familiar.

Not only are there real towns in *Bearheart*, but many of the characters are based on real people. Vizenor uses a generous amount of hyperbole, but the essence of these characters are borrowed from people he knows. For instance, Lilith Mae Farrier is the subject of a biographical sketch in Vizenor's collection of essays, *Wordarrows*.

As Vizenor puts it in the acknowledgments to *Bearheart*:

> Many of the characters in these stories about trees and masks and bear visions are real people with fictional names. Charles Lindbergh, President Jimmy Carter, N. Scott Momaday, and John Clement Beaulieu, among other visitors and presidents and tribal heroes who are mentioned in the word wars, are fictional characters with real names.[43]

What is the result of placing trickster in the highly specific chronotope of the postmodern novel? For one thing it humanizes him and makes him more vulnerable. If mythic verism stretches the laws of nature as we conceive them in our Western paradigm, it is also verisimilar in that it makes the hero more man than god, or *manido* to use the Anishinaabe word. Manabozho, for all his silliness and buffoonery, was a spirit not a human. Despite his ability to dream himself out of trouble and translate himself to the next world, Proude is a man. He patterns himself on the trickster hero of his tribe's mythology, doing his best with what magic and wit he can muster to lead his people through a hostile country.

Proude is not the only trickster figure in *Bearheart*; in fact, he is really half the trickster. The other half is Bigfoot, Benito Saint Saint Plumero. Splitting the trickster figure is not without precedent in myth and literature: Prometheus (the "forethinker" who tricked the gods and stole their fire) and his brother Epimetheus (the "afterthinker" who was tricked by Zeus into taking in Pandora and her box) represent both sides of the trickster.

Proude represents the trickster in his positive role as culture hero. Leading the pilgrims as they cross America, he resembles the Manabozho who kills the Windigo and Evil Gambler, who brings the Anishinaabe fire and saves mankind on his raft during the great flood.

Like Manabozho Proude is always on the move. It is true that he was originally reluctant to leave his home in Minnesota and was driven from the reservation by collusion between the federal government that wanted the trees and a corrupt tribal chief. Whatever the impetus, however, once Proude starts his travels he doesn't stop, traversing western America until he finally escapes into the fourth world.

Like Manabozho Proude survives by his wits rather than by brute force. His creed is to outwit but never to kill evil. He departs from this in the case of the evil gambler, who kills himself when Proude defeats him. But inconsistency is part of the trickster's nature, and myth decrees that the trickster be the cause of the Gambler's death.

Like Manabozho, Proude has the ability to change shapes. Rather than becoming a hare, however, he becomes a bear and in that shape escapes from the third world into the fourth. He floats through the corner window in Pueblo Bonito past the rising winter solstice sun to the world above this one. In his discussion of chronotopes Bakhtin has observed that there is a tendency in mythological narratives to change the horizontal axis of time into a vertical axis of space when discussing Golden Ages or Paradises.[44] This is certainly true of tribal myth.

Whatever the similarities, Proude's powers are more diminished than Manabozho's. He defeats the evil gambler, but not until Lilith Mae Farrier dies. He also fails to protect Belladonna Darwin Wintercatcher (who dies at the hands of the hunters and horsebreeders of Orion) or Bishop Parasimo (who is killed by the Fast Food Fascists) or Little Big Mouse (torn apart by the cripples and lepers). To be sure there is much violence in myths, but in the mythic chronotope such events are often reversible. In some versions of the Gambler myth the gambler's victims are restored from death; in the novelistic chronotope of *Bearheart* time and events are irreversible.

In fact, although Proude fights the good fight and ultimately escapes evil himself, he appears painfully vulnerable. Nowhere is this more apparent then at the end when Bigfoot seduces his wife Rosina, who Proude leaves behind when he ascends to the next world. Although Proude's ascent seems to be a personal triumph there is an odd sense of loss accompanying it; Proude seems to be losing his identity as a trickster. The trickster is traditionally a priapic figure, having sex anywhere, anytime, with anything, but we hear nothing of Proude's sexual exploits. Toward the end of the novel, when what is left of the band of pilgrims reaches the Walatowa Pueblo,[45] two sacred Jemez clowns reproach Proude for losing his sex urge: "You speak fine thoughts from the heart paths but who will take your little cock in hand mister proud and lust with you. . . . Your wife has forgotten the feeling of your rude prize . . ."[46]

Rosina apparently expects more passion from a trickster since she betrays Proude for Bigfoot. Bigfoot first has Rosina play with his penis then forces her to commit fellatio. Although the act begins involuntarily Rosina dissolves like the ingenue at a movie kiss. While she and Bigfoot are occupied, however, Sister Eternal Flame strangles Bigfoot. The narrator never tells us that Proude leaves Rosina behind because she has been unfaithful or defiled, but the feeling is somehow there. The book ends on an elegiac note with Rosina finding bear tracks in the snow and following them to where they end at the rim of the mesa.

Bigfoot clearly represents the negative side of the trickster. He is like Manabozho, the menace who kills his brother and marries his sister, the buffoon who tries to share a meal with the trees and gets stuck between branches, who tries to fly like a bird but falls to the ground.

Bigfoot is a mixedblood who views himself as a "trickster clown, a new contrarion down on my luck."[47] He is a small man of huge parts, outsized feet which "moved in the grass like huge rodents,"[48] and a huge penis, President Jackson, which he uses to service the women of the Scapehouse for Weirds and Sensitives.

Although most versions of the trickster stories in print today have been cleaned up by missionaries, other prudes who recorded them, or publishers who packaged them as tales for children, traditionally trickster was known for his uncontrollable sexual appetite. Manabozho, as mentioned above, commits incest; Sendeh, the Kiowa trickster, injures himself having sex with the whirlwind; and Wakdjunkaga, the Winnebago trickster, sends his penis across the lake to rape the chief's daughter then transforms himself into a woman to marry the chief's son.

Bigfoot is solidly in this tradition. His most outrageous act is the seduction of Rosina, but he has been quite active sexually before that. He sits under the table of the Weirds and Sensitives, caressing them as they dine on stuffed kitten. The love of his life is a bronze statue in a Saint Paul pond, which he steals and moves to a shrine in the cedar woods. When an onanistic white man defiles the statue, Bigfoot castrates the man and strangles him with the man's own private parts.

Tricksters seldom die in myth or literature. When they do the reader's expectations seem to be violated. For instance, in the second book of Ostap Bender's adventures, *The Twelve Chairs*, Ilf and Petrov's trickster has his throat cut. The authors never say why, but possibly Soviet censors decreed that this sort of social parasite must be dispatched so as not to encourage amoral behavior in easily swayed readers. Bender fails in his scam in Mel Brooks' movie version of the novel, but he is alive and up to his old tricks as the film ends.

In myth tricksters occasionally die (in the Cheyenne tale "The Sharpened Leg," Coyote starves to death), but it is understood by teller and audience that trickster will be alive in the next episode.[49] One difference between a novel like *Bearheart* and a group of tales or myths is that *Bearheart* has a beginning, middle and end and tales can be told in any order. An exception are the Winnebago trickster myths, which are arranged in a cycle. At the end of the cycle trickster abandons his foolishness and remembers the purpose for which he was sent to earth— helping the Winnebagos to cope with supernatural enemies. Finally he ascends to the world above. The end of *Bearheart* is similar. Bigfoot, the negative, evil buffoon part of trickster, dies; the good part, Proude, ascends to the next world.

Vizenor borrows the concept of interlocutors in discourse from Bakhtin, saying that the "'interlocutors' in the trickster narratives are the author, the narrator, the characters and audience."[50] In *Bearheart* Vizenor writes like a trickster, creating a narrator who is a professed trickster, telling a story of tricksters, all with the purpose of turning the audience into tricksters.

Vizenor writes like a trickster in several ways. He is fighting those whose values he despises, but he fights them obliquely with wit rather than directly with confrontation. Vizenor's formulation of the trickster's creed, as expressed by Third Proude Cedarfair, is "Outwit but never kill evil. . . . The tricksters and warrior clowns have stopped more evil violence with their wit than have lovers with their lust and fools with the power and rage . . ."[51] Vizenor's weapon is satire and humor; he plays the clown while launching his attacks.

Secondly, Vizenor plays with language and like the trickster and warrior clown he plays with it and fights it at the same time through the trope of catachresis. Catachresis, the deliberate misuse of words or mixing of metaphors, for example, "Measure most of our lives in darkness, the bear and me, count in silence our faces on the dawn . . . turning out miles and miles of heirship records at small federal desks, under the slow motions of government forearms . . ."[52] is Vizenor's way of winking at the reader and fighting the limits of language. He is aware that you can't break out of the prisonhouse of language, but catachresis is his way of kicking at the walls.

Vizenor's narrator in *Bearheart* is Saint Louis Bearheart, a minor functionary in the Heirship Division of the B.I.A. The novel has a frame: in the preface Bearheart explains that while ostensibly tracing tribal inheritances for the Bureau, he has been working on a novel, *Cedarfair Circus: Grave Reports from the Cultural Word Wars*. He gives this novel to a young urban radical with the American Indian Movement who breaks in on him while she is occupying the B.I.A. building. Bearheart first has sex with her then gives her his novel to read. What she reads, we read.

We don't see much of Bearheart, but what we do see establishes him clearly as a trickster. He has spent his life defying white authority while ostensibly working within the system. He has sex with the only woman we see him with. He is a free spirit who thinks for himself and despises the cliches of AIM as much as those of the U.S. Government.

In regard to characters, there seems little point in repeating the description of Proude and Bigfoot as tricksters. As for readers, by reading the narrative of the trickster, told by the trickster, they are manipulated into being tricksters who will share Vizenor's, Bearheart's and Proude's outrage at the current state of things and will join them in the fight against evil, using wit rather than violence.

Notes

1. Simon Ortiz, Paula Gunn Allen and Annette West, among others, have written Coyote poems which have obvious resemblances to trickster narratives, but which I cannot discuss here.

2. M. M. Bakhtin, *The Dialogical Imagination* (Austin: University of Texas Press, 1986) 84.

3. Tzvetan Todorov, *Mikhail Bakhtin: The Dialogical Principle* (Minneapolis: University of Minnesota Press, 1984) 83.

4. Bakhtin 85.

5. Gerald Vizenor, *The People Named the Chippewa* (Minneapolis: University of Minnesota Press, 1984) 7.

6. Bakhtin 115.

7. Jeanne L'strange, *Chippewa Tales* (Los Angeles: Wetzel Publishing, 1928) 15.

8. Bakhtin 90.

9. Bakhtin 90.

10. Bakhtin 91.

11. Sister Bernard Coleman, Ellen Frogner, and Estelle Rich, *Ojibwa Myths and Legends* (Minneapolis: Ross and Haines, 1962) 62ff.

12. John G. Neihardt, *Black Elk Speaks* (Lincoln: University of Nebraska Press, 1961) 81

13. Niehardt 7.

14. Neihardt 217.

15. Coleman 70, 70, 76.

16. Sister Laurina Levi, *Chippewa Indian Folklore* (New York: Writer's Press, 1978) 26.

17. Bakhtin 262.

18. Barnouw, Victor, *Wisconsin Chippewa Myths and Tales* (Madison: University of Wisconsin Press, 1977) 41.

19. Barnouw 14.

20. Theodore Beaulieu, ed., *The Progress* May 19, 1888: 1.

21. Gerald Vizenor, *Summer in the Spring* (Minneapolis: Nodin Press, 1981) 121, 116, 111.

22. Beaulieu, May 19, 1888: 1.

23. Beaulieu, May 12, 1888: 1.

24. Ian Watt, *The Rise of the Novel* (Berkeley: University of California Press, 1964) 32, 32, 14.

25. James, Henry, *The Future of the Novel* (New York: Vintage, 1956).

26. Watt 10.

27. Bakhtin 225.

28. Bakhtin 169.

29. Gerald Vizenor, "Trickster Discourse," paper presented at the School of American Research, Santa Fe, Jun. 1986: 5.

30. Bakhtin 172.

31. Bakhtin 172.

32. Gerald Vizenor, *Darkness in Saint Louis Bearheart* (Saint Paul: Truck Press, 1978) 147.

33. Bakhtin 168.

34. Bakhtin 169.

35. Bakhtin 170.

36. Gerald Graff, "The myth of the postmodernist breakthrough," *Tri-Quarterly* 26 (Winter 1973): 384.

37. Vizenor, "Trickster," 4.

38. Vizenor, "Trickster," 6.

39. Vizenor, "Trickster," 6.

40. Vizenor, "Trickster," 8.

41. Vizenor, "Trickster," 5.

42. Vizenor, *Darkness*, 67.

43. Vizenor, *Darkness*, xxi.

44. Bakhtin 148.

45. Walatowa is Momaday's name for Jemez in *House Made of Dawn*.

46. Vizenor, *Darkness*, 233.

47. Vizenor, *Darkness*, 79.

48. Vizenor, *Darkness*, 43.

49. Barry Lopez, *Giving Birth to Thunder, Sleeping with his Daughter* (New York: Avon, 1981) 115ff.

50. Vizenor, "Trickster," 7.

51. Vizenor, *Darkness*, 11.

52. Vizenor, *Darkness*, vii.

9

"Ecstatic Strategies":
Gerald Vizenor's Darkness in Saint Louis Bearheart

LOUIS OWENS

A few years ago, teaching a course in the American Indian novel, I discovered that three of my students had gone to a dean to complain about me. My offense: I had included Chippewa author Gerald Vizenor's *Darkness in Saint Louis Bearheart* in the class syllabus. The students were women and they were Indians, mixedbloods like myself of fairly indeterminate quantum. The complaint: *Bearheart* painted a false and degrading picture of Native American people. The outrageous novel included homosexual and transexual Indians, and everyone—particularly those of us living in Los Angeles on the edge of Hollywood—knew that Indian people were never such. The novel included Indians who were lustful, bestial, violent, sadistic, greedy and cowardly, and the three women who had grown up in Los Angeles but wore plastic beads and spoke of Mother Earth a great deal all knew that real Indian people could never be like that. Finally, the humor of *Bearheart* was undeniably sick, including a gratuitous amount of truly shocking sexual violence and, more serious yet, making fun far too often of "Indianness."

I was disappointed. The novel also contained Indian characters—the central protagonist in particular—who were transcendent in their goodness, wholeness, wisdom and courage. The novel was a scathing expose of white hypocrisy, brutality, genocidal, ecological murder and greed. And I had gone so far as to require the class to read Paul Radin's *The Trickster*, in which the archetypal trickster was not only explained by such a luminary as Carl Jung but was shown in action in the Winnebago Trickster Cycle. There, in traditional material, was a trickster lustful and avaricious, a sexually rapacious shapeshifter of appetite so boundless he would devour himself. Scatalogical references abounded. No taboo or more' was safe from trickster's tests. We had discussed this trickster, but somehow a connection had been missed by three of my twenty-three students.

Puzzling it out and talking with the students, I came finally to what must pass as an illumination. Not the sexual violence, not the "holosexuality" of Bishop Omax Parasimo's metamasks or the transexuality of Pio the mammoth parawoman clown, not the irrepressible "President Jackson" of Saint Plumero the double saint clown, not even the vile Evil Gambler or his mixed-blood horde had truly upset these students. It was trickster himself who was at fault, the trickster who challenges us to reimagine moment-by-moment the world we inhabit. Trickster challenges definitions of the self and, concommitantly, the world defined in relation to that self.

Darkness in Saint Louis Bearheart, like all of Vizenor's fictions, is a trickster narrative, a post-apocalyptic allegory of mixedblood pilgrim clowns afoot in a world gone predictably mad. This postmodern pilgrimage begins when Proude Cedarfair—mixedblood Anishinaabe shaman and the fourth in a line of Proude Cedarfairs—and his wife Rosina flee their Cedar Circus reservation accompanied by seven clown crows as the reservation is about to be ravaged for its timber by corrupt tribal officials. The nation's economy has collapsed due to the depletion of fossil fuels, and the government and tribal "bigbellies" lust after the Circus cedar.

As the pilgrims move westward toward the vision window at Pueblo Bonito, place of passage into the fourth world, their journey takes on ironic overtones in a parody not merely of the familiar allegorical pilgrimage a la *Canterbury Tales* but more pointedly of the westering pattern of American "discovery" and settlement. Very early in their journey, Proude and Rosina are joined by an intense collection of misfits, both mixedblood and white. Benito Saint Plumero, or Bigfoot, is a mixedblood clown and "new contrarion" descended from "the hotheaded political exile and bigfooted explorer, Giacomo Constantino Beltrami."[1] Bigfoot's pride, in addition to his huge feet, is an enormous and exuberantly active penis named President Jackson by the appreciative sisters in the "scapehouse of weirds and sensitives," a retreat founded with federal funds by thirteen women poets from the cities. Another pilgrim, Pio Wissakodewinini, "the parawoman mixedblood mammoth clown," has been falsely charged with rape and sentenced to a not-quite-successful sex change. Inawa Biwide, "the one who resembles a stranger," is sixteen, "an orphan rescued by the church from the state and the spiritless depths of a federal reservation housing commune" (71). Inawa Biwide will quickly become the novel's apprentice shaman, eventually following Proude Cedarfair into the fourth world. Rescuer of Inawa Biwide from the state is Bishop Omax Parasimo, wearer of metamasks which allow him to pass from Bishop to Sister Eternal Flame and other transexual metamorphoses. Justice Pardone Cozener, a minor figure in this pilgrimage of the outraged and outrageous, is an "illiterate law school graduate and tribal justice . . . one of the new tribal bigbellies . . . who fattened themselves overeating on expense accounts from conference to conference" (74). Justice Pardone is in love with Doctor Wilde Coxwaine, the bisexual tribal historian also along on this journey westward.

One of four consistently female characters journeying with Proude is Belladonna Darwin-Winter Catcher, the daughter of Old John Winter Catcher, Lakota shaman, and Charlotte Darwin, a white anthropologist. Conceived and born at Wounded Knee, Belladonna is a victim of rigid world views. Other female pilgrims include Little Big Mouse, "a small whitewoman with fresh water blue eyes" who rides in foot holsters at the waist of the giant Sun Bear Sun, "the three hundred pound seven foot son of the utopian tribal organizer Sun Bear" (74), and Lillith Mae Farrier, the white woman who began her sexual menage with two dogs while teaching on an Indian reservation.

Unarguably the most radical and startling of American Indian novels, *Darkness in Saint Louis Bearheart* is paradoxically also among the most traditional of novels by American Indian authors, a narrative deeply in the trickster tradition, insisting upon community versus individuality, upon synchretic and dynamic values versus the cultural suicide inherent in stasis, upon the most delicate of harmonies between man and the world he inhabits, and upon man's ultimate responsibility for that world.

The fictional author of this novel-within-a-novel is old Bearheart, the mixedblood shaman ensconced in the Bureau of Indian Affairs offices being ransacked by American Indian Movement radicals as the book begins. Bearheart, who as a child achieved his vision of the bear while imprisoned in a B.I.A. school closet, has written the book we will read. "When we are not victims to the white man then we become victims to ourselves," Bearheart tells a female radical with her chicken feathers and plastic beads. He directs her to the novel locked in a file cabinet, the "book about tribal futures, futures without oil and governments to blame for personal failures." To her question, "What is the book about?" Bearheart answers first, "Sex and Violence," before adding, "Travels through terminal creeds and social deeds escaping from evil into the fourth world where bears speak the secret languages of saints" (xii–xiv).

"Terminal creeds" in *Bearheart* are beliefs which seek to fix, to impose static definitions upon the world. Such attempts are destructive, suicidal, even when the definitions appear to arise out of revered tradition. Third Proude Cedarfair expresses Vizenor's message when he says very early in the novel, "Beliefs and traditions are not greater than the love of living" (11), a declaration repeated near the end of the novel in Fourth Proude's statement that "The power of the human spirit is carried in the heart not in histories and materials" (214).

"In trickster narratives," Gerald Vizenor has written, "the listeners and readers imagine their liberation; the trickster is a sign, and the world is 'deconstructed' in a discourse."[2] *Bearheart* is such a liberation, an attempt by this most radically intellectual of American Indian authors to free us from romantic entrapments, to liberate the imagination. The principal target of this fiction is the sign "Indian," with its predetermined and well worn path between signifier and signified. Vizenor's aim is to free the play between these two elements, to liberate "Indianness."

While the authorial voice explains that Rosina "did not see herself in the abstract as a series of changing ideologies" (35), most of the pilgrims in this narrative, to varying degrees, do indeed suffer from the illness of terminal creeds. Bishop Omax Parasimo is "obsessed with the romantic and spiritual power of tribal people" (71), a believer—like those students so disturbed by this novel—in the Hollywood version of Indianness. Matchi Makwa, another pilgrim, chants "Our women were poisoned part white," leading Fourth Proude to explain, "Matchi Makwa was taken with evil word sorcerers" (55).

Belladonna Darwin-Winter Catcher, the most obvious victim of terminal creeds, attempts to define herself as "Indian" to the exclusion of her mixedblood ancestry and, more fatally, to the exclusion of change. "Three whitemen raped me," she tells Proude, "three evil whitesavages." Upon learning she is pregnant Proude replies, "Evil does not give life" (65). Belladonna does not heed the warning Proude offers when he says, "We become the terminal creeds we speak . . ." (143).

When the pilgrims come to Orion, a walled town inhabited by the descendants of famous hunters and western bucking horse breeders, Belladonna is asked to define "tribal values." Belladonna replies with a string of clichés, stating, "We are tribal and that means that we are children of dreams and visions . . . Our bodies are connected to mother earth and our minds are part of the clouds . . . Our voices are the living breath of the wilderness. . . ." A hunter replies, "My father and grandfathers three generations back were hunters. . . . They said the same things about the hunt that you said is tribal. . . . Are you telling me that what you are saying is exclusive to your mixedblood race?" Belladonna snaps, "Yes!" adding, "I am different than a whiteman because of my values and my blood is different . . . I would not be white." She blithers on, contradicting much of what we have witnessed thus far in the novel: "Tribal people seldom touch each other. . . . We do not invade the personal bodies of others and we do not stare at people when we are talking . . . Indians have more magic in their lives than whitepeople . . ." (190–91).

A hunter responds: "Tell me about this Indian word you use, tell me which Indians are you talking about, or are you talking for all Indians . . ." (191). Finally, after trapping Belladonna in a series of inconsistencies and logical culs-de-sac, he asks the question which cuts through the dark heart of the novel: "What does Indian mean?" When Belladonna replies with more clichéd phrases, the hunter says flatly, "Indians are an invention. . . . You tell me that the invention is different than the rest of the world when it was the rest of the world that invented the Indian. . . . Are you speaking as an invention?" (191). Speaking as a romantic invention indeed, a reductionist definition of being that would deny possibilities of the life-giving change and adaptation at the center of traditional tribal identity, Belladonna is further caught up in contradictions and dead-ends. The hunters and breeders applaud and then give the young mixedblood her "just desserts": a cookie sprinkled with a time-release alkaloid poison. "Your mixedblood friend is a terminal believer and a victim of her own narcissism," a breeder says to the pilgrims (194).

Belladonna Darwin-Winter Catcher represents what Vizenor has described in an interview as the "invented Indian." In the interview, Vizenor confesses his satirical, didactic purpose:

"I'm still educating an audience. For example, about Indian identity I have a revolutionary fervor. The hardest part of it is I believe we're all invented as Indians. . . . So what I'm pursuing now in much of my writing is the idea of the invented Indian. The inventions have become disguises. Much of the power we have is universal, generative in life itself and specific to our consciousness here. In my case there's even the balance of white and Indian, French and Indian, so the balance and contradiction is within me genetically. . . . There's another idea that I have worked into the stories, about terminal creeds. I worked that into the novel *Bearheart*. It occurs, obviously, in written literature and in totalitarian systems. It's a contradiction, again, to balance because it's out of balance if one is in the terminal condition. This occurs in invented Indians because we're invented and we're invented from traditional static standards and we are stuck in coins and words like artifacts. So we take up a belief and settle with it, stuck, static. Some upsetting is necessary."[3]

Belladonna is obviously inventing herself from "traditional static standards." In its association with both beauty and deadly nightshade, Belladonna's very name hints at her narcisistic dead-end. That the belladonna, or nightshade, plant is also associated historically with witchcraft implies the nature of evil witchery according to Native American traditions: the misuse of knowledge for the benefit of the individual alone rather than for the community as a whole. Her mixed-blood surname, "Darwin," calls to mind also the scientist most responsible in the popular consciousness for the substitution of random event, or evolutionary chance, for a world of imagined structure and order. In the wake of Darwinian evolution, man was made capable of imagining himself as victim—pawn of chance—rather than creator and controller. According to the Darwinian origin myth, as conveyed to the modern mind through the vehicle of naturalism, powerless man inhabits an imagined world antithetical to that evoked in Native American origin myths in which men and women share responsibility for the creation and safeguarding of the world. In her attempt to define herself and all Indians according to predetermined values, Belladonna has foresaken such responsibility in favor of a definition of the Indian as victim and static artifact.

Belladonna illustrates the result of a long process. Out of James

Fenimore Cooper's gothic last Mohican, the romantic residue of a vanishing civilization, grew the late nineteenth-century naturalistic phenomenon of the helpless (and thus unthreatening) "vanishing American," which in turn became in the twentieth-century the Indian as quintessential modernist victim. Writers have embraced joyously the Indian as the deracinated, powerless and pathetic figure so essential to the modernist predicament, inventing the Indian only to doom him, a contrivance illustrated splendidly by Faulkner's Chief Doom and the general confusion of Chickasaws and Choctaws in Faulkner's fiction. It remained at mid-century for an Anglo contrarion clown such as Ken Kesey to upset the machinery of naturalism and the invented vanishing American when he allowed Chief Bromden ("Broom") to hurl the control panel through the window and escape from the great machine in the trickster novel *One Flew Over the Cuckoo's Nest.* For Kesey, as for Vizenor, essential to the healing and freeing are responsibility and laughter.

Belladonna is a victim of her own words. As Proude explains, "We become our memories and what we believe. . . . We become the terminal creeds we speak . . ." (143).

Chance, random event, would deny the responsibility of individuals for the world they inhabit, a denial not part of the traditional tribal world view. When the pilgrims arrive at What Cheer, Iowa to gamble for fuel with Sir Cecil Staples, the "monarch of unleaded gasoline," Proude declares flatly that "Nothing is chance. . . . There is no chance in chance. . . . Chances are terminal creeds" (107). With chance, responsibility diminishes, a criticism the novel's author voices early in the novel:

> Tribal religions were becoming more ritualistic but without visions. The crazed and alienated were desperate for terminal creeds to give their vacuous lives meaning. Hundreds of urban tribal people came to the cedar nation for spiritual guidance. They camped for a few days, lusted after their women in the cedar, and then, *lacking inner discipline, dreams, and personal responsibilities,* moved on to find new word wars and new ideas to fill their pantribal urban emptiness. (12, emphasis added)

At the What Cheer Trailer Ruins, the pilgrims encounter additional victims of terminal creeds, the Evil Gambler's mixedblood horde: "the three mixedbloods, dressed in diverse combinations of tribal vestments and martial uniforms, bangles and ideological power patches and armbands. . . . Deep furrows of ignorance and intolerance stretched across their unwashed foreheads" (99). In an experience common to Native Americans, the three killers feel themselves to be the victims of white America. Cree Casket, the "mixedblood tribal trained cabinet maker with the blue chicken feather vestments," tells the pilgrims, "I was trained in the government schools to be a cabinet maker, but all the cabinets were machine made so making little wooden caskets made more sense" (101). Cree Casket, we discover, is also a necrophiliac. Carmine Cutthroat, described by Justice Pardone as "the red remount . . . with the green and pink stained chicken feathers," cannot speak, the Papago and Mescalero mixedblood having had hot lead poured down his throat by "seven whitechildren" while he slept. Willie Burke, the "Tliingit and Russian mixedblood" with a "compulsive need to kill plants and animals and trees," is rendered unconscious by Pio before he has a chance to tell his story of victimage. Doctor Wilde Coxwaine, examining the three mixedbloods, labels them "Breathing plastic artifacts from reservation main street," declaring, ". . . here stand the classic hobbycraft mannikins dressed in throwaway pantribal vestments, promotional hierograms of cultural suicide" (100).

Even the Evil Gambler himself is a victim of modern America, having been kidnapped from a shopping mall and raised in a big-rig trailer on the road, his upbringing a distillation of the peripatetic American experience. Being raised outside of any community, Sir Cecil has no tribal or communal identity; he exists only for himself, the destructive essence of evil witchery. From being doused repeatedly with pesticides, he has become pale and hairless, a malignant Moby Dick of the heartland. He explains, "I learned about slow torture from the government and private business. . . . Thousands of people have died the slow death from disfiguring cancers because the government failed to protect the public" (123). Sir Cecil, the Evil Gambler, is the product of a general failure of responsibility to the communal or tribal whole.

Among the trailer ruins Lillith Mae Farrier is selected to gamble for fuel with Sir Cecil, the Evil Gambler reminiscent of the traditional evil gambler in American Indian mythologies. Because she "did not know the rituals of balance and power," because she has not been properly prepared according to tradition for her contest with the Evil Gambler, Lillith loses and destroys herself (112). Proude then tosses the four directions in competition with Sir Cecil and, because chance plays no part in Proude's vision, the Gambler loses and is condemned to death by Saint Plumero. Sir Cecil complains to Proude: "The pilgrims wanted gasoline which is part of the game, but you want to balance the world between good and evil. . . . Your game is not a simple game of death. You would change minds and histories and reverse the unusual control of evil power" (126).

From the Trailer Ruins, the pilgrims, whose postal truck soon runs out of gas, travel westward on foot, encountering hordes of deformed stragglers on the broken highways. This host of cripples and monsters are, in the words of Doctor Wilde Coxwain, "Simple cases of poisoned genes," all ravaged by pesticides, poisoned rain, the horrors of the modern technological world. The authorial voice describes this national suicide:

> First the fish died, the oceans turned sour, and then birds dropped in flight over cities, but it was not until thousands of children were born in the distorted shapes of evil animals that the government cautioned the chemical manufacturers. Millions of people had lost parts of their bodies to malignant neoplasms from cosmetics and chemical poisons in the air and food.

Insisting blindly on identifying the cripples as romantic figures, Little Big Mouse is attacked and torn to pieces by a mob of technology's victims.

Following the canonization of Saint Plumero, a ceremony making Bigfoot a "double saint," the pilgrims arrive at Bioavaricious, Kansas and the Bioavaricious Regional Word Hospital where terminal creeds—language whose meaning is fixed, language without creative play—are the goal of the hospital staff. In an attempt to rectify what is perceived as a national breakdown in language, the scientists at the word hospital are using a "dianoetic chromatic encoder" to "code and then reassemble the unit values of meaning in a spoken sentence" (163). We are told that with

> regenerated bioelectrical energies and electromagnetic fields, conversations were stimulated and modulated for predetermined values. Certain words and ideas were valued and reinforced with bioelectric stimulation. (164)

The endeavor at the word hospital suggests what Michel Foucault has labeled an intention "to programme . . . to impose on people a framework in which to interpret the present."[4] This attempt to create an impossibly pure "readerly" prose stands in sharp contrast to the oral tradition defined in a description of life among *Bearheart's* displaced just a few pages earlier:

> Oral traditions were honored. Families welcomed the good tellers of stories, the wandering historians of follies and tragedies. Readers and writers were seldom praised but the travelling raconteurs were one form of the new shamans on the interstates. Facts and the need for facts had died with newspapers and politics. Nonfacts were more believable. The listeners traveled with the tellers through the same frames of time and place. The telling was in the listening. . . . Myths became the center of meaning again. (158)

In the oral tradition a people define themselves and their place in an imagined universe, a definition necessarily dynamic and requiring constantly changing stories. The listeners recreate the story in the act of hearing and responding. As Vizenor himself has written elsewhere, "Creation myths are not time bound, the creation takes place in the telling, in present-tense metaphors."[5] Predetermined values represent stasis and thus cultural suicide. French critic Roland Barthes says simply, "the meaning of a work (or of a text) cannot be created by the work alone. . . ."[6] And in *Trickster Discourse*, Vizenor quotes Jacques Lacan who warns us not to "cling to the illusion that the signifier answers to the function of representing the signified, or better, that the signifier has to answer for its existence in the name of any signification whatever."[7]

Impressed by the word hospital, Justice Pardoner and Doctor Wilde Coxwaine remain at Bioavaricious while the remaining pilgrims journey onward toward New Mexico. As they move westward the pilgrims and sacred clowns meet fewer deformed victims of cultural genocide until finally they encounter the modern pueblos of the Southwest and a people living as they have always lived. At the Jemez Pueblo, the Walatowa Pueblo of N. Scott Momaday's *House Made of Dawn*, the pilgrims encounter two sacred Pueblo clowns who outclown with their traditional wooden phalluses even Saint Plumero himself. The clowns direct Proude and the others toward Chaco Canyon and the vision window where, finally, Proude and Inawa Biwide soar into the fourth world as bears at the winter solstice.

A great deal is happening in *Darkness in Saint Louis Bearheart*, but central to the entire thrust of the novel is the identification by the author, Vizenor, with trickster, the figure which mediates between oppositions, or as Vizenor himself quotes in *Trickster Discourse:* "embodies two antithetical, nonrational experiences of man with the natural world, his society, and his own psyche. . . ." Citing Warwick Wadlington, Vizenor stresses the duality of trickster's role as on the one hand "a force of treacherous disorder that outrages and disrupts, and on the other hand, an unanticipated, usually unintentional benevolence in which trickery is at the expense of inimical forces and for the benefit of mankind."[8]

In one of the epigraphs to *Earthdivers,* Vizenor quotes Vine Deloria's declaration that life for an Indian in today's world:

> "becomes a schizophrenic balancing act wherein one holds that the creation, migration, and ceremonial stories of the tribe are true and that the Western European view of the world is also true. . . . the trick is somehow to relate what one feels to what one is taught to think."

About this balancing act, Vizenor himself says in the preface to this same collection of trickster narratives:

> The earthdivers in these twenty-one narratives are mixedbloods, or Métis, tribal tricksters and recast cultural heroes, the mournful and whimsical heirs and survivors from that premier union between the daughters of the woodland shamans and white fur traders. The Métis, or mixedblood, earthdivers in these stories dive into unknown urban places now, into the racial darkness in the cities, to create a new consciousness of coexistence.[9]

For Vizenor, trickster is wenebojo (or *naanabozho,* manibozho, nanibozhu, etc.), "the compassionate tribal trickster of the woodland anishinaabeg, the people named the Chippewa, Ojibway. . . ."[10] This is not, according to Vizenor, the

> "trickster in the word constructions of Paul Radin, the one who 'possesses no values, moral or social . . . knows neither good nor evil yet is responsible for both,' but the imaginative trickster, the one who cares to balance the world between terminal creeds and humor with unusual manners and ecstatic strategies."[11]

This compassionate trickster—outrageous, disturbing, challenging as he is—is the author of *Bearheart.* Vizenor says in the interview: "When I was seeking some meaning in literature for myself, some identity for myself as a writer, I found it easily in the mythic connections."[12] Central to these mythic connections is trickster, the shapeshifter who mediates between man and nature, man and deity, who challenges us to reimagine who we are, who balances the world with laughter.[13] Near the end of *Darkness in Saint Louis Bearheart*, Rosina and Sister Eternal Flame (Pio in the late Bishop's metamask) encounter three tribal holy men "who had been singing in a ritual hogan. It was the last morning of a ceremonial chant to balance the world with humor and spiritual harmonies. . . . The men laughed and laughed knowing the power of their voices had restored good humor to the suffering tribes. Changing woman was coming over the desert with the sun" (239).

Coming over the desert with the sun, from east to west, is Rosina herself, who, like Proude, has achieved mythic existence here near the end. "During the winter," we are told in the novel's final line," "the old men laughed and told stories about changing woman and vision bears." Translated through trickster's laughter into myth, Proude and Inawa Biwide and Rosina have a new existence within the ever-changing stories, the oral tradition. Contrary to the idea of the Indian as static artifact invented over the past several centuries, adaptation and change have always been central to American Indian cultures, responses which have enabled tribal cultures to survive. For all peoples Vizenor seems to argue, but for the mixedblood in particular, adaptation and new self-imaginings are synonymous with psychic survival. Those who would live as inventions, who, like Belladonna, would define themselves according to the predetermined values of the sign "Indian," are victims of their own terminal vision. Bearheart's mocking laughter is their warning.

Notes

1. Gerald Vizenor, *Darkness in Saint Louis Bearheart* (Saint Paul, Minnesota: Truck Press, 1978) 68–69. Subsequent references to this novel will be identified by page number in the text.

2. Gerald Vizenor, *The Trickster of Liberty* (Minneapolis: University of Minnesota Press, 1988).

3. Neal Bowers and Charles L. P. Silet, "An Interview with Gerald Vizenor," *Melus*, 8:1 (Spring 1981): 45–47.

4. Michel Foucault, "Film and Popular Memory," interview by Martin Jordin, *Radical Philosophy* 11 (1975): 29. Quoted in Vizenor's "Trickster Dis-

course: Comic Holotropes and Language Games," paper presented at the School of American Research, Santa Fe, Jun. 1986: 9.

5. Gerald Vizenor, *Earthdivers: Tribal Narratives on Mixed Descent* (Minneapolis: University of Minnesota Press, 1981) xii.

6. Roland Barthes, *Critical Essays*, trans. Richard Howard (Evanston: Northwestern University Press, 1972) xi.

7. Vizenor, "Trickster," 4.

8. Vizenor, "Trickster" 2–3.

9. Vizenor, *Earthdivers*, xii.

10. Vizenor, *Earthdivers*, xii.

11. Vizenor, *Earthdivers*, xii.

12. Bowers and Silet 42.

13. Chance, on the other hand, forms the essential spirit of trickster himself, who "liberates" the mind in comic discourse" as Vizenor declares in his prologue to *The Trickster of Liberty*, a unified collection of Vizenor's trickster narratives published by the University of Minnesota Press. As is suggested in the discussion of *Bearheart's* "Bioavaricious Regional Word Hospital," the liberating impulse of chance is vital to the creative play of language, though in a Native American world-view man cannot concede control of his destiny to an illusion of incomprehensible chance or victimage but must accept ultimate responsibility as co-creator of his world and wield language as a means of articulating his own identity within that world.

10

Metalanguages

ELAINE A. JAHNER

Metalanguages, with their capacity to totalize or destabilize, construct or deconstruct, have evoked responses of cautious wariness on the part of most critics of American Indian oral or written literatures. Among the best critics, this caution derives from an intelligently informed awareness of how easily a way of life gets broken into data to satisfy someone's need for a particular form of scholarly tidiness. It also derives from knowledge of how critical language is always thoroughly implicated in philosophical traditions whose relationships to the native literatures of this continent are what we question, not what we want to assume as the origin of our descriptive categories. Critics of tribal literatures, whatever their race, ordinarily think and write with more than the scholarly audience in mind. They think in terms of communities, urban or reservation, where traditions live on, their origins in a barely imaginable history and their current existence showing a determination not to face the world on terms dictated entirely by a dominant culture. So the critic, by definition educated in that very dominant culture as is the creative writer, believes in the possibility of using language to mediate among what we still call different traditions, even though many traditions have been interwoven and the very act of mediation on the part of writer and critic becomes one more variable in shaping the traditional process. For the writer and critic the engagement with whatever language is meant for public consideration and debate becomes a process of trying to perform at the limits of language and culture, where it is less a matter of answering questions than it is one of performing the questions themselves.

Gerald Vizenor, delightfully aware of the possibilities of this twentieth-century critical frontier, has given us images that allow us to move from abstractions to a metaphorically mixed play of language, to a veritable carnival of images that constitutes the intersection where traditions that have somehow persisted through time and change meet the very forces of externally induced change.

> Holding forth at the spacious treelines with the bears and the crows, the best tellers in the tribes peel peel peel peel their words like oranges, down to the last navel, Mimicked in written forms over winter now, transposed in mythic metaphors, the interior glories from oral traditions burst in conversations and from old footprints on the trail. . . .
> The reader remembers footprints near the treeline, near the limits of understanding in written words, but the trail is never marked with printed words. The trail is made as a visual event between imaginative creators, tellers, and listeners: we hold our breath beneath the surface, the written word, but we know that respiration and transpiration are possible under water.[1]

During the last two decades many critics have joined in the process of tracking those conversations and metaphors—often extended into songs and poems and even novels—that show the oral traditions living beneath the surface of the written word that is our stock in trade. Much of our critical endeavor has been to work out instructions on how to breathe beneath the surface of the written word because most of us have been trained to walk on top of these particular waters. One example of how to breathe freely, diving or surfacing as needed, has consistently inspired critic and creative writer alike. It is N. Scott Momaday's *The Way To Rainy Mountain*.

Now, twenty years after its completion, the questions posed by this literary performance with its several voices, its drawings, its framing poems and essays are taking on new significance as critics from diverse intellectual traditions turn their attention to what Wlad Godzich has characterized as two basic and related issues for today's international critical enterprise. He mentions "the conception of the subject as the organizer and sense-maker of lived experience, and the challenge posed to forms of Western thought by the liberation movements of the past forty years."[2]

Momaday's book is a performance, a dialogue with tradition by a scholar whose critical acuity assures him a place within mainstream critical history and a poet whose gift allows him to bring even the simplest language to revelation. This book dramatizes the tensions and intensities of one effort to situate the subject as sense-maker of lived experience that would otherwise disappear into an inaccessible past. Momaday wrote of this journey as a way of appropriating his own Kiowa-Apache tradition, and it exemplifies how a contemporary individual, living multiple cultural traditions, might use his own self-reflective powers to move from one way of confronting and using personal and collective memory into another. To the degree that such an effort remains possible, it stands as a particularly realized challenge to the "forms of Western thought," and it coexists with and within those very forms.

Momaday's book is a carefully structured compilation of myth, legend, historical and personal commentary. As Momaday has explained, the process of writing the book was part of a conscious effort to understand "the way in which myths, legends, and lore evolve into the mature condition of expression which we call 'literature.'"[3] In order to explore the way oral narrative develops into written form Momaday established a principle of narration that he terms "elaborate and experimental." The principle involves three distinct narrative voices so that each section of Kiowa myth is followed by historical commentary and a personal response.

As he juxtaposes mythic, historical and personal narrative Momaday establishes himself as the one addressed by voices from his own past and he allows himself to be called back to what is primal, situated literally in that territory where the Kiowas began their journey toward their distinct cultural identity and situated psychologically in those emotions and linguistic responses that Momaday has located as starting points for his own journey toward artistic identity. As we follow the personal voice in its reactions to the force of the mythic and historical, we observe how primordial perception is altered by memory. It gradually leads to awareness of the social, then on to violence, breakup and survival, ending with a precise historical and geographical situating of the conditions for survival east of his grandmother's house. He understands that the "shadow" of the gravestone on which his grandmother's name is written and which her "name defines" exists within his very being; her death is a call to his living in the continuity of his Kiowa past, however that continuity may be realized in his life.

Momaday's book has much of the power of drama. It transposes the performance possibilities of oral literature into a realized progression showing how myth and history can call forth his own creative responses. Readers, too, become members of an audience, listening to the old myths and meditating on Momaday's framing commentaries. Properly attended performances evoke a whole range of possible responses among audience members; and if the audience happens to include literary critics their responses will derive from their own beliefs about what literature is and can do. In such a situation criticism is less a matter of one-sided interpretation than of stating what Momaday's effort can evoke among different participants in his unique performance. Therefore, I have added a chorus of possible responses from different critical perspectives. I stress the word *response* because it is meant to sidestep notions of imposition that would subsume one way of thinking under the categories of another. I have juxtaposed ideas from major critics with quotations from Momaday's book in order to trace the significance of Momaday's thought in ways that are consonant with the form and spirit within which he wrote.

Today's critics of American Indian literatures are not included among my major critics because I am attempting to establish foundations for further work that would set their work into systematic relation with critics from outside their subdivision of critical inquiry. Exclusion of specialists in tribal literatures is not a rejection of the fine work of the last two decades. Rather, it is meant to emphasize a conviction that American Indian writers and critics have nurtured questions within their particular range of attentiveness that deserve spirited give-and-take with proponents of other critical positions. During the course of that exchange we may discover that there is greater international significance to diving beneath written surfaces and tracking footprints at the treeline of human understanding than we might have guessed.

My commentaries to the juxtapositions of Momaday's text and those of other critics suggest some of the terms of the critical exchange that might occur if critics from within the field of American Indian literatures were to engage in sustained and persistent dialogue with those major international figures whose work has been reshaping the terms of critical discourse during the years when critics of American Indian literatures have grown in number and have developed ways of thinking about literature that are rooted in distinct tribal traditions.

I am writing this imagined critical exchange twenty years after the first sections of *The Way To Rainy Mountain* were published. Less than two years later Momaday's novel *House Made of Dawn* won the Pulitzer Prize and reminded the world that American Indian writers are continuing voices in American and world literature. Since that time there has been an intensification of creative and critical writing that owes much to the events of twenty years ago. Anniversaries call for celebration. This orchestrated exchange is written in a celebratory spirit. At its beginning I quote Momaday ". . . let me hold to the way and be thoughtful in my going."[4]

N. Scott Momaday

The journey began one day long ago on the edge of the northern Plains. It was carried on over a course of many generations and many hundreds of miles. In the end there were many things to remember, to dwell upon and talk about. . . .

It is a whole journey, intricate with motion and meaning; and it is made with the whole memory, that experience of the mind which is legendary as well as historical, personal as well as cultural. And the journey is an evocation of three things in particular; a landscape that is incomparable, a time that is gone forever, and the human spirit, which endures. The imaginative experience and the historical express equally the traditions of man's reality. Finally then, the journey recalled is among other things the revelation of one way in which these traditions are conceived, developed and interfused in the human mind.[5]

Carlos Fuentes

Parallels, analogies: history is never the same, but we do share a historical destiny, or at least the memory of experience and the resonance of fate.

That is why we cannot dismiss the art and life of pre-Columbian antiquity as irrelevant to our deeper cultural and political search today. Art, power and death come together in the images of the past which were once the images of the future, and which we consign to a dead past only at the risk of having them reappear, one day as a surprising, uncontrollable or unrecognizable future.

The art—the stone, the sculpture, the form, the poetry—have outlived death, power, and religion, and are still with us, in the hushed respect of museums, in the clamorous throb of the marketplace, but also in the faces and the hearts of all of us in Latin America.

If we cannot have a future without a past, how are we to integrate that past into our future? The answer is: by giving both of them the time of the present.[6]

Commentary

The first voice in this critical exchange is that of a Latin American, Carlos Fuentes. As statesman and diplomat, Fuentes knows the contrariness of the present as it is regularly manifested through political ironies. As a novelist, critic and essayist he senses with particular fullness the diverse forms through which the past survives into the present even when, as is the case with this hemisphere's Indian cultures, political powers have sought to break the continuity between past and present.

In the article quoted here, Fuentes gives special attention to the Aztec Empire:

> by disregarding the living past of others or disfiguring it for their own political purposes, the Aztecs courted a future similar to the one they had imposed on others; they were repaid in kind by the Spanish who attempted to obliterate the Indian past. But the Indian world was able to reconquer itself through the power of its moral heritage and its artistic creations: all that had survived Aztec political necessity then went on to survive Spanish political necessity." (343)

Moral heritage and artistic creations—for Fuentes these have a staying power that persists, that remains ever the living past's threshold to a forbidden future. Artistic creation embodies the moral heritage, formalizes it, encodes it in ways that elude conquerors and allow communal recollection.

Coding invites decoding. The precise forms of the past are reminders that the very act of presenting or participating in the performance of any particular tradition was an enactment and interpretation of values, achieving the transformation of those values into personal ideals. Or as Umberto Eco states in his study of symbolic language, "A code is not only a rule which *closes* but also a rule which *opens*. It not only says 'you must' but says also 'you may' or 'it would also be possible to do that.' If it is a matrix, it is a matrix allowing for infinite occurrences, some of them still unpredictable, the source of a game."[7]

Fuentes plays with images and events from history, pulling their possibilities into the present, trying to make them serve his overtly political dream of a culturally pluralistic future. He does not quickly rationalize history. That would be using the intellect to idealize history and free it from its terrible concreteness, from the specifics of experience that allow it to exist as connected to details of daily life in the present. Nor does he shun rational consideration at its proper stage in the development of his thought.

For him the rational turns quickly to the political imperative or ideal. He gathers definite forms and sensually specific memories from cultures seldom linked together and he turns his project into a task:

> The future can only be a creative community if it belongs to a shared past: remember the future, it happened once. It is happening all the time, your future is in the rediscovery of an Aztec temple, in the persistence of a Hebrew legend, in the sound of the rain on the uneven pavements of Venice: you cannot have a future without these. . . . If we are to have a future, it will depend on the growing presence of cultures long relegated to insignificance because they did not participate in the truths proper to the triumphalist West. (351)

Both Momaday and Fuentes depend upon the artist to address practical aspects of helping cultures long kept outside the boundaries of political power and intellectual credibility to find their proper place in Fuentes' revised map of future influence. Viewed from this perspective, all the formal characteristics of Momaday's writing achieve exemplary status. They are in themselves coded responses to the call of the past.

The Russian writer Marina Tsvetaeva has described qualities of human exchange that can help us approach the intensely personal sense of history characterizing writers like Momaday and Fuentes and allows history to have such a hold on their creative aspirations. "To continue," she says, "is, after all, to put to the test." She reminds us that in every exchange, including that between past and present, there are elements of longing and fears of emptiness. "Longing (the cut to the quick) arises when the giving is not completed by that other person or by me, by us. Emptiness arises when the giving goes too far to one unworthy."[8]

Momaday and Fuentes present history as that means by which people continue in longing beyond death itself. The present also longs and seeks itself in its reply to the past that comes coded in words remaining from people who put their own pasts to the test and merited continuity. Emptiness is the fear, perhaps it is the overriding fear, because it presupposes a moral dimension to giving and receiving that demands worthiness on the part of giver and receiver.

As Fuentes notes traces of Aztec ancestors in the facial bones of people in Mexico, he presents concrete traces of the past motivating longing. As Momaday tries to shape a literary event which will allow him to listen to the dead, he demonstrates the animating potential of longing. In remaining so close to personal experience gained in definite times and places, he forges a link with the past that is indisputably part of his own living and responsible creative imagination. The past becomes intuitively present through those sensually explicit sets of associations that have been woven through time. They form a network of connotations linking definite landmarks to definite myths and legends with their aura of emotional specificity. These examples of oral literature, having been told by people whom he knew, whose intonations of voice echo in his memory, become literary evidences of longing incarnated and personalized. They are evidences of a tradition that has been tested in each succeeding generation so that what is useful and life-giving has become the motive for continuity.

Although these authors' longing is basically an emotion, it can not be assuaged by emotional means alone. It requires an intellectual response that allows the act of listening to the past to achieve its communicative potential. The act of listening must be formal, structured, channeled. If this is true for any response to history that recognizes that the response itself is rooted in one's own psychological history, it is even more imperative in a minority context where history has been kidnapped by conquerors and its voices muffled in an effort to induce an emptiness that could be filled by the dominant people's past. Among such peoples the act of listening to the past is approached with extraordinary care as they seek responsible evidence of what they perceive to be an endangered gift. That the past stares back from one's own mirror is a constant motive for a kind of commemorative recovery of ancestors that anticipates self-acceptance. The same image of self reflected in any mirror reflects multiple and conflicting historical pasts and creates an imperative to situate listening so that the voices of the past do not become an indistinguishable cacophony. *The Way To Rainy Mountain* is one such situating.

The juxtaposition of Fuentes' and Momadays' commentaries on the ways one moves through space and time to bring elements of the past into the shaping of the present calls attention to the structure of those acts of attention. No single analytic method can elucidate both the texts or objects to which this attention is directed and the quality of attention directed to them. Attentiveness is a matter of method and methods allows accountability and social force. Method as a mode of addressing a text or an object, which is always moved from one context to another, presupposes beliefs about why and how we make such moves. Altogether, these become the unavoidable foundations of theory. Momaday's journey to Rainy Mountain uses no language we ordinarily deem theoretical; nevertheless, a realized theoretical stance is implicit in it. In its structure and content it illustrates a traditional mode of textual interpretation. It examines the possibilities of transferring that mode from oral to written texts. As writing, it necessarily reaches out to other national and international contexts of writing.

Momaday divides his journey to Rainy Mountain into three parts: The Setting Out, The Going On, The Closing In. Setting features of various major critics' explicit theoretical agendas next to Momaday's should reveal much of what is implicit in Momaday's work. Sometimes this disclosure will come about through the way that Momaday stands in contrast to major theorists, sometimes through goals that generate closely comparable acts of attention. What I begin here is partial indeed. It could go on and on. The Closing In of this journey remains in the future and depends on the inclusion of many more traditions.

N. Scott Momaday

In one sense, then, the way to Rainy Mountain is preeminently the history of an idea, man's idea of himself, and it has old and essential being in language. The verbal tradition by which it has been preserved has suffered a deterioration in time. What remains is fragmentary: mythology, legend, lore, and hearsay—and of course, the idea itself, as crucial and complete as it ever was. That is the miracle. (4)

Jacques Derrida

. . . it must be recognized that in *Being and Nothingness, The Sketch of a Theory of the Emotions,* etc., the major concept, the theme of the last analysis of the irreducible horizon and origin is what was then called 'human reality'. As is well known this is a translation of Heideggerian *Dasein.* A monstrous translation in many respects, but so much the more significant. . . .

Certainly the notion of 'human-reality' translated the project of thinking the meaning of man, on a new basis, if you will. If the neutral and undetermined notion of 'human reality' was substituted for the notion of man, with all its metaphysical heritage and the substantialist motif or temptation inscribed in it, it was also in order to suspend all the presuppositions which had always constituted the concept of the unity of man.[9]

Commentary

Momaday's assertion that "the idea" survives "crucial and complete" even when the verbal tradition in which it was preserved has suffered fragmentation is the starting point for his journey which recovers the idea through a particular quality of attentiveness to the verbal tradition. What is this idea that allows for the kind of listening to the past that Momaday dramatizes in *The Way To Rainy Mountain?* Momaday himself has used the word often enough so that we can infer its sense from its various contexts before comparing it to other exemplary uses of the same word in order to suggest a kind of continuity and activity within specific traditions.

His most startling use of the word is in his essay "The Man Made of Words." There he defines so basic a matter as American Indian identity as an idea: "an Indian is an idea which a given man has of himself. And it is a moral idea, for it accounts for the way in which he reacts to other men and to the world in general. And that idea, in order to be realized completely, has to be expressed."[10]

Read apart from their context, Momaday's words could be understood as implying a complete domination of the intellectual over the inherited elements of racial identity. In context, though, we come to understand that the intellectual with its creative potential is but the means of realizing the inherited. Each requires the other. In the same essay Momaday returns to this point, turning it into a question with broader significance than specific racial identity.
"What is the relationship between what a man is and what he says—or between what he is, and what he thinks he is?" Momaday's answer to his own question invokes the idea again.

Generally speaking, man has consummate being in language, and there only. The state of human *being* is an idea, an idea which man has of himself. Only when he is embodied in an idea, and the idea is realized in language, can man take possession of himself. In our particular frame of reference, this is to say that man achieves the fullest realization of his humanity in such an art and product of the imagination as literature—and here I use the term "literature" in its broadest sense. This is admittedly a moral view of the question, but literature is itself a moral view and it is a view of morality.

For Momaday "the idea," insofar as it can be thought of apart from language in which it always realizes itself, is an active intentionality shaping and interpreting language. It belongs both to time and to place; for *where* one is shapes a fundamental relationship between self and land that, in turn, leads to a particular way of formulating that relationship in language that corresponds to the matching of self and place. Such correspondence may reach through time to take into account how someone else used language in similar circumstances and therefore, the forms by which language is preserved through time become the means of contact between persons responding similarly to place and circumstance.

Momaday states his sense of the personal and geographic aspects of the dynamics of a tradition much more vividly and concretely. He describes how his own act of writing about tradition required his concrete, imaginatively realized memories of the woman Ko-Sahn whose own experience forged an immediate link between a particular landscape and a particular legend. He dramatizes an experience that was part of his writing "The Man Made of Words," the essay that has been so fundamental a statement of American Indian esthetics. What he realized as he wrote came to him almost as a vision or fundamental revelation; and as he describes what he understood, he stresses how central is the direct personal memory to his sense of the idea as the dynamic of continuity. He claims that his writing had reached an impasse when suddenly he saw the Kiowa woman Ko-sahn before him.

> "But all of this, this imagining," I protested, "this has taken place—is taking place in my mind. You are not actually here, not here in this room." It occurred to me that I was being extremely rude, but I could not help myself. She seemed to understand.
>
> "Be careful of your pronouncements, grandson," she answered. "You imagine that I am here in this room, do you not? That is worth something. You see I have existence, whole being in your imagination. It is but one kind of being, to be sure, but it is perhaps the best of all kinds. If I am not here in this room, grandson, then surely neither are you."
>
> "I think I see what you mean," I answered meekly. (51)

Momaday's idea requires the same dynamics of transmission as the more structured oral literary genres. It achieves its present existence only if it is passed on from person to person and interpreted by each person in the chain of transmission as a way of making sense of contemporary experience. The constantly repeated interpretive act implicit in the dynamics of oral transmission is essential to the life of the idea which in transmission animates imagining in mind after mind. It continues from person to person, attaining its fullness not through its statement in abstract, logical form but through its activity of allowing entry to older forms of the imagination of which it is an originating force that lives on as the origin is reincarnated in the lives of individuals. "[Storytelling] is a process in which man invests and preserves himself in the context of ideas" (56).

If the process of transmission that supports the life of the idea is that of the oral tradition, the idea itself is not necessarily exclusive to the oral tradition. That is the point of Momaday's literary journey which exists in some intermediate position between the oral and the written traditions. Its epistemological foundations (its idea) are firmly within what has been continued through the oral traditions. Its particular realization is in the written mode. If the definitive notion is that of an act of attention in which one remains the addressee, the listener, and in which one receives words in a context and through formal means that are determined by a concrete historical situation, the oral/written dichotomy is secondary. The relationship between the speaker and the listener is primary as is the quality of the imaginative response. Momaday's great contribution is to show that the structure of this act of attention can become the subject and the object of writing. The listener becomes the writer through a particular kind of listening which is reflected in a form and style of writing that compares to little else in world literature. His literary journey is indeed experimental and transitional.

Momaday's idea turns out to have a mode of existence quite different from the notion of the idea that dominates the development of European philosophy. But before considering how this mode of existence allows for a particular kind of continuity, we must note that Momaday's idea shares with European philosophy that semantic core which refers to an act of cognition. In each case, *what* is known is transferrable to the registers of logical discourse. The differences lie in judgments about the degree to which logical discourse can effect an *adequate* communication of that knowledge. If the means whereby one comes to know something is inextricably bound to what one knows, logical discourse effects only a very partial transfer of any knowledge except that gained through its own means. The traditional knowledge

Momaday seeks has been transmitted through performative and meta-phoric modes of discourse, so immersion in those same modes is essential to all aspects of recovery including the cognitive. In cultures whose specific epistemological traditions remain secure, unthreatened from the outside, cognitive growth can occur without translation to purely analytical and logical levels of discourse. The culture's tropo-logical resources can encompass the cognitive, the affective and the commemorative. Such epistemological innocence is now like the lost Garden of Eden. The critical enterprise is now one of seeking meta-languages to describe the different epistemological traditions that char-acterize nations and regions. But if the metalanguages are a recent de-velopment limited more or less to scholars, the question of how to describe the differences is as old as contact and negotiation. The tribal peoples of this continent learned quickly that simply translating from their languages into English was inadequate. As so many voiced so often "words work differently" in the two traditions and these differ-ences are systematic, affecting every aspect of communication, sepa-rating people far more effectively than mountain ranges or oceans or deserts.

The more philosophically minded members of tribes on this conti-nent quickly sensed that how one came to know something not only separated them from those with whom they tried to negotiate treaties but was important to the possibilities ethnic survival itself. Translating what they sensed into terms that might communicate interculturally was impossible because such translation requires knowledge of two ways of knowing, but beyond that it requires that the issue itself make sense to the people to whom it is being addressed. Until the twentieth century, few European intellectuals radically questioned their own epistemological foundations.

Twentieth-century philosophy has so consistently foregrounded the question of how one knows that it has become the century's dominant theme. The stage has been set so that characters from different tradi-tions can speak to each other, asking questions that made no sense in earlier philosophical settings. The characters may still talk past each other, but such failures to communicate can now become the focus of the exchange as scholars address why the failures occur and what such failures may tell us about how to refine our means of intercultural communication. Today, we wonder about the possible terms of co-existence among diverse ways of knowing. Such wondering inevitably gets transferred to political registers.

Jacques Derrida is one scholar who has refused to pay unthinking homage to the idea and helped teach the world to question it. His constant and radical meditations on the human tendency to bow down before an idea have altered the way many think about language, even those who disagree with him. True to the most fundamental vocation of philosophy, he questions the very origins of ideality and he always does so within the intricacies of the language that carried forward the metaphysical traditions of the Western world.

Coexistence cannot work well without some awareness of why there is coexistence rather than assimilation. That is why Derrida's impact on critical and philosophical thinking is situated in relation to Momaday's presentation of the idea which survives as a way of knowing. Derrida is engaged in a process which seeks the hidden implications of the way European philosophy has formulated its ideas. Through his intricate tracings of how European thought has often seemed to be working toward one goal while simultaneously reinforcing its contrary, he is concentrating the attention of critics on the process of knowing. By deferring the closure that logic demands, Derrida makes the act of criticism into a refusal of the idea as defined by European philosophy. After such a refusal the critic is left to concentrate on the rhetorical mazes which are evidences of how European tradition has become what it is. Derrida's writing is an exercise in European self-knowledge with the goal kept always just out of reach of the exercise itself. But if Derrida refuses to allow the presence of the idea to guide his enterprise, it is because once accepted as the guide, the idea dominates. So Derrida addresses the idea by trying to keep it beyond the reach of his philosophical language. It is powerfully present by its absence. It is present in the way that darkness makes light a presence. And by keeping the idea as it has come to exist in European philosophy, always just beyond the grasp of what he is writing and thinking, Derrida is helping to shape an awareness within European philosophy of how the idea of the idea is a force shaping the modes of any discourse. As we watch the power of the Derridean insight capture the imagination and intellectual curiosity of critics around the world, we can also see critics pursue that initial insight in directions that seem barely consistent with its starting points in the European tradition. But as the pursuit intensifies, so does the emphasis on the act of writing or communicating as constituting a force in and of itself. If subordinated prematurely to the domination of the idea, it becomes a repressed force, a continuing generative force for transformations that will never be amenable to the control of the idea. If the idea's control within the generation of discourse always brings about that which exceeds its possible control, it also raises the question of whether or not that dynamic might be an analogue to what happens in the political realm where the idea is also made into an instrument of control. On this single point Derrida's insights and those of Fuentes converge. Both worry about what might one day reappear from out of collective repression as "a surprising, uncontrollable or unrecognizable future." Derrida has addressed this possibility, though, in ways quite unlike those of Fuentes.

For Derrida, any force that affects meaning while eluding formulation in philosophical language works as a pressure upon language, motivating an analysis of language that proceeds in the hope of noting those points where the pressure has shaped language use. Such points allow us some insight into what it is to live within language which is always being affected by what is outside it. One such "outside" is the unconscious as presented by Freud. Another, more immediately germane to this particular exercise, is that outside shaped by insiders' knowledge that cultures have developed beyond the boundary of what has shaped the "inside" of European conceptual categories. This second boundary, unlike the first, is not absolutely impermeable. But crossing its borders is no mean feat. There is always the likelihood that the crossing may be an illusion, an hallucination appearing to satisfy the desires of the weary traveler who moves forward in and through language.

Simply because the border exists people are compelled to think about it, and that awareness motivates a questioning that moves within and through the space defined by the linguistic/conceptual terrain in which we exist. Such questioning, now popularly known as deconstruction, moves one closer and closer to the limits of our philosophical homelands.

Derrida's descriptions of this border and its impact on European philosophy are vivid and clear in *Margins of Philosophy*:

. . . the discourse on anthropos, philosophical anthropology . . . [must have] as its theme, must feel bearing down on its borders the insistent weight of this difference, which is of an entirely other order than that of the internal or intraphilosophical differences of opinion which could be freely exchanged herre. Beyond these borders, what I call the philosophical *mirage* would consist as much in perceiving philosophy—a more or less constituted and adult philosophy—as in perceiving the desert. For this other space is neither philosophical nor desert-like, that is barren. If I recall this obvious fact, it is also for another reason: the anxious and busy multiplication of colloquia in the West is doubtless an effect of that difference which I just said bears down, with a mute, growing and menacing pressure, on the enclosure of Western colloution. The latter doubtless makes an effort to interiorize this difference, to master it, if we may put it thus by affecting itself with it." (113)

But what about people like Momaday whose lives have moved back and forth between ways of knowing and being? Is Momaday's "idea" a threshold allowing him to cross back and forth across the boundary of difference? And finally, if such movement across philosophical and cultural boundaries is deemed possible, does it presage a new stage in the European journey toward self-knowledge, one that is dependent on preserving and nurturing what access to difference remains after the insistent imposition of European ways of thinking throughout the world? Does it mean that the radically self-reflective gestures of Edmund Husserl and Martin Heidegger, which Derrida cites as turning points in European philosophy, have helped to create the beginnings of what Derrida has called "a worldwide historico-philosophical situation" in which "the fundamental conceptual system produced by the Greco-European adventure"[11] can coexist nonviolently with other systems?

Derrida's writing presents these questions; it does not provide answers to them. But Derrida's awareness of the questions has motivated the agenda whose ongoing realization has made him the world's preeminent philosopher. What I present so schematically is explicated with care and graceful precision in his essays. Certain threads recur, identifiable colors in each new tapestry. The role of the unconscious is most systematically developed in his essays on Freud and in the essay entitled "Differance."[12] The impact of cultures which developed outside the boundaries established by the European philosophemes is most concisely set forth in "The End of Man" a five-part essay in *Margins of Philosophy*. To this must be added "Violence and Metaphysics"[13] in which Derrida cogently analyzes the position of Jewish intellectuals who "live in the difference between the Jew and the Greek, which is perhaps the unity of what is called history." Whether or not Momaday could be said to be living "the difference" between the Kiowa and the Greek is undoubtedly one of the questions that is generated by Derrida's impact on contemporary thought. And Derrida's own thought teaches us the complexities attendant upon any attempt to answer the question. We may debate these within the context of whether or not it is possible to retain alternatives when political realities continue to make the European conceptual system into a world-wide system, endorsed by international political organizations and by educational institutions which help to create, maintain and impose the discursive realizations of the European agenda.

As we debate, we do well to remember certain lines Derrida wrote in his essay "Violence and Metaphysics" where he describes the thought of Emmanuel Levinas as a thought which

> without philology and solely by remaining faithful to the immediate, but buried nudity of experience itself, seeks to liberate itself from the Greek domination of the Same and the One (other names for the light of Being and of the phenomenon) as if from oppression itself—an oppression certainly comparable to none other in the world, an ontological or transcendental oppression, but also the origin or alibi of all oppression in the world. (83)

However we work out issues of coexistence of diverse pasts moving into the future, that dream of Fuentes and of Momaday, the realities of power in today's world require us to attend to the ways in which scholars like Derrida lead everyone to a rethinking of what is involved in the European project of self-examination.

N. Scott Momaday

VII The years went by, and the boy still had the ring which killed his mother. The grandmother spider told him never to throw the ring into the sky, but one day he threw it up, and it fell squarely on top of his head and cut him in two. He looked around, and there was another boy, just like himself, his twin. The two of them laughed and laughed, and then they went to the grandmother spider. She nearly cried aloud when she saw them, for it had been hard enough to raise the one. Even so, she cared for them well and made them fine clothes to wear (30).

Julia Kristeva

There is one inevitable moment in the movement that recognizes the symbolic prohibition and makes it dialectical: *laughter*. Practice as we have defined it, posits prohibitions, the ego, "meaning," etc. and makes them dialectical, and *laughter* is the operation that attests to this mechanism. . . .

Baudelaire emphasizes the contradictory structure of laughter which embraces an infinite "pride" and "misery" and rebels against theological authority. . . . Although laughter thus indicates one of the internal laws governing meaning, only a few rare philosophers can become the *subject* of laughter (whereas anyone can be its *object*). It is above all the "artist" who must accomplish, in each of his actions, what the instant of laughter reveals to the philosopher only in rare privileged moments. Consequently Baudelaire writes that laughter "comes into the class of all artistic phenomena which indicate the existence of a permanent dualism in the human being—that is the power of being oneself and someone else at one and the same time" Laughter is thus merely the *witness of a process* which remains the privileged experience of the "artist": a sovereignty (of the subject and of meaning, but also of history) that is simultaneously assumed and undermined.[14]

Commentary

Each of Momaday's sections presenting tradition's three voices calls for its own commentary and response. Although I rather arbitrarily choose only one for special attention, it is treated both in terms of its specific dimensions and in relation to Momaday's general technique of juxtaposing the mythic, historical (legendary) and personal voices. By simply juxtaposing the voices rather than incorporating them into a narrative structure, Momaday can preserve his own role as addressee. His own conventions dictate that the mythic and historical speak *to him* before they speak *through him*. This receptivity becomes the condition for a remembering which is disciplined and selective of what this one tradition evokes in him because it is called forth by only those images, events and words that are commemorated in Kiowa lore. Momaday's own mediation is shown to have been premeditated as the collective memory becomes personal memory.

This specific episode describes how the child of the sun and the earth woman breaks his grandmother's prohibition and literally becomes two. He is twinned.

Twins, those ubiquitous presences in world mythology, come into Momaday's narrative just before he confronts the power of words as linked to custom, to that incarnation of their power through the small things people do over and over again. Duality is antecedent to custom.

Twins exemplify a particular relationship of sameness and difference that has in many societies become the mythological image for unity existing between contrasting social structures which give rise to structures of exchange. Thus, all exchanges originate in an intuition of twinness.

Against this background of structured exchange, sameness and difference an otherwise confusing historical voice makes its own kind of sense. The historical section refers to Mammedaty's ownership of horses, those beings which facilitated all forms of exchange. "Mammedaty owned horses. And he could remember that it was essentially good to own horses; that it was hard to be without horses."

The personal voice for this section reminds us that we all know a doubling of self; it is one step in the psychological process whereby we enter our symbolic heritages. We have all experienced that moment in which the image of self is reflected back to us and becomes the occasion for self-reflection. We also know that such self-reflection is always threatened and so we empathize with Momaday's description. "Once from the limb of a tree, I saw myself in the brown water; then a frog leaped from the bank, breaking the image apart."

Throughout Momaday's presentations on twins one sound rises from the text and colors the meaning of events. It is the sound of the twins' laughter, their reaction to seeing themselves as double. It is the sound used to summon the critic situated in relation to this section of Momaday's text. Whatever critic relates to this section must provide ways of speaking about texts that are consonant with that instinct for the nature of narrative that Leslie Silko gave to her character Tayo in the novel *Ceremony.* "He cried the relief he felt at finally seeing the pattern, the way all the stories fit together—the old stories, the war stories, their stories—to become the story that was still being told."[15]

Major critic Julia Kristeva is consistently alert to any story "still being told" and manages to retain a place within her theoretical writing for ways in which any "story" will be shaped but not entirely determined by a whole range of social as well as personal elements. She questions the way scholars, particularly anthropologists, establish equivalencies between social symbolism and artistic creation. She never denies fundamental relations between the two; she accepts these relations and adds to them. She gives an expanded theoretical basis to the artist's intuited sense that there is something dangerously wrong about the easy imposition of meaning that occurs when symbols are interpreted in ways that make culture seem like predetermined programming in which individual differences and choices have no inaugural significance.

She establishes her own distinction between poetry and the sacred, assigning poetry a role in the individual's response to the sacred and its particular intervention in daily life. In her scheme of things the symbolic formalizes the sacred. Poetry "works on," moves through and "threatens" the symbolic, thus keeping the symbolic vital, part of the total process whereby individuals can relate to the culture's symbolic possibilities without being dominated by them (*Revolution* 72). The individual's recognition that such separation from determining form is possible evokes laughter, real laughter, the artist's laughter.

Couched in mythic language, the entire episode of the twins explores comparable realizations about relationships to the sacred. The twins are trouble. Prohibitions exist to be tested. They come from the sky and their very presence on earth is a consequence of a broken prohibition. They are creators and mediators; as such they can go between the meanings encoded through prohibitions and use the prohibition as a creative force.

For Kristeva, the writer "in the strongest sense of the word" is such a mediator, going between the meaning that any given instance of language imposes and that which can be found in that same language when one allows personal instincts and desires to motivate creative play that adds to and subtracts from given meanings.

Her theoretical elaborations allow us to expand our thinking about the importance of Momaday's making himself the receiver of the call implied in the mythic and historical voices, a call which allows him to discover the appropriate words of response. If, for Kristeva, the poetic word is always "polyvalent and multi-determined," and if it "adheres to a logic exceeding that of codified discourse," it can discover itself only within the confines of codified discourse. Following the lead of Mikhail Bakhtin she examines the consequences of looking at all texts as performances with a writing subject, an addressee and an exterior text, all having their role in the production of meaning. Her statements about how the word functions in such a context of interpretation could sum up Momaday's endeavor. "The word as minimal textual unity thus turns out to occupy the status of mediator, linking structural models to cultural (historical) environment, as well as that of regulator, controlling mutations from diachrony to synchrony, i.e., to literary structure.[16]

Laughter, duality, mediation, passage from the mythic to the historical to the personal. Momaday and Kristeva both are challenged by the possibilities meditation on these experiences keeps revealing. The points at which their meditations converge and diverge suggest the uses of contemporary semiotic theory—modified by psychoanalytic insights—for discussing the relationships between the interpretive systems implicit in the way the tribes defined the genres of their oral literatures and structured the transmission process and the interpretive systems that semioticians are making explicit.

N. SCOTT MOMADAY

Rainy Mountain Cemetery

Most is your name the name of this dark stone.
Deranged in death, the mind to be inheres
Forever in the nominal unknown,
The wake of nothing audible he hears
Who listens here and now to hear your name.

The early sun, red as a hunter's moon,
Runs in the plain. The mountain burns and shines;
And silence is the long approach of noon
Upon the shadow that your name defines—
And death this cold, black density of stone.[17]

FREDERICK GODDARD TUCKERMAN

Hymn Written For the Dedication of a Cemetery

Beside the River's dark green flow,
   Here where the pinetrees weep,
Red Autumn's winds will coldly blow
   Above their dreamless sleep:

Their sleep, for whom with prayerful breath
   We've put apart today
This spot, for shadowed walks of Death,
   And gardens of decay.

This crumbling bank with Autumn crowned,
   These pining woodland ways,
Seem now no longer common ground;
   But each in turn conveys

A saddened sense of something more:
   Is it the dying year?

Or a dim shadow, sent before,
Of the next gathering here?

Is it that He, the silent Power,
Has now assumed the place.
And drunk the light of morning's hour
The life of Nature's grace? [18]

DONALD PEASE

American Renaissance writers, I claim, wished to avoid a civil war by returning America to agree-upon relations, thereby restoring to America a common life all Americans could share. Restoring these relations meant reminding Americans of the agreements that made them possible, which meant reminding nineteenth-century Americans of the hopes, ideals and purposes they shared with their ancestors. It meant restoring their relationship with the nation's past, and involved an acknowledgment of a living tradition of cultural ideals, begun in the past but demanding realization and renewal by subsequent generations. Such a collective memory would remind individuals of the memorable life they shared with everyone else in the community. Moreover, a commemorative attitude, insofar as it demanded that an individual come to terms with separation through the connective tissue of memory, would replace the superficial bonds of self-interest and restore an interest in the general weal at a time in which secession threatened the nation.

In turning the visionary compacts reestablished in nineteenth-century literature into [my] subject . . . my intention is not to isolate them within that time period but to suggest that these compacts await renewal as a way of liberating us from the general crisis in cultural legitimation ruling the days of our present lives. [19]

Commentary

As a critic N. Scott Momaday has been primarily identified with American Indian literatures. But he has also written about nineteenth-century mainstream literature. He edited the complete poems of Frederick Goddard Tuckerman and he has published an article on Emily Dickinson. Therefore, we can not help but wonder how his dual literary heritage may inform his experience of the literary process, whether that process be creative writing or critical reading. In order to end this critical exchange within the developing context of general American literature, I turn to Momaday's own contributions to nineteenth-century criticism. Some of the influence of nineteenth-century writers seems inscribed in the formal structure of the poem he uses to end *The Way To Rainy Mountain*.

With its regular versification, rhyme scheme and formal dignity, all so different from other poetry being written during the decade of the sixties, "Rainy Mountain Cemetery" recalls earlier writers, even to a degree Tuckerman. We learn the quality of Momaday's particular regard for Tuckerman when we read the final introductory paragraph he wrote for his edition of Tuckerman's poems.

> If Tuckerman is to emerge completely in our literature, he had best be revealed for the right reasons. There are two in particular. First he stands in historical opposition to the mainstream of nineteenth-century American Romanticism. That fact ought now to account for his renown as, for the better part of a century, it has accounted for his anonymity. Tuckerman's intellectual and literary isolation will bear careful investigation, for it constitutes a valid literature in itself. Second, Tuckerman's poems are valuable in their own right. They are the best possessions of a man whose vision is keen and whose judgment is sound (xxviii).

Reevaluations of American Renaissance writing have not yet achieved any renewal of interest in Tuckerman. As Momaday discusses Tuckerman's positions, he situates Tuckerman's "historical opposition" in contrast to Emerson. As he does so, we glimpse Momaday's own historical opposition. Even if Tuckerman's poems remain as obscure as ever, the dynamics of the differences among nineteenth-century writers are proving important to our twentieth-century assessment of our literary and cultural heritage.

Momaday establishes the contrasts between Tuckerman and Emerson by using Emerson's essay "Nature" to focus these differences. First, he contrasts Tuckerman's implicit and exemplary recommendations to solitude with Emerson's explicit, moralistic ones. Then he addresses what he considers the major premise of the Emersonian ideal—the belief that "the landscape is a barometer of moral change." Emerson used details of nature to express moral attitudes, Tuckerman used them for their own sake. "Unlike Emerson, [Tuckerman] perceived that the determination of 'worth in the population' requires a moral judgment which the landscape, no matter how the intelligence views it, cannot reflect." Finally Momaday brings in the Emersonian idea that "intuition is superior to intellection," and he quotes the well known passage in which Emerson declares "I become a transparent eyeball; I am nothing; I see all; the currents of the Universal Being circulate through me; I am part or parcel of God" (xxiv–xxv).

Momaday's response to this famous passage is particularly important in the light of his own heritage. The popular stereotype of the American Indian assigns to all tribes a relationship to nature close to that of the popular interpretation of Emerson's mysticism and in so doing the stereotype dissolves the historical particularity of tribal life. Momaday limits his interest to the aesthetic and for him Emerson's view:

> suggests a thorny problem in aesthetics. The mystical experience is ineffable. It cannot occur per se in literature, but must be validated, rendered objectively, given the aesthetic distance of description by a third person. When it is not so validated, it is sure to result in the kind of unfortunate metaphor exemplified by Emerson's "transparent eyeball."

According to Momaday, Tuckerman approaches nature with more integrity. "Tuckerman appreciates fully the anomalies of the natural world: light and shadow, here and there, appearance and reality. The importance of that appreciation in nineteenth-century American poetry cannot easily be overestimated" (XXV).

How might we view a configuration of voices like those of Momaday, Tuckerman and Emerson today? In sketching one answer to this question we also outline a basis for Momaday's critical position on a major American author, and by extension we demonstrate what is implicit in the interpretive systems which have survived along with specific tribal traditions. Within these traditions there are critical attitudes (but not developed critical languages) that can be a valuable means of situating major canonical writings. I began this orchestration of critical voices by setting major critics in relation to American Indian writing in order to show how just such an exchange can bring American Indian writing into the international critical discussion. I will end by demonstrating that American Indian writing need not always be the object of critical inquiry; it can also generate critical positions. The particular uses of the past that necessitate a situating of self amid the concrete demands and insights of the present are always culturally determined. As long as the present remains culturally heterogeneous, different pasts will be addressed from these diverse sites. These sites, though, are not just a plurality of discrete differences, they are pluralities of pluralities. Today to be American Indian is to be a member of a definite tribe, but it includes seeking a relationship between the tribal American heritage and the other heritages that have become bound to that tribal history. Through the years general American history and the canonical works of American and world literature have acquired many specific histories. A Lakota Sioux woman with whom I team-taught for ten years had an abiding love of Shakespeare that was every bit as much a part of her Lakota heritage as her knowledge of Lakota oral literature because her love of Shakespeare and her methods of interpreting his work were shaped by the same cultural stances as those which shaped her knowledge of Lakota oral literature. Her Shakespeare mediates between England and the Rosebud Sioux Reservation in South Dakota. Only she could tell me how such mediation is possible.

With a critic as attuned to general American tradition as Momaday, the mediation takes on intellectual implications of the highest order. His reading of Emerson or Tuckerman is not that of a Richard Poirier or a Harold Bloom, nor perhaps could it ever be. Yet Momaday's Emerson or Tuckerman impacts American thought and sensibility as much as theirs. The argument, so obvious when stated directly, needs to be made because minority critics are so often limited to minority writers. Clearly their perspective on these writers is a crucial and irreplaceable one for the many reasons suggested by this article. But their perspective on canonical writers is equally irreplaceable. In a critical world, aware not only of the existence of minority literary traditions but also of traditions of minority interpretation of majority literatures, their perspectives should be viewed as crucial. We need to examine the Momaday, Tuckerman and Emerson configuration, and we can profitably do so in relation to other critical views of Emerson which place him in relation to the general literary historical agenda.

In his book *Visionary Compacts: American Renaissance Writings in Cultural Context* Donald Pease explicates readings and uses of Emerson's texts that reveal why Emerson appears to work against a project like Momaday's. But Pease goes further and finally discovers a distance in Emerson that accommodates Momaday's resistances and allows us to see his objections to Emerson as critically productive in comprehensive ways. Emerson's project, like Momaday's, in part responds to a desire to come to terms with his ancestors. According to Pease, "Emerson felt overshadowed by the achievements of his ancestors, his brothers, his predecessors, and his culture. For the young Emerson, life in culture felt like a moral rebuke" (205).

Emerson took an opposition that is a fundamental part of European philosophy—that of form and substance—and made it a doctrine of self-reliance. The substance or the spirit of the past remains a valuable necessity, but such is not the case with the specific forms in which this spirit has been realized. Creating new forms is the task of self-reliant individuals. Within this way of thinking "Emerson distinguishes the power resulting in the ancestors' achievements from the ancestors' persons" (205). This is precisely the move that Momaday resisted. For Momaday, it is the ancestors' personal and hence moral commitment to remaining living elements in tradition's chain of transmission that is the primary gift of the past. The dominant culture has regularly destroyed the ancestors' achievements. It can not, however, destroy the memory of their persons and that memory, even more than the achievements themselves, motivates Momaday's own achievements and personal development.

In his essays Emerson pursued his own ideas relentlessly, driving many of them beyond the limits he perceived for them. Pease maps that pursuit. Inheritor of an entire catalogue of European conceptual oppositions, Emerson's integrity allowed no easy resolutions of these oppositions. Such questioning was, in fact, incumbent upon him as an American seeking to be something other than European. He confronted the impasses implicit in this own ways of structuring his essays, and he turned the difficulties into motives for metaphors that served his own needs. "Emersonian metaphor" is an earned characterization designating a particular development of metaphor as a cognitive instrument, one that derives from a sense of American history.

Pease describes the nature and purpose of these metaphors. They "assert the self-transcending, metaphorical"—in short, relational—quality of all things. In his view each existent must relate to another before it can possess its own significance. Within the Emersonian structure of relationship, self-reliance gets transmuted into "spirit"-reliance with spirit speaking through nature. The voice of the writer modulates into an impersonation of nature.

When he describes writing as an activity where "I gain my point, I gain all points, if I reach my companion with any statement which teaches him his own worth," Emerson equates writing with the activity of transferring this spirit or natural genius, visible between his "point" and a companion's worth, from himself to a reader. Reducible neither to Emerson nor to his reader, this genius quickly universalizes itself into all points precisely because it cannot be limited to any single entity. We

180

require the "transparent eyeball" to imagine this spirit or genius, just as we need the law of nature to describe it. The influence at work in *Nature* does not require a self-other opposition wherein Emerson would prove his originality by surpassing (or repressing) the worth of another writer (or reader). Influence charges the space between writer and reader with the power of nature's laws. The words in this space can be said to belong neither to Emerson nor to his readers but to the quotable proverbs in which nature has recorded its laws. (232–233)

According to the way that Pease reads him, Emerson finally privileges the role of active listening. So does Momaday. This analysis of Emerson presents a common ground for Momaday's and Emerson's agendas, but differences remain and can be charted outward from this common ground. Emerson's proverbs owe little, nothing fundamental, to a specific culture's person-to-person transmission, to the historical contexts wherein meaning is adapted as the proverb labels a definite experience. Momaday's traditional forms owe everything to that historical and personal context. Momaday lives and writes by treasuring the "shadow" that the name of his grandmother (and through her all his ancestors) "defines" in death. If "the mind to be inheres / Forever in the nominal unknown," it nevertheless listens. Hearing nothing audible, it "listens" with the eye, seeing the shadows defined by the real names of real ancestors, passing on one of the many histories to which Momaday is heir. Nature in Momaday as in Emerson is that which resists reduction to any self-other opposition, but for Momaday nature's voice is incorporated into the human voice so that nature is not quite the mystical force it is for Emerson. As Momaday claimed, the mystical intuition needs the validating distance of the interpreting voice which is always that of a real human being. Momaday can appreciate why, in so many tribal cultures, visionary experiences were revealed first to holy men skilled in interpreting the visions in terms that were amenable to cultural ideals. Emerson's writing is implicitly opposed to such third person interpretation.

This discussion of differences between Emerson and Momaday has shifted from the effects of a popularly misunderstood doctrine of self-reliance to their uses of metaphor to recuperate a relationship to nature and hence to ancestors. The relationship sketched between them is inscribed within the very substance of the literary history of this nation. Emerson interpreted from Momaday's position attains new force and significance, just as does Momaday when viewed from the Emersonian stance. Very little in *The Way To Rainy Mountain* relates directly to canonical works of American literature. Noting the traces of Emerson and Tuckerman in the framing poems is about as far as one can safely go without becoming extraordinarly ingenious. But because a method of interpretation is implicit within *The Way To Rainy Mountain*, these implicit interpretive moves can be made explicit and then applied to other traditions. Such movement across cultural boundaries is by no means unprecedented. Momaday himself has frequently cited his interest in the career and writings of Isak Dinesen, the writer who came to understand traditional interpretive and storytelling processes through her experiences of African traditions. Her own writing, though, became an exploration of the dynamics of the Danish traditions. The lived sense of one past can become a threshold to other pasts. And movement across thresholds is two-way.

Conclusion

These juxtapositions and brief commentaries on possible avenues of exchange between critical positions that are not routinely brought into relation with each other are designedly partial and suggestive. The critical discourses so briefly situated in this critical performance on a literary performance represent continuing means allowing international access to literary possibilities. Within this international context, American Indian literature encompasses a range of practices and responses that is, in and of itself, a testing of these critical discourses and engaging in that testing can refine the possibilities of the critical enterprise as well as adding new dimensions to the reading of American Indian literatures.

As noted at the beginning of this exercise, critics of this continent's tribal literatures have exercised admirable caution in using critical fads and have avoided hasty applications of partially understood positions. They have, instead, concentrated primarily on developing culturally based commentaries on specific traditions, and they have sought to present the needed background to readers allowing them to situate texts within their tribal literatures and histories. Now we seem to be at a stage in our century's theoretical development where the work so carefully done by those committed to American Indian literatures can find its place within the broader critical enterprise without necessarily adopting new positions or critical languages. Both sides are experiencing a need for the other, and genuine exchange can occur far more regularly than has been the case to date.

Critics of Native American literatures, through their insistence on remaining in touch with the ways in which texts reflect specific cultural traditions, have collectively achieved remarkable insights into the possibilities of textual adaptation to changing demands upon those traditions. The major American Indian creative writers have given us texts which reflect these adaptations in highly sophisticated forms. To return to the issues presented by Wlad Godzich and quoted earlier in this paper, all the creative writers and most of the critics give us new critical angles on "the conception of the subject as the organizer and sense-maker of lived experience, and the challenge posed to forms of Western thought by the liberation movements of the past forty years."

Both of the areas given theoretical positioning in Godzich's overview serve as perspectives (accepted narrative orderings) that can structure and guide historical and critical analysis needed to represent the immediacy, the precisely sensuous detail and the poetic force that are part of the continuing significance of those texts. Such critical interpretation can animate theory allowing it to go beyond its currently narrow range of analysis—narrow only in the sense that its dynamic derives from the need to overcome through analysis the restraints placed upon it by its own particular history. Such necessary, even admirable narrowness, establishes the conditions of its own expansion when it enables critics to pay more informed attention to texts outside any single historical trajectory. Critics have shown how critical discourse is always implicated in its own history, and they have shaped a vocabulary to show how criticism must establish itself as a conscious part of the dynamic shaping the very cultural phenomena which it analyzes and articulates. Now the question remains as to how to use that critical self-consciousness to guide a relationship between theory and the kinds of texts which have traditionally remained outside its purview because they bear the marks of a contrasting historical dynamic.

We can use texts to show how culture imposes order upon lived experience and, indeed, such demonstration has been the purpose of considerable scholarly writing in all disciplines affected by the major anthropological models of our century. The problem with much of this scholarship is that it often declares that attention to the individual is theoretically insignificant. Sensitively detailed evidence of any individual subject resisting or appropriating imposed order of any kind was minimized or excised from historical narrative and social scientific description. The individual found among the pages of social scientific narrative is almost always bound by rules of description and analysis created by whoever controls those levels of discourse which achieve enough political prestige to affect the language. Until recently even criticism of American Indian literatures was bound to social scientific criteria rather than literary ones. Now that we are adding more specifically literary and aesthetic insights to those that are most amenable to social scientific analyses, we can correct some of the imbalances of the past. The individual is always part of literature.

People resist all forms of extinction, including homogenization. And so we have texts of varying degrees of sophistication which in culture after culture tell us about someone's need to situate the self in and through language. We do not lack texts. We lack the qualities of attentiveness that allow us to learn from them.

Contemporary theory is carefully building new frameworks of informed attentiveness. No doubt we have far to go but it is an endeavor now well started. The most helpful research is that which presents and criticizes the notion of the subject as a linguistic and hermeneutic category, thus permitting a consideration of the subject that subsumes other crucial categories—such as race—keeping all analysis firmly based within the acknowledged (and therefore explicit) critical assumptions of a given social and historical configuration. American Indian writers and critics have consistently done just this. As my brief analysis of Momaday was meant to suggest, writers like him—and there are many more writers that I might have chosen as the focus of this analysis—have achieved far more than many have yet begun to suspect.

Notes

1. Gerald Vizenor, *Earthdivers* (Minneapolis: University of Minnesota Press, 1981) 165–66.

2. Michel de Certeau, *Heterologies* (Minneapolis: University of Minnesota Press, 1986) viii.

3. N. Scott Momaday, "Man Made of Words," *Indian Voices: The First Convocation of American Indian Scholars* (San Francisco: American Indian Press, 1970) 58.

4. N. Scott Momaday, *The Names* (New York: Harper and Row, 1964) 156.

5. N. Scott Momaday, *The Way To Rainy Mountain* (Albuquerque: University of New Mexico Press, 1969) 3.

6. Carlos Fuentes, "Remember the Future," *Salmagundi* (Fall, 1985, Winter 1986) 344–45.

7. Umberto Eco, *Semiotics and the Philosophy of Language* (Bloomington: Indiana University Press, 1986) 187.

8. *Marina Tsvetaeva, A Captive Spirit: Selected Prose* (London: Virago Press, 1983) 115.

9. Jacques Derrida, *Margins of Philosophy* (Chicago: University of Chicago Press, 1982) 115.

10. N. Scott Momaday, "The Man Made of Words," 56.

11. Jacques Derrida, *Of Grammatology* (Baltimore: Johns Hopkins University Press, 1976) 82.

12. Jacques Derrida, *Speech and Phenomena* (Evanston: Northwestern University Press, 1973) 129–60.

13. Jacques Derrida, *Writing and Difference* (Chicago: University of Chicago Press, 1978) 79–153.

14. Julia Kristeva, *Revolution in Poetic Language* (New York: Columbia University Press, 1984) 222–223.

15. Leslie Marmon Silko, *Ceremony* (New York: Viking Press, 1977) 246.

16. Julia Kristeva, *Desire in Language* (New York: Columbia University Press, 1980) 65, 66.

17. N. Scott Momaday, *The Way To Rainy Mountain* (Albuquerque: University of New Mexico Press, 1969) 89.

18. Frederick Tuckerman, *The Complete Poems of Frederick Goddard Tuckerman* (New York: Oxford University Press, 1965) 79.

19. Donald Pease, *Visionary Compacts: American Renaissance Writings in Cultural Context* (Madison: University of Wisconson Press, 1987) x–xi.

11

Trickster Discourse:

Comic Holotropes and Language Games

GERALD VIZENOR

The anthropos games

Cultural *anthropologies* are monologues with science; moreover, social science subdues imagination and the wild trickster in comic narratives. These anthropologies are at last causal methodologies and expiries, not studies of anthropos, human beings or even natural phenomena; rather, anthropologies are remains, reductions of humans and imagination to models and comparable cultural patterns—social science is institutional power, a tragic monologue in isolation.

The tribal trickster is a liberator and healer in a narrative, a comic sign, communal signification and a discourse with imagination. These anthropologies and tribal tricksters are not structural binaries; social science is a trope to power, the trickster is a language game in a comic narrative.

Comic holotropes

Naanabozho, the woodland tribal trickster, is a *holotrope*, a comic holotrope, and a *sign* in a language game; a communal sign shared between listeners, readers and four points of view in third person narratives.

The trickster is androgenous, a comic healer and liberator in litera- ture; the *whole figuration* that ties the unconscious to social experi- ences. The trickster sign is communal, an erotic shimmer in oral tradi- tions; the narrative voices are holotropes in a discourse. The author, narrator, characters and audience are the signifiers and comic holo- tropes in trickster narratives. In this discourse the signified becomes a comic *chance* in oral presentations; however, in translated narratives the signified is rehearsed in hermeneutics and structural lections, causal theories and comparative models in social science.

Robert Scholes and Robert Kellogg construe that in addition to the three points of view, "as a narrative becomes more sophisticated, a fourth point of view is added by the development of a clear distinction between the narrator and author. Narrative irony is a function of dis- parity among these three or four viewpoints."[1]

The trickster is a semiotic sign; not cultural material or discovered elements that are recomposed to endorse invented models in social sci- ence. Paul Watzlawick argues that what is considered to be the real world, what is discovered, "is an invention whose inventor is unaware of his act of invention . . . the invention then becomes the basis of his world view and actions."[2] The most "accepted construction of reality," he writes, "rests on the supposition that the world cannot be chaotic— not because we have any proof for this view, but because chaos would simply be intolerable."[3]

Roy Wagner argues that "anthropology exists through the idea of culture," which is an invention, an intrusion and a tragic monologue with science.

> The study of culture *is* culture. . . . The study of culture is in fact *our* [dominant material] culture; it operates through our forms, creates in our terms, borrows our words and concepts for its meanings, and re- creates us through our efforts. [The dominant culture] is a vast accumu- lation of material and spiritual achievements and resourses stemming from the conquest of nature and necessary to the continuance of this effort.[4]

The trickster summons agonistic imagination in a narrative, a lan- guage game, and livens chaos more than bureaucracies, social science models or tragic terminal creeds; the comic holotrope is a consonance of narrative voices in discourse.

Warwick Wadlington argues that the trickster straddles oppositions and "embodies two antithetical, nonrational experiences of man with the natural world, his society, and his own psyche: on the one hand," he explains that there is "a force of treacherous disorder that outrages and disrupts, and on the other hand, an unanticipated, usually unintentional benevolence in which trickery is at the expense of inimical forces and for the benefit of mankind."[5]

Structuralism, structural linguistics and various semantic theories reveal more about trickster narratives (the texture of the language and the structure of sentences) than do theories in social science, such as behaviorism, functionalism and new materialism that have dominated the academic interpretations of tribal cultures. The emphasis here, however, is semiotics, the reader, the listener or audience, and the consciousness of signs in literature (signs, myths, and metaphors) than on linear and causal theories or on ontological idealism; semiotics that locates *being* in discourse.

Stein Haugom Olsen writes that "the *signifier* and the *signified* are two aspects of the *sign* which can be abstracted for theoretical purposes but which in practice belong together like the recto and verso of a sheet of paper."[6] The trickster is a sign, a communal signification that cannot be separated or understood in isolation; the signifiers are acoustic images bound to four points of view, and the signified, or the concept the signifier locates in language and social experience, is a narrative event or a translation. The listeners and readers become the trickster, a sign, and semiotic being in discourse; the trickster is a comic holotrope in narrative voices, not a model or a tragic figuration in isolation.

Jacques Lacan, however, liberates the signifier; the comic holotrope in trickster narratives. Lacan warns not to "cling to the illusion that the signifier answers to the function of representing the signified, or better, that the signifier has to answer for its existence in the name of any signification whatever."[7]

The narrative voices or comic holotrope, the signifier in a trickster narrative, is signified in *chance*. The trickster is a semiotic sign, closer in connotation to an iconic sign than to the arbitrary symbolic signification or causal representation in semiotic theories. The trickster sign wanders between narrative voices and comic chance in oral presentations.

Geoffrey Strickland points out that signs are defined "by means of their differences from one another."[8] The trickster is never the same in oral and translated narratives; however, these differences are resolved in comic holotropes and discourse in modern literature. The trickster has a real voice, a mythic and communal voice in imagination; but in translation the isolated voice or representation of the trickster is neither real nor mythic. Even so, "an image is what we make of it, and what we make of an acoustic image is determined by the concept for which it stands."[9] In another connection Marshall Blonsky argues that "images *do* things, operate for real interests although they are themselves, struck with unreality."[10] The trickster is real in those who imagine the narrative, in the narrative voices.

Tropes are figures of speech; here the trickster is a sign that becomes a comic holotrope, a consonance of sentences in various voices, ironies, variations in cultural myths and social metaphors. Comic holotropes comprise signifiers, the signified, and signs, which in new critical theories provide a discourse on the trickster in oral narratives, translations and modern imaginative literature. This *sui generis* discourse is named "mythic verism" in this discourse, which assumes that the theoretical arbitrariness of signs has been resolved in comic holotropes. Tzvetan Todorov explains that "discourse is not simply an adding together of sentences: it is, itself, one great sentence."[11] That great sentence in trickster narratives is communal, a comic holotrope. While there are similarities to theories in structuralism, the comic holotrope is more than the unexpected harmonies that survive even the worst translations; it is a discourse, not an isolated element in mythic structures or social science models.

Verisimilitude is the appearance of realities; mythic verism is discourse, a critical concordance of narrative voices, and a narrative realism that is more than mimesis or a measure of what is believed to be natural in the world. Stein Haugom Olsen explains that "naturalism and verisimilitude need not be measured against reality. It can simply be measured against what is natural with the world of the work. . . ."[12] The trickster is imagination, an agonistic sign in narrative voices; mythic verism is a concordance, the discourse we choose to hear and believe in literature. Paul Ricoeur writes, "For my part, I hold that to search for concordance is part of the unavoidable assumptions of discourse and communications."[13]

Emile Benveniste argues that the

> semiotic sign exists in itself, and establishes the reality of the language, but it has no particular application; the sentence, an expression of the semantic, can *only* be particular. With the sign, we come to the intrin-

sic reality of the language; with the sentence, one is in contact with what lies outside language. . . .[14]

The trickster is a sign, comic holotropes are narrative voices, and mythic verism is discourse and critical concordance. "We can conclude then that, with the sentence, we leave the domain of language as a system of signs and enter another world, that of language as an instrument of communication, whose expression is discourse."[15]

Roy Wagner, however, argues that a "trope can be elicited but not defined," while "a sign can be defined precisely, and can be assigned discrete functions in an exact science of semiotics."[16] These precise interpretations, these "discrete functions" would trammel comic holotropes and our imagination in trickster narratives. The trickster as a comic holotrope is a sign that "exists in itself . . . with no particular application."

In his studies of Mikhail Bakhtin, Todorov explains that "human utterance" is an interaction and the context "belongs to history." The utterance is similar to a sentence, both are discourses. "The most important feature of the utterance . . . is its *dialogism*" or the "intertextual dimension," which means that "all discourse is in dialogue with prior discourses on the same subject. . . . There is no utterance without relation to other utterances, and that is essential."[17] The comic holotrope is a "dialogism" in these "translinguistic" theories of discourse. The trickster is a comic discourse, a collection of "utterances" in oral traditions; the opposite of a comic discourse is a monologue, an utterance in isolation, which comes closer to the tragic mode in literature and not a comic tribal world view.

Bakhtin explains in translation that "no utterance in general can be attributed to the speaker exclusively; it is the *product of the interaction of the interlocutors* . . . the whole complex social situation in which it has occurred."[18] The interlocutors in the trickster narratives are the author, narrator, characters and audience. These points of view, these utterances are *dialogism*, or the relation to other utterances. "Discourse lives, as it were, beyond itself, in a living impulse toward the object," which in this instance is the trickster; "if we detach ourselves completely from this impulse," as social science has done in the translations of oral narratives and the comic trickster, "all we have left is the naked corpse of the word, from which we can learn nothing at all about the social situation or the fate of a given word in life. *To study*

191

the word as such, ignoring the impulse that reaches out beyond it, is just as senseless as to study psychological experience outside the context of that real life toward which it was directed and by which it is determined." [19]

The language game

The trickster is a chance, a comic holotrope in a postmodern language game that uncovers the distinctions and ironies between narrative voices; a semiotic sign for "social antagonism" and "aesthetic activism" in postmodern criticism and the avant-garde, but not "presence" or ideal cultural completion in narratives. Charles Russell argues that postmodern identities are "recast in terms of the essential workings of language, especially of the play of variance and difference, and the shifting grounds of all discourse." The conception of "being" as an ideal "ontological presence," he writes, is a radical change to semiotics which "denies presence and completion. Being, known through and as discourse, is experienced as the field of free play. . . ." One side of "postmodern creation is expressed in the acceptance, even glorification, of play, chance, indeterminacy, and self-conscious performance." [20]

The trickster and comic liberator craves chance in agonistic imagination to lessen the power of social science and bourgeois humanism; in postcolonial translations, where tokens are secured, the trickster is cornered in a lexical ruse, a cold recitation in semantic dioramas. This comic liberator is a healer in language games, chance and postmodern imagination; the trickster, as a semiotic sign, "denies presence and completion," that romantic "vital essence" in tribal representations, and the instrumental language of social science.

Naanabozho, the woodland trickster, is a social antagonist in a comic holotrope but not a ritual sign; not a ceremonial, a spectacle or a seasonal festival. The trickster is not a structural code or an invitation to the arcane. The trickster is a comic sign not a trope to power in social science. The myth of objectivism was established on tribal cultures; anthropologists, archaeologists and others, with state subsidies, have published thousands of articles and monographs. This predacious research became an imperative voice in public institutions; the doctrines and taxonomies on tribal encounters have been rewarded with doctorates and academic tenure, the tropes to power in social science.

Material cultures are possessed and continue to be manipulated in museums; tribal identities are revised with new theories and abstract "discoveries" that never heal and never lead to liberation. Tribute to the tribes has seldom been much more than postcolonial and racial overcompensation with smooth adjectives. On the other hand, there are innumerable sentimental scholars and culture hobbyists enchanted by abstruse emblems and assumed tribal values. The romantic "transvaluation of roles," as the sociologist Robert Bellah points out, "that turns the despised and oppressed into symbols of salvation and rebirth is nothing new in the history of human culture, but when it occurs, it is an indication of new cultural directions, perhaps of a deep cultural revolution." [21] The trickster summons agonistic imagination in a comic holotrope to a discourse on the revolution in semiotic signs.

Michel Foucault argues that there is a "battle for and around history going on at this very moment. . . . The intension is to programme, to stifle what I've called 'popular memory'; and also to propose and impose on people a framework in which to interpret the present." [22]

At the same time there are those inspired by the aesthetics and politics of modernism. The trickster in modernist literature was invented to be an individual, or at least the metaphor of individualism; this image supported the notion of the vanishing tribes. Certain individuals survived discoveries, lethal pathogens, studies and relocations (but not their cultures) and were assimilated as exceptional in modern aesthetic and political theories. The stoic "savage" survived in literature and emulsion; invented, painted and photographed by postcolonial adventurers; the modern individual was then interpreted as the structural opposition to bourgeois democracies. The "savages" were separated from their social experiences, reinvented as racial emblems and then isolated, abstracted, revised and used in literature as ideologies to oppose bourgeois materialism.

The trickster, however, is a communal sign, comic discourse, and does not represent aesthetic modernism in narratives or the glorification of isolated individualism. Fredric Jameson asserts that the "great modernisms were . . . predicated on the invention of a personal, private style, as unmistakable as your fingerprint, as incomparable as your own body. But this means that the modernist aesthetics is in some way organically linked to the conception of a unique self and private identity, a unique personality and individuality, which can be expected to generate its own unique vision of the world. . . ." [23] This unique individualism has been rendered to compare tribal cultures; the trickster was associated with cultural roles and other inventions that permeate social science research.

Charles Russell writes that the

> glorification of "man" and the assumed sanctity of individual iden-
> tity . . . now are attacked as untenable ideological strictures. Individual
> identity is shown to be a fiction, having no center, no clear boundaries.
> Instead, we are found to be constructs of discrete elements of social
> discourse. . . .
>
> Society is perceived as a fictive framework of ideological codes which,
> like all semiotic systems, are grounded in nothing more than human
> desire and fear but which appear to have the authority of essential truth.
> As such, social values and systems of order are subject to critical de-
> mystification and deconstruction, through which the embattled individ-
> ual may perceive his or her conceptual freedom.[24]

In trickster narratives the listeners and readers imagine their liberation; the trickster is a sign and the world is "deconstructed" in a discourse.

Science and narrative knowledge

Roland Barthes compares science and literature. He writes, "For science, language is merely an instrument which it chooses to make as
transparent, as neutral as possible. . . ."[25] The trickster is a comic sign
not a paratragic instrument; language in science immures the trickster
and incises comic holotropes with structural binaries. Barthes asserts
that literature is

> alone today in bearing the entire responsibility for language; for though
> science needs language, it is not, like literature, *within* language. . . .
> Science speaks itself; literature writes itself; science is led by the voice,
> literature follows the hand; it is not the same body, and hence the same
> desire, which is behind the one and the other.

The trickster is "within language" and not a neutral instrument that
reveals codes and structural harmonies in tribal cultures. The trickster
is a sign and a patent language game in a narrative discourse; science is
language closure, a monologue in theoretical contention.

Jean-François Lyotard is more precise on the language games in science and the postmodern condition in the new human sciences. He writes:

> Scientific knowledge requires that one language game, denotation, be retained and all others excluded. A statement's truth-value is the criterion determining its acceptability. . . . Scientific knowledge is in this way set apart from the language games that combine to form the social bond. Unlike narrative knowledge, it is no longer a direct and shared component of the bond. But it is indirectly a component of it, because it develops into a profession and gives rise to institutions, and in modern societies language games consolidate themselves in the form of institutions run by qualified partners.[26]

The trickster is a comic narrative in the same language game that accommodates science as a variation in discourse, but "the opposite is not true," as Lyotard points out, because the

> scientist questions the validity of narrative statements and concludes that they are never subject to argumentation or proof. He classifies them as belonging to a different mentality: savage, primitive, underdeveloped, backward, alienated, composed of opinions, customs, authority, prejudice, ignorance, ideology. Narratives are fables, myths, legends, fit only for women and children. At best, attempts are made to throw some rays of light into this obscurantism, to civilize, educate, develop. . . . We all know the symptoms. It is the entire history of cultural imperialism from the dawn of Western civilization.[27]

Lyotard concludes that it is important to recognize this special form of imperialism, the "demand for legitimation." However, he points out that the "problem of legitimation is no longer considered a failing of the language game of science."

Paul Feyerabend argues that when anthropologists "collected and systematized" tribal cultures, the scientific emphasis was on the "psychological meaning, the social functions, the existential temper of a culture," while the "ontological implications" were disregarded.[28] Feyerabend contends that, to the anthropologists who transformed tribal cultures, the "oracles, rain dances, the treatment of mind and body," and the trickster narratives in this instance

> *express* the needs of the members of a society, they *function* as a social glue, they *reveal* basic structures of thought, they may even lead to an

increased *awareness* of the relations between man and man and man and nature but without an accompanying *knowledge* of distant events, rain, mind, body. Such interpretations were hardly ever the result of critical thought—most of the time they were simply a consequence of popular antimetaphysical tendencies combined with a firm belief in the excellence . . . of science.

Louis Sass suggests that "the facts of social science are not facts at all but interpretations of interpretations."[29]

The power in social science research is intractable because it is located in institutions; that power is heard and endured but tribal resistance is reduced to new measures in academic language games. Translations of narratives and the comparative studies of tribal myths are not the least revisions of power and knowledge in social science. Alan Sheridan, in *Michel Foucault: The Will to Truth*, construes that

> power and knowledge are two sides of the same process. Knowledge cannot be neutral, pure. All knowledge is political not because it may have political consequences or be politically useful, but because knowledge has its conditions of possibility in power relations.[30]

The trickster is a comic liberator in a narrative and the sign with the most resistance to social science monologues: if not in narrative discourse the trickster is "released" as an "object" in translation. Victor Barnouw, for example, asserts that the trickster is a real person, but his assertion reveals power relations over the culture he has studied and invented in social science; his interpretations subdue the comic discourse and holotropes in trickster narratives.

The trickster is disembodied in a narrative; the language game transmutes birds and animals with no corporeal or material representations. The trickster is a communal sign, a comic holotrope and a discourse; not a real person or a tragic metaphor in an isolated monologue.

The trickster narrative situates the participant audience, the listeners and readers, in agonistic imagination: there, in comic discourse, the trickster is being, nothingness and liberation; a loose seam in consciousness; that wild space over and between sounds, words, sentences and narratives; and, at last, the trickster is comic shit.

Naanabozho and coprophilia

Victor Barnouw collected trickster narratives and published them in *Wisconsin Chippewa Myths & Tales.* He writes that from "these stories we can learn something about the belief systems of the people who told and listened to them." Barnouw asserts that the trickster "was a real person whom they respected although they also laughed at his antics."

The short narratives that follow were selected from several translated parts of the origin myth to review the theoretical interpretations and to continue the argument that the trickster is a fictional character, a semiotic sign, a comic holotrope and a discourse in a tribal language game.

The story that I'm going to tell you won't be about this earth. It will be about a different world. There were only two people living in this other world: an old lady and her daughter. . . .

The old lady's daughter used to go every day into the woods to find something that she could use for food. This was in the summer. She got those early berries in the spring. That was their food. She went into the woods to pick the berries all day long, picking here and there.

Then one day somebody saw her traveling all alone by herself in the woods. That person seemed to take a liking to her. He even wanted to marry her. He knew what to do. When she was out berrying one nice hot day, when there was no wind, at noon-time, she heard a noise like a gust of wind. She looked around in the direction of the noise and saw a wind coming. When the wind reached her, she couldn't pull her dress down for some time, until the gust of wind went by. She didn't think anything of it, because no one was there to see her. She started picking berries again. . . .

It wasn't long afterwards that the girl found out that something else was going to happen. She left that place where she and her mother had been living and went into the woods. There she gave birth to some children—three of them. The first looked just like a human baby boy. After it was born, she held him in her arms. Then she heard a voice from somewhere telling her to put her baby on the ground. She didn't do it. After the person whose voice she heard got tired of waiting for her to put her baby down, he spoke to her again, "You don't want to do what I told you to do—put your baby on the ground. If you had done that, your baby would have got up and walked. But since you don't want to do that, it will be a year from the time that he is born that he will be able to walk." That's the way that people of this earth would have done from the time that they were born. They would have walked right away, just like animals. The Indian could have done that too.

Then the next baby was born. This one didn't have human features exactly, but he looked like a human baby to some extent. Just a little while later another one was born. This one didn't look like a human child. This one was a stone. . . . Sometimes when I go into the woods I see this stone. It's a very hard stone. I'm just telling you what I heard. It doesn't say that this woman took her babies home. . . ."

The trickster ran:

he heard a big noise coming behind him. He knew just what it was that was coming. It was the water that was coming. He looked around for a big high hill. He found one. He ran to the top of a hill where a big pine tree was standing. That's where Wenebojo [Naanobozho] stopped. In a short time the water got up to the top of the hill. When he saw the water coming that high, he climbed right up to the top of the tall pine tree. He said to the tree, "Brother, stretch yourself to twice the length you are now." The tree did that. Then he climbed some more. This tree stretched four times. That's how long it was. Then the tree told Wenebojo that he couldn't do any more for him. That was as high as he could go. But then the water stopped. Wenebojo was standing on the top of the tree. He had his head back, and the water was up to his mouth. Pretty soon Wenebojo felt that he wanted to defecate. He couldn't hold it. The shit floated up to the top of the water and floated around his mouth.

After a while Wenebojo noticed that there was an animal in the water. This animal was playing around. Wenebojo couldn't see the animal, but he knew that it was there. He tried to look around. Then he saw several animals—beaver, muskrat, and otter. Wenebojo spoke to the otter first, "Brother," he said, "could you go down and get some earth? If you do that, I will make an earth for you and me to live on. . . ."[31]

Tom Badger told these stories through an interpreter, his wife, to Victor Barnouw forty-two years ago at Lac du Flambeau in Wisconsin. Barnouw delivered his interpretations in isolation, as an anthropologist; he rendered a tribal language game into power theories, linear social structures, and carried on an autistic monologue with science. There is no discourse with the narrative artist.

Barnouw is outrageous in his evaluations of the narrator, a nonpareil monologue with science:

Tom Badger was a reserved, intelligent, mild-mannered man in his seventies. . . . I gave him a Rorschach Test and collected two Draw-a-

Person drawings. . . . there was evidence of emotional dependency and also some confusion about sex. . . . The two interpretations suggest the existence of repression, which is also suggested by the origin myth, with its avoidance of women and sex and its recurrent oral and anal themes. [32]

There is a distinction between the author, a collective and agonistic imagination, and the narrative artist who quotes the trickster, the wind, a tree, and comments on the mythic verism of the narrative: "I'm just telling you what I heard," the narrator told the translator and anthropologist. Here the narrator intrudes in discourse, a first person divergence in a third person narrative, an ironic intrusion. What is being told in the past tense is known to the sophisticated narrator.

Ann Jefferson writes that the "preterite" is the

tense which guarantees causality, the linking of the chain of events lead- ing to a solution, and the promise of the revelation of truth. . . . The third person and the preterite have in common the ability (albeit a ques- tionable one) to speak of the world without calling into question the na- ture of that speech. [33]

Social science theories abase the comic holotropes in trickster nar- ratives. The narrator and trickster are separated in translation; the points of view in narrative discourse and that "clear distinction be- tween narrator and author," are denied. The trickster is measured in causal roles and the narrative is compared to other translations. Barnouw for example declares, "Since myths may be, in part, caution- ary tales, the appearance of certain motifs may indicate tabooed be- havior." His suppositions burden the trickster sign, end comic dis- course in a language game and demand legitimation.

Karl Kroeber, editor of *Traditional Literatures of the American In- dian*, writes that "anthropologists and folklorists whose disciplines are not directed toward appreciation of superior artistry, usually play down, or ignore, the individual distinction of creative accomplishment in ethnographic material." [34]

Dennis Tedlock, an enlightened translator and interpreter of tribal narratives, points out that "storytellers can talk *about* stories, but their observations and speculations come from accumulated experience at hearing and telling stories, not from the recollection of a lesson plan." [35] Tedlock explains that the

teller is not merely repeating memorized words, nor is he or she merely giving a dramatic "oral interpretation" or "concert reading" of a fixed script. We are in the presence of a *performing art*, all right, but we are getting the *criticism* at the same time and from the same person. The interpreter does not merely play the parts, but is the narrator and commentator as well.[36]

Barnouw, in the introduction to the narratives, writes that the "best way to highlight the distinctive features in the folklore of a society is to compare it with the folklore of another society which has contrasting features in social structure or family type." This method is an autistic monologue with social science. Naanabozho, he wrote, "was a real person whom they respected." Later however he noted that the trickster "seems to be neither a human being nor a god, but something of both."[37] Barnouw listened and recorded what he heard, but there is no evidence that the anthropologist responded or participated in a narrative discourse on the trickster. His monologue on the narratives, at best, is a "lesson plan."

The Anishinaabe [Chippewa] "origin myth seems to make the point that it is difficult to live with others; then one becomes tied down to people who are slower than oneself. . . . There is an implicit regret that children take so long to mature and reach independence, whereas animals can walk shortly after birth." Barnouw contends that the trickster "seems to be happiest when he is completely alone."[38] Here, interpretation is linear, a causal distortion and outside the narrative concordance. The trickster is a comic holotrope in a language game and a discourse that narrative artists mind and social scientists manipulate and pretend to understand. The trickster is a tribal sign, communal in various narrative voices, mythic verism is a narrative and artistic event but there is no concordance in the instrumental language of science. The tribal sign is inherited and liberated in literature but not in social science models that deduce "real" and "functional" worlds.

"And yet a real world exists," writes Geoffrey Strickland. "The study of language is not a denial of reality but one of the means to a more realistic view of the world."[39] The studies of language are the studies of the trickster in spoken and written narratives.

Walter Ong, in *Orality and Literacy*, argues that "oral speech" is "natural to human beings" and rises "out of the unconscious" as does the comic sign in trickster narratives. "The process of putting spoken language into writing is governed by consciously contrived, articulable rules. . . . Thought is nested in speech, not in texts," is a notion that would invite deconstruction criticism. "The spoken word is always an event, a movement in time, completely lacking in the thing-like repose of the written or printed word. . . ." He concludes that "writing and print isolate."[40] The trickster is a communal sign, a comic holotrope in a narrative discourse, oral or written in translation. Social science as an instrumental language game becomes "articulable rules" in translation and interpretations; the isolation of "writing and print" is intentional in the monologue with science.

Jacques Derrida is critical of structural linguistics and the "logocentric tradition" that confers privileged status to the spoken word and phonological theories. The origin of language is writing, not the spoken word. Derrida announces that "there is no linguistic sign before writing."[41] Naanabozho is a sign in translated narratives, and at the same time the trickster is a comic deconstructionist in social science. The trickster was created with bears and crows, imagined in narrative voices, and has survived taxonomies with the crow, translations, structural models, transvaluations with the bear, in a language game that is spoken and written; comic discourse shimmers with the crows and bears over dead metaphors and isolated monologues, the tragic monologue with science.

Roland Barthes, however, observes that

> writing is in no way an instrument for communication, it is not an open route through which there passes only the intention to speak. . . . writing is a hardened language which is self-contained and is in no way meant to deliver to its own duration a mobile series of approximations. It is on the contrary meant to impose, thanks to the shadow cast by its system of signs, the image of a speech which had a structure even before it came into existence.[42]

Barnouw points out that there "seems to be more emphasis on the anal zone in the folklore" of the Anishinaabe than in other tribal cultures.

> Freudians find an explanation for the "anal character" in severe early toilet training, but one would not expect to find strict toilet training in a "nomadic" tribal culture.
>
> On the other hand, perhaps we should not see the presence of anal motifs as something surprising or pathological. After all, an interest in feces is natural and understandable. . . .

Barnouw reminds the reader that in "modern flush toilets, feces are quickly spirited away and disappear, but a hunter who defecates on the earth is literally closer to his feces, and they have more permanence for him."[43] Barnouw imposes structural binaries in his interpretations; the hunter and the modern flush toilet are dubious undertows. Savagism and civilization, a common structural theme, has inspired more lucid racialism.

Barthes blurs the structural models, a "liberation from 'the binary prison.' To anyone who does not get into the binary categories of ordinary social reference," and the trickster does not, "the Neutral is the only nonimprisoning hope." Barthes stands "for many-sided meanings, for the oscillation of value, for metamorphosis,"[44] and he must stand for the comic trickster, the deconstruction reader. The death of the author is the birth of the reader, and the death of social science is the birth of the trickster in modern literature.

> Through the Text the reader becomes a writer, producing meaning; the reader produces writing of his own only as a response to a previous experience of a Text. Critics are perhaps to be defined, Barthes suggests, in the same way as other writers—as "those who read *in order to* write."[45]

The trickster author becomes the narrator, and narrative voices, the comic holotrope in a discourse; the trickster author never died but a mock death in a monologue with science.

Elizabeth Bruss, in "Theory of Literature Becomes Theory as Literature," notes that the

> *author* turns out to be a misnomer: not a divine creator, not even a divine creation, but a secular invention and an economic convenience. . . . By replacing the relationship between text and source with an infinite intertextual circuit, literary theory has, in effect, enormously expanded the powers and responsibilities of the reader.[46]

Alan Dundes on an analogous theme advanced coprophilia to record levels; he declared:

> Despite the lack of a great number of actual excremental myths, the existence of any at all would appear to lend support to the hypothesis that men do think of creativity in anal terms, and further that this conception is projected into mythical cosmogonic terms.

Dundes rests his hypothesis on two assumptions: "The existence of a cloacal theory of birth, and the existence of pregnancy envy on the part

of males."[47] Dundes does, however, explain in part the "failure of anthropology" to make "notable advances in myth studies." There is a
"rigid adherence to two fundamental principles," he writes:

> A literal reading of myth and a study of myth in monocultural context.
> The insistence of most anthropologists upon the literal as opposed to the
> symbolic interpretation, in terms of cultural relativism as opposed to
> transcultural universalism, is in part a continuation of the reaction
> against nineteenth-century thought, in which universal symbolism in
> myth was often argued, and in part a direct result of the influence of two
> dominant figures in the history of anthropology, Boas and Malinowski.
> Both these pioneers favored studying one culture at a time in depth, and
> both contended that myth was essentially nonsymbolic.[48]

Here again anthropologists secure an uncertain monologue with science and other anthropologists, but not a discourse with the tribal cultures that were reduced to theories in their studies.

Naanabozho is shit in a comic holotrope and so is Martin Luther;
this is a real connection between trickster narratives, dubious the-
ologies and hagiographies, which provides a more interesting discussion on shit than the rather prudish monologues by anthropologists.
"'It's as I've often said,' Luther told his wife, 'I'm like a ripe *freck* [shit]
and the world's like a gigantic *arschloch* [asshole].' But if Luther thought
he didn't belong in the world's asshole," Martin Pops writes in "'The
Metamorphosis of Shit,'"[49] "he [Luther] thought the Devil belonged in
his. For the Devil is not just the materialized lord of the world and the
flesh, but, as Norman O. Brown has argued, the hallucinated displacement of Luther's own anality. Like a quixotic knight of faith,
Luther met him in theological combat, daily and strenuous. Doctrine
failing to convince, Luther repulsed him with a fart, a turd, or the
sight of his naked backside." The trickster does no less in literature to
heal and balance the world; Barnouw, Dundes and other theorists burdened with coprophilia would have done much better to construe shit
as a universal comic sign than to bind the literal malodor in social science monologues.

Naanabozho could not escape his own shit; the earth was not *his* shit
because he invited several animals to dive down and return with
some earth. "If you do that," said the trickster with shit as high as his
mouth, "I will make an earth for you and me to live on." In several
other narratives, however, the trickster created humans from shit.
William Jones collected a narrative about a beautiful tribal woman

who spurned the men in her tribe. Several wanton suitors constructed a handsome man with shit, dressed him in fine clothes and directed him to the woman. She was smitten with love at the sight of him, an outsider; she followed him to the end of the trail where he melted down to a heap of shit.[50] Modern variations on this narrative turn anthropologists into cloacal tropes to power, shit mounds at the end of the trail in social science.

Norman Mailer seems to understand the trickster and shit as a comic sign in literature. In "The Metaphysics of the Belly" he recommends a bowel inspection "because feces are the material evidence of the processes of communication within us." Comic shit is a smooth sign and shit floats in trickster narratives, but when the "communication within us" is blocked, when the comic holotrope is ruined with literal shit, "the odors and shapes are tortured, corrupt, rich, fascinating . . . even tragic."[51]

The trickster as healer

In *The Trickster: A Study in American Indian Mythology* Paul Radin reviews the trickster as the "presence of a figure" and as a "theme or themes" which are told in various cultures. Radin seems to present the trickster as an "aesthetic presence" in narratives; this is modernism, and in a sense a celebration of individualism. On the other hand, Barnouw declared that the trickster was a "real person" and "neither human being nor a god, but something of both." The trickster is not a presence or a real person but a semiotic sign in a language game, in a comic narrative that denies presence. The sign is communal and the narrative is a discourse; individualism is isolation, a tragic mode, in the instrumental language of social science.

Radin declares that the trickster is

> at the same time creator and destroyer, giver and negator, he who dupes others and who is always duped himself. He wills nothing consciously. At all times he is constrained to behave as he does from impulses over which he has no control. He knows neither good nor evil yet he is responsible for both. He possesses no values, moral or social, is at the mercy of his passions and appetites [and yet,] through his actions all values come into being. . . .
>
> Laughter, humour and irony permeate everything Trickster does. The reaction of the audience in aboriginal societies to both him and his

exploits is prevailingly one of laughter tempered by awe. . . . Yet it is difficult to say whether the audience is laughing at him, at the tricks he plays on others, or at the implications his behaviour and activities have for them.[52]

In his essay on the psychology of the trickster Carl Gustav Jung construes:

> Since all mythical figures correspond to inner psychic experiences and originally sprang from them, it is not surprising to find certain phenomena in the field of parapsychology which remind us of the trickster. . . .
>
> In picaresque tales, in carnivals and revels, in sacred and magical rites, in man's religious fears and exaltations, this phantom of the trickster haunts the mythology of all ages, sometimes in quite unmistakable form, sometimes in strangely modulated guise.[53]

Jung names the trickster an "archetypal psychic structure of extreme antiquity." Enriched with psychic structures and narrative stemmata, the tribal trickster shimmers and crosses the limina into universal consciousness. The comic sign is not denied in instrumental languages.

Jung, however, asserts that the trickster as a "collective figure gradually breaks up under the impact of civilization, leaving traces in folklore which are difficult to recognize."[54] He must assume an inert trickster, an erroneous assertion because the narrator imagines the trickster and the characters are active in a narrative discourse. The trickster is a sign, a healer and comic liberator in narratives, not an artifact or a real victim in historical summaries; rather than a trace element, suppose the tribal trickster is atavistic, a revenant holotrope in new and recurrent narratives. Moreover, the trickster is a communal sign in imagination, a comic holotrope and a discourse that endures in modern literature.

Jung observes that the

> trickster is a primitive "cosmic" being of *divine-animal* nature, on the one hand superior to man because of his superhuman qualities, and on the other hand inferior to him because of his unreason and unconsciousness. He is no match for the animals either, because of his extraordinary clumsiness and lack of instinct. These defects are the marks of his *human* nature. . . .[55]
>
> The trickster is a collective shadow figure, an epitome of all the inferior traits of character in individuals. And since the individual shadow is never absent as a component of personality, the collective figure can construct itself out of it continually. . . . In the history of the collective

as in the history of the individual, everything depends on the development of consciousness. This gradually brings liberation from imprisonment in . . . consciousness, and is therefore a bringer of light as well as healing.[56]

Trickster Metaphors and Models

In the context of literary theory models extend into uncertain situations constructed over measured words, signs and sentences; the models lean uneven with too much intension. Elizabeth Bruss points out that models and metaphors initiate "a process of trial and error, which leads to a reorientation of our own approach and a reorganization in how we see a given subject matter."[57] Trickster narratives are tested models in social science; instrumental interpretations are used to compare cultures. The trickster is dead in models and mock tragedies in the same manner that a comic sign or metaphor is dead when overused, overrun and insolated in a monologue with science.

In his anthropological studies on humor and laughter, which include a chapter on the trickster, Mahadev Apte establishes his model with two axioms. Humor, he writes, "is by and large culture based," and with unabashed arrogance he asserts that "humor can be a major conceptual and methodological tool for gaining insights into cultural systems."[58] The trickster is a semiotic sign in written narratives, a comic sign that "wanders" in universal signification. Humor, however, or at least the humor that heals, is closer to the oral tradition and bound to a specific culture. The second axiom is an isolated monologue with science, the paratragic model that compares narratives as material.

Apte argues that his research on the trickster is definitional and concerned with how to separate the trickster from "other related concepts." He describes and compares invented cultures and models but asserts that he does not choose one definition of the trickster over another. Here are three model definitions:

E. W. Voegelin describes the tricksters in "prose narratives as animal-human beings who are typically 'greedy, erotic, imitative, stupid, pretentious, deceitful' and whose thievery and deceitfulness benefit people. . . ."

M. L. Ricketts agrees and "adds that the trickster is a restless wanderer and does not distinguish between friend and foe in carrying out his pranks."

R. Abrahams believs that "the trickster is the most paradoxical of all characters in traditional narratives and his outstanding characteristic is his lack of morals. . . . The concepts of jesters, fools, clowns, and morons all basically derive from the broad, general notion of trickster."[59]

Apte and others who have compared definitions of tribal tricksters seem to assume a literal "presence" of the trickster and measure imagination and narrative behavior in human terms—causal and with literal motivations. In his summaries Apte names traits—the trickster is cruel, stupid, does not resist temptation, lacks control, mocks and ridicules and "his inability to recognize things as they are or to identify his surroundings frequently leads him into trouble, as do other actions." Apte imposes structuralist theories when he writes that the "overall personality that emerges from the trickster tales incorporates opposites of all kinds."[60] Once more, the trickster is not a structural opposite or an element in a tragic model; the trickster is a comic sign, neither a real person nor a character with "aesthetic presence."

Apte seems to ascertain that "rarely are individuals with such opposing traits to be found in human societies." However, he returns to the notion of a real person. He writes that tricksters

> appear to be disorderly, chaotic personalities. They also manifest extremely inappropriate and socially deviant behavior and actions. Their acts are aberrant by any cultural standards, making the tricksters misfits in human societies because of their refusal to abide by the established sociocultural norms. . . . The incongruities associated with tricksters, in other words, are biological, psychological, and sociocultural.[61]

Apte holds his descriptions close to social science models, too close to imagine tricksters as comic signs in narratives; he asserts that in "American Indian prose narratives, little attention has been given in the past to context, function, and performance of verbal art, while texts are overemphasized in folklore research."[62]

In his article on the forms of prose narratives William Bascom points out that classifications are not "particularly interesting," at the same time he contributes his own interpretations of tribal narratives, his own monologue with social science because folklore "needs clarification" and because the field "has so long been plagued by inconsis-

---

tent and contradictory definitions." To that end he contributes definitions of three forms of prose narratives:

> Folktales are prose narratives which are regarded as fiction. . . .
> Myths are prose narratives which, in the society which they are told, are
> considered to be truthful accounts of what happened in the remote
> past. . . .
> Legends are prose narratives which, like myths, are regarded as true
> by the narrator and his audience, but they are set in a period considered
> less remote, when the world was much as it is today.[63]

Bascom concedes that myth, legend and folktale are not the "only
major categories of prose narratives" and are not proposed as "univer-
sally recognized categories." He asserts that these are "analytical concepts" which can be applied "cross-culturally even when other systems
of 'native categories' are locally recognized."[64] His categories are tropes
to power; monologues with social science. Moreover, he declares that
the Anishinaabe are the "only society reported to lack fictional prose
narratives," and "apparently have no folktales."[65] Bascom bases his assertion on the published observations of other anthropologists; he did
not hear the aural stories of tribal people.

In his studies of bourgeois perceptions, Donald Lowe points out that
written languages "preserved knowledge after the act of speech and beyond the lapse of memory." He argues that in oral cultures "hearing
surpasses seeing as the most important" of the senses; the assimilation
of knowledge in an aural performance without the "mediation of the
eye." Once in print, however, there is an emphasis on content; what is
known from what is heard in an oral culture is "detached from the
knower."[66] Even those anthropologists who *hear* stories rather than
read cultures must overturn the aural performance in their translations
and publications—the separation of the knower from a tribal discourse.

Naanabozho is overheard as a comic holotrope; heard but not seen
in an aural performance the trickster fashions an anthropologist with
shit to show that the tribe has "fictional prose narratives" and the
comic mind to transform the obvious.

Notes

1. Robert Scholes and Robert Kellogg, *The Nature of Narrative* (London:
Oxford University Press, 1966) 240.

2. Paul Watzlawick, ed. *The Invented Reality* (New York: W. W. Norton, 1984) 10.

3. Walzlawick 63.

4. Roy Wagner, *The Invention of Culture* (The University of Chicago Press, 1981) 16.

5. Warwick Wadlington, *The Confidence Game in American Literature* (Princeton University Press, 1975) 15.

6. Stein Haugom Olsen, *The Structure of Literary Understanding* (Cambridge University Press, 1978) 17, 18.

7. Vincent Leitch, *Deconstructive Criticism* (New York: Columbia University Press, 1983) 11. Jacques Lacan in "Sign, Symbol, Imagery," defines the sign as an obstacle "to the grasp of the signifier. . . . The sign presupposes the someone to whom one makes a sign or something. The shadow of this someone obscured the entry into linguistics. . . . The sign makes language the basis of abstracts and the means of discussion." In *On Signs*, ed. Marshall Blonsky (Baltimore: Johns Hopkins University Press, 1985) 201–09.

8. Geoffrey Stickland, *Structuralism or Criticism?* (Cambridge University Press, 1981) 13.

9. Strickland, 16.

10. Marshall Blonsky, *On Signs* (Baltimore: Johns Hopkins University Press, 1985) XLVI.

11. Tzvetan Todorov, "Language and Literature" *The Structural Controversy*, ed. Richard Macksey (Baltimore: Johns Hopkins University Press, 1970) 130. Quot. Stein Haugom Olsen, *The Structure of Literary Understanding* 17.

12. Olsen 76.

13. Paul Ricoeur, *Time and Narrative*, vol. 2 (The University of Chicago Press, 1985) 28.

14. Emile Benveniste, *Problèmes de linguistique générale*. Trans. Geoffrey Strickland *Structuralism or Criticism?* (Cambridge University Press, 1981) 18.

15. Benveniste 134.

16. Roy Wagner, *Symbols That Stand for Themselves* (The University of Chicago Press, 1986) 128.

17. Tzvetan Todorov, *Mikhail Bakhtin: The Dialogical Principle*, trans. Wlad Godzich, *Theory and History of Literature*, vol. 13 (Minneapolis: University of Minnesota Press, 1984) 60.

18. Todorov 30.

19. Mikhail Bakhtin, *The Dialogic Imagination*, ed. Michael Holquist, trans. Caryl Emerson and Michael Holquist (Austin: University of Texas Press, 1981) 292.

20. Charles Russell, *Poets, Prophets, and Revolutionaries: The Literary Avant-garde from Rimbaud Through Postmodern* (New York: Oxford University Press, 1985) 248.

21. Robert Bellah, *The Broken Covenant: American Civil Religion in Time of Trial* (New York: Seabury, 1975) 106.

22. Michel Foucault, "Film and Popular Memory," interview by Martin Jordin *Cahiers du Cinema* (London: *Radical Philosophy* 11, 1975) 24–29.

23. Fredric Jameson, *The Anti-Aesthetic Essays on Postmodern Culture*, ed. Hal Foster (Bay Press, 1983). Quot. "Modernism and its Enemies," by Hilton Kramer, *The New Criterion*, March 1986, 2.

24. Russell 247.

25. Roland Barthes, "From Science to Literature," *The Times Literary Supplement*, 1967. Reprint. *The Rustle of Language*, trans. Richard Howard (New York: Hill and Wang, 1986) 4.

26. Jean-François Lyotard, *The Postmodern Condition: A Report on Knowledge*, trans. Geoff Bennington and Brian Massumi (Minneapolis: University of Minnesota Press, 1984) 25.

27. Lyotard 27.

28. Paul Feyeraband, *Science in a Free Society* (London: Verso Editions, 1978) 77.

29. Louis Sass, "Anthropology's Native Problems," *Harper's*, May 1986: 52.

30. Alan Sheridan, *Michel Foucault: The Will to Truth* (London: Tavistock Publications, 1980) 220.

31. Victor Barnouw, *Wisconsin Chippewa Myths & Tales* (Madison: The University of Wisconsin Press, 1977) 13–15, 38. The spelling of *Naanabozho* and other *Anishinaabe* words conforms to entries in *Ojibwewi-Ikidowinan: An Ojibwe Word Resource Book*, ed. John Nichols and Earl Nyholm (Saint Paul: Minnesota Archaeological Society, 1979). Manabozho, Nanabush and Winnebozho, are other transcriptions for the name of the woodland tribal trickster.

32. Barnouw 61.

33. Ann Jefferson, *The Nouveau Roman and the Politics of Fiction* (Cambridge University Press, 1980), p. 30–31, 99.

34. Karl Kroeber, ed. *Traditional Literature of the American Indian: Texts and Interpretations* (Lincoln: University of Nebraska Press, 1981) 17.

35. Dennis Tedlock, *The Spoken Word and the Work of Interpretation* (Philadelphia: University of Pennsylvania Press, 1983) 15. First published in *Traditional Literatures of the American Indian*, ed. Karl Kroeber (Lincoln: University of Nebraska Press, 1981).

36. Tedlock 236.

37. Barnouw 51.

38. Barnouw 48.

39. Strickland 127.

40. Walter Ong, *Orality and Literacy: The Technologizing of the Word* (London: Metheun, 1982) 74.

41. Leitch 29.

42. Roland Barthes, *Writing Degree Zero* (New York: Hill and Wang, 1968) 19.

43. Barnouw 241.

44. Helen Vendler, "The Medley Is the Message," *The New York Review of Books*, May 1986: 48.

45. Vendler 46.

46. Elizabeth Bruss, *Beautiful Theories: The Spectacle of Discourse in Contemporary Criticism* (Baltimore: Johns Hopkins University Press, 1982) 63, 66.

47. Alan Dundas, "Earth-Diver: Creation of the Mythopoeic Male," *American Anthropologist*, 64 (1962). Reprint. *Sacred Narrative*, ed. Alan Dundas (Berkeley: University of California Press, 1984) 278.

48. Dundas 271.

49. Martin Pops, "The Metamorphosis of Shit," *Salmagundi*, 56 (Spring 1982): 29.

50. William Jones, *Ojibway Texts*, vol. 7 (Leyden: American Ethnological Society, 1917).

51. Norman Mailer, "The Metaphysics of the Belly," *The Presidential Papers* (New York: Putnam, 1963). Quot. Martin Pops "the Metamorphosis of Shit," *Salmagundi*, 56 (Spring 1982): 60.

52. Paul Radin, *The Trickster: A Study in American Indian Mythology* (New York: Schocken Books, 1972) xxii–xxiv.

53. Carl Gustav Jung, "On the Psychology of the Trickster Figure," *The Trickster*, by Paul Radin (New York: Schocken Books, 1972) 200.

54. Jung 202.

55. Jung 204.

56. Jung 209, 211.

57. Bruss 58.

58. Mahadev Apte, *Humor and Laughter: An Anthropological Approach* (Ithaca: Cornell University Press, 1985) 16.

59. Apte 224.

60. Apte 216.

61. Apte 230.

62. Apte 321.

63. William Bascom, "The Forms of Foklore: Prose Narratives," *Sacred Narrative: Readings in the Theory of Myth*, ed. Alan Dundas (Berkeley: University of California Press, 1984), 8, 9.

64. Bascom 10.

65. Bascom 25.

66. Donald Lowe, *History of Bourgeois Perception* (Chicago: University of Chicago Press, 1982) 3, 4, 7.

Notes on Contributors

KIMBERLY BLAESER, an enrolled member of the Minnesota Chippewa Tribe from the White Earth Reservation, graduated from the College of St. Benedict in Minnesota. She received her Ph.D. at the University of Notre Dame. A recipient of a Francis C. Allen Fellowship, she studied at the Newberry Library's D'Arcy McNickle Center for the History of the American Indian. She is an assistant professor in Native American Literatures in the English department at the University of Wisconsin, Milwaukee.

ELAINE JAHNER is professor of English and Native American Studies at Dartmouth College. Her recent research and publications have been part of an effort to show how texts, once perceived as marginal to established literary concerns, can provide a critical perspective that allows for transformations of interpretive traditions. She has specialized in American Indian literatures and languages and she has translated traditional texts for publication in addition to her critical studies of modern literature.

KARL KROEBER, Mellon Professor of Humanities at Columbia University, has also served as chairman of the Department of English and Comparative Literature there and has taught at the University of Wisconsin, Madison (where he served as associate dean of the graduate school) and at the University of Washington. A recipient of Fulbright, Guggenheim, and NEH fellowships, he is the author of more than 100 articles and reviews. His twelfth book, *Romantic Fantasy and Science Fiction*, was published by Yale. Since 1977 he has served as editor of *Studies in American Indian Literatures*.

ARNOLD KRUPAT lives and works in New York. A member of the literature faculty at Sarah Lawrence College, he teaches a revisionist version of American literature and writes on Native American subjects in relation to American culture and society. He has published a novel, *Woodsmen, or Thoreau and the Indians*, and a study of Native American autobiography, *For Those Who Come After*, along with theoretically oriented articles in numerous journals. With Brian Swann he has edited *I Tell You Now: Autobiographical Essays by Native Americans* and *Recovering the Word: Essays on Native American Literature*.

LOUIS OWENS is Professor of Literature at the University of California, Santa |

Cruz. He is the author of *Other Destinies: Understanding the American Indian Novel,* two novels and numerous essays on American literature as well as stories and nonfiction articles.

GRETCHEN RONNOW teaches in the English Department at Wayne State College. She has published in *Al-'Arabiyya, a Journal of Teachers of Arabic* and in the *Native Press Research Journal;* she has also written book reviews for *Western American Literature* and the *American Indian Quarterly.*

JAMES RUPPERT teaches English at the University of Alaska, Fairbanks. He has published articles on contemporary American Indian literature and comparative essays on American and American Indian literatures. His introduction to the life and work of D'Arcy McNickle was published as part of the Western Writers Series.

ROBERT SILBERMAN is Associate Professor of Art History and Chairman of Film Studies at the University of Minnesota. A regular contributor to *Art in America,* he has written articles and reviews for many other publications, primarily on film, photography and contemporary art. He is currently writing a book on American political films.

ALAN VELIE teaches American Indian literature at the University of Oklahoma. He is the author of *Four American Literary Masters.* He edited an anthology of traditional and contemporary Indian literature and has also published essays on Shakespeare, folklore and critical theory.

GERALD VIZENOR is professor in the Ethnic Studies Department at the University of California, Berkeley. He has published critical essays on Native American literatures, narrative histories and several novels, including *Dead Voices, Griever: An American Monkey King in China,* and *Darkness in Saint Louis Bearheart.* He has taught Native American literature at the University of Minnesota and at the University of Oklahoma.

INDEX

Index

death of, 135–36; definitions of,
206–8; dual aspects of, 133–35; as
fictional character, 197–204; as
healer, 187, 204–6; and individualism, 193; as liberator, 131, 144,
187–88; sexual appetite of, 135; as
sign, 131, 187, 189; and social science
monologues, 196; tribal, 122, 151
Trickster, The (P. Radin), 142, 204–5
"Trickster Discourse" (G. Vizenor),
131–33, 150, 151
tricksterism, and contemporary conditions, 35
trickster narratives, 103, 142–50
trickster novel, 121–37
Trickster of Liberty, The (G. Vizenor),
153 n13
trickster signature, xi
truth: distinguished from error, 59; and
knowledge, 85
Tsvetaeva, Marina, quoted, 161
Tuckerman, Frederick Goddard, 175–
76; contrasted with Emerson, 177–78
Twelve Chairs, The, 135
twins, concept of, 172–74
Tyler, Stephen, quoted, 4–5

"Uncle Tony's Goat" (L. M. Silko), 60,
67 n11
unconscious, Derridean view of, 170
unity, illusion of, 70
usages, particular, 35–36

values, dominant, 68 n15
"vanishing tribes," notion of, 10, 193
Velie, Alan, 68 n14
Veogelin, E. W., quoted, 206
verbal links, 45
verisimilitude, 190
"Violence and Metaphysics" (J. Derrida), 170, 171
Visionary Compacts (D. Pease), 179–82
Vizenor, Gerald, 103, 121–37; quoted,
20, 131–32, 133, 144, 146, 150,
151–52, 156; writes as trickster,
136–37, 150–52. *See also titles of individual works*

voice: literary, 63; normative, 65; personal, 60; plurality of, 65, 157, 172
voices, 71
Voices of the Rainbow, 68 n14

Wadlington, Warwick, quoted, 188–89
Wagner, Roy, quoted, 188, 191
Watkins, Floyd, quoted, 19
Watts, Ian, quoted, 128
Watzlawick, Paul, quoted, 12, 188
Way to Rainy Mountain, The (N. S.
Momaday), 39–54, 156–59; as au-
thor's quest for identity, 48–53,
157–58; form of, 41–42; and literary
canon, 182; and literary criticism,
158–84; as performance, 157; pro-
logue of, 40–41; reader response to,
42–44; and structural polyphony,
47–48; structure of, 44–47; theoretical stance of, 163
White, Leslie, 19
White Earth Agency, 126
"whole truth" models, 11
Williams, Raymond, 68 n15
Winnebago Trickster Cycle, 136, 142
Winter in the Blood (J. Welch), 101,
118 n9; trickster figure in, 121, 122
Wisconsin Chippewa Myths and Tales,
197–204
witchcraft, 70, 146
Woman, and women, 81–82
Wood, Michael, 105
Wordarrows (G. Vizenor), 133
words: functions of, 72, 73, 174; power
of, 20; as presence, 78
"word wounds," 72
"work in movement," 42, 43–44,
47–48. *See also* open works
world view: comic v. tragic, xiii, 6, 9;
Native American, 153 n13; tribal, 131
wound, Lacanian concept of, 82
Wright, James, xiii, 63
writer, as mediator, 174
writing, compared to telling, 61–62

Yellow Raft in Blue Water, A (M. Dorris), 119 n15